PEASANTS, WARRIORS, AND WIVES

PEASANTS  WARRIORS

AND WIVES

Popular Imagery in the Reformation

KEITH MOXEY

 The University of Chicago Press · Chicago and London

KEITH MOXEY, professor of art history at Barnard College, and Columbia University, is the author of *Pieter Aertsen, Joachim Beuckalaer, and the Rise of Secular Painting in the Context of the Reformation* and coeditor, with Norman Bryson and Michael Holly, of *Visual Theory: Painting and Interpretation.*

The University of Chicago Press, Chicago 60637
The University of Chicago Press, Ltd., London
© 1989 by The University of Chicago
All rights reserved. Published 1989
Printed in the United States of America

98 97 96 95 94 93 92 91 90 89 54321

Library of Congress Cataloging in Publication Data

Moxey, Keith P. F., 1943–
    Peasants, warriors, and wives : popular imagery in the Reformation
    Keith Moxey.
        p.   cm.
    Includes index.
    ISBN 0-226-54391-9
    1. Printed ephemera—Germany—Nuremberg—History—16th century.
2. Wood-engraving. German—Germany—Nuremberg.   3. Wood-engraving—16th century—Germany—Nuremberg.   4. Reformation and art—Germany—Nuremberg.   5. Social classes in art.   6. War in art.
7. Marriage in art.   I. Title.
NE958.3.G3M68   1989   88-37668
769′.4994332—dc19   CIP

To Patrick

The Present continually hovers before the backward looking glance, because it is by the aid of analogies drawn from the life of today—however little this may be consciously before the mind—that we reach the causal explanation of the events of the past. But what is still more important is that we always, either voluntarily or involuntarily, relate the course of past events to the complex of effects which lies before us in the present, and that we are constantly drawing either special or general conclusions from the past and making use of them in our task of shaping the present with a view to the future.

Ernst Troeltsch, *Protestantism and Progress*

Contents

Illustrations

Preface

This book assembles a number of separate essays written over several years. Chapter 3, "Festive Peasants and Social Order," was written while I was a fellow at the Center for Advanced Study in the Visual Arts at the National Gallery of Art in Washington, D.C., during the academic year 1980–81. I am deeply grateful to Henry Millon and Shreve Simpson for making my stay such a productive and pleasant experience. The text benefited from the suggestions of Donald Posner, Natalie Davis, Walter Gibson, Fedja Anzelewski, and Rosalind Krauss, to whom I am most grateful. It was originally published in *Simiolus* 12(1982): 107–30 and appears here by kind permission of the editors.

The research for chapters 4 and 5, "Mercenary Warriors and the 'Rod of God'" and "The Battle of the Sexes and the World Upside Down," was carried out in Germany with the support of a grant from the Humboldt Foundation during the academic year 1982–83. The foundation proved unusually helpful, and I should like to express special thanks to Thomas Berberich and to Ingrid Praetzel-Friauf. During my stay in West Berlin, Fedja Anzelewski, my sponsor, placed the facilities of the print room of the West Berlin museums at my disposal and assisted me in ways too numerous to describe. I am most deeply grateful to Thomas Gaehtgens, director of the Art Historical Institute of the Free University, and his wife Barbara, who helped me deal with the practical difficulties of making a life in a foreign city. Among my Berlin friends I must thank Ranier Hausherr for his kindness and Bernd Lindemann for his friendship in acting as my guide to the fascinating culture of the divided city. Versions of these chapters were delivered as talks at several scholarly meetings and institutions in the years 1984–86 and incorporate helpful suggestions made by a variety of individuals. Among the most useful were those proposed by Natalie Davis, Erik Midelfort, Larry Silver, and Sandra Hindman. Some of this work was published as "The Function of Secular Woodcuts in Nuremberg Culture of the Sixteenth Century" in *New Perspectives on the Art of Renaissance Nuremberg,* ed. Jeffrey Chipps Smith (Austin, 1985), pp. 63–81.

A faculty seminar, "Historical Interpretation," held at the University of Virginia under the leadership of Ralph Cohen was of great assistance in formulating the theoretical approach to the interpretation of the images discussed in this book. I also want to thank my former colleague David Summers for his willingness to engage in innumerable discussions and debates about these matters.

Most of the book was either written or rewritten while I was a sesquicentennial fellow at the University of Virginia during the academic year 1986–87. I am much indebted to the university for its generous support. Holly Wright, who read the manuscript at an early stage, pointed out major problems in the argument of chapter 2 and made helpful comments throughout. Peter Parshall saw it later and made me rethink parts of the Introduction. Michael Holly read the entire manuscript before publication and had a number of useful suggestions.

I especially thank Jan Piet Filedt Kok for his help in obtaining photographs of rare prints and Charlotte Bowen for typing many drafts as well as the final text.

There is one further most important debt to acknowledge: to my son Patrick for his company over many years.

Introduction

The woodcuts that are the focus of the following chapters have been largely ignored by art historical scholarship. Beyond pioneering efforts by connoisseurs to establish which masters were responsible for which prints, there has been relatively little interest in discussing their subject matter and the significance it may have had for German society in the sixteenth century. In large part this neglect is the result of the works' having been excluded from what is generally called "art." The failure to recognize sixteenth-century woodcuts as a legitimate subject for the more ambitious forms of art historical analysis undoubtedly stems ultimately from the prominence ascribed to the discussion of artistic form in art historical studies since the nineteenth century. Our current ideas about the nature of "art" were formed under the influence of the concept of the "aesthetic." According to Kant's *Critique of Aesthetic Judgment,* works of art had the ability to promote a "disinterested" appreciation in the viewer. The beautiful was not merely the agreeable but the necessary—it consisted not of what merely pleased the individual but of what had the potential to please universally.[1] In defining the "aesthetic" as a universal concept, one that could be identified in works of art of all ages, Kant chose to ignore the vast differences that characterize the subjects they represent in favor of an analysis of their formal qualities. Consideration of such characteristics as form and color proved more amenable to the development of a universally applicable concept of the aesthetic than the analysis of subject matter, which was far too susceptible to historical change to serve as the foundation for a general theory. The result was a theory of the aesthetic that was notable for its ahistoricism. The preeminence of form in this definition of the aesthetic decisively shaped the development of German art history in the nineteenth century. The view that the true subject of the discipline was the discussion of artistic form rather than content prevailed when, under the influence of Hegel, it became possible to identify artistic forms with the notion of "style."[2] The idea of style as the configuration adopted by artistic forms in different historical periods enabled art historians to pursue an essentially ahistorical analysis of artistic forms in the guise of history.

Late medieval German woodcuts have had no place in the canon of aesthetic worth built upon the imposition of such values. With notable exceptions, they are characterized by a formal simplicity that distinguishes them from the media of sculpture, painting, and engraving, all of which were affected sooner and more completely by the introduction of the formal intricacies associated with the art of the Italian Renaissance. It is no surprise, for example, that the work of Albrecht Dürer, an artist who deliberately sought to acquire the idealizing and illusionistic qualities of his Italian contemporaries, should have become the yardstick against which the work of other artists was judged. Dürer's role as the exponent of an art form that was self-conscious about the theoretical principles that determined its stylistic characteristics made his work accessible to ideas about art shaped under the influence of the nineteenth-century notion of the aesthetic.[3] His contemporaries and followers, on the other hand, whose graphic work often fails to exhibit the interest in formal problems that characterizes his own, have been consigned to oblivion. In describing Aby Warburg's fascination with Reformation broadsheets, for example, Ernst Gombrich wrote: "But however important this type of imagery may be for our knowledge of the mentality of the period and the specific way in which it visualized the powers which ruled its destiny, is there a connection between these coarse and ugly prints and the art of the period?"[4]

One consequence of the imposition of anachronistic aesthetic values on the artistic production of the late Middle Ages has been the classification of woodcuts as "mass art" or "folk art."[5] It has often been claimed, for example, that the woodcut medium, which was first developed in the fifteenth century, is one of the earliest forms of folk art.[6] This folk art has proved capable of multiple definitions. It has been viewed as the vestigial remains of art forms once popular at a higher level of society; as the expression of the artistic values of the "people"; and as art produced for the lower classes by those in positions of power.[7] By viewing sixteenth-century woodcuts as folk art, for example, it was possible to regard them as the equivalent of the mass media of the nineteenth century. This perspective has proved particularly misleading for the study of woodcuts and broadsheets produced in the context of the Reformation. It suggested that the flood of anti-Catholic propaganda was an expression of popular sentiment.[8] More recent studies of such imagery have been much more cautious, suggesting that, far from being expressions of popular opinion, such prints were actually the means by which the reformed attitudes of the middle and upper classes could be disseminated to as broad an audience as possible.[9]

In attempting to understand the artistic character of late medieval woodcuts, it is important to see through the distinction between "high art" and "low art" that has been imposed on them by the notion of the aesthetic. Unlike the modern period, the Middle Ages had no such notion, nor even a category for "art."[10] While this situation, of course, did not mean that aesthetic experiences were unknown or that certain cultural artifacts were not viewed in ways analogous to the ways we approach works of art today, it does mean that these concepts do not coincide with one another. According to the medieval view, form and function were indissolubly united. What made an object beautiful was as much the way it fulfilled its cultural function as its formal appearance.[11] One contributed to the other to produce an experience in which these dimensions of the work of art could not be distinguished. Any effort to understand the nature of medieval art therefore must take into consideration the notion of cultural function. The brief given the visual arts following the second council of Nicea (A.D. 787) was that images should on the one hand provide the worshiper with an aid to devotion and on the other serve as a means of instruction.[12] As formulated in Gregory the Great's famous letter to the bishop of Marseilles, the second point equated the painted image with the written word: "For what the written book conveys to those who read it, that also painting conveys to the uninstructed folk who contemplate it."[13] The woodcuts considered here participate in the second of these cultural functions. Although secular in the subject matter, they resemble religious art of a didactic nature both in being intimately related to texts and in their use as a form of indoctrination.

If this book is to avoid invoking anachronistic aesthetic criteria as the basis for selecting works of art for art historical discussion, then I need to provide some account of the principles by which I chose the medium as well as the subjects or themes dealt with in the following essays. The medieval aesthetic, together with the value it ascribed to the cultural function of the work, animated the production of woodcuts as much as that of paintings or buildings. However, this does not mean they were all once regarded as possessing equivalent aesthetic merit. Indeed, in focusing on woodcuts I have deliberately chosen one of the least expensive forms of late medieval art. In an age when the materials used in executing art served as a metaphor of the importance of its cultural function and thus as a way of establishing its aesthetic merit,[14] a work printed on paper was among the least valued forms of artistic production.

The intention underlying this project should not be misunderstood. This is not an attempt to rescue valuable works of art from unwarranted neglect and promote them into an aesthetic canon sanctioned by tradition. Far from choosing on aesthetic grounds—that is, either on the basis of aesthetic values we share today or in light of the aesthetic values of the period, I selected the woodcut medium because its very lack of aesthetic value made it cheap to produce and acquire. Rather than articulating the personal beliefs or ambitions of particular patrons or illustrating the theological tenets of the faith, as was the case with painting and sculpture in this period, woodcuts were produced with an eye to sales in an anonymous marketplace. The public quality of the arena in which woodcuts were bought and sold implies that its representations must have been accessible to a large proportion of the population. The intent underlying this analysis, therefore, has less to do with the aesthetic status of the woodcuts than with the social transactions they enabled.

The imagery of German woodcuts in the first half of the sixteenth century is both rich and varied. In the wealth of subject matter represented, biblical narratives and devotional images mingle with Catholic and Lutheran satires as well as with subjects taken from ancient history and mythology, from folklore and fable. Such images coexist with battle scenes, sieges, triumphal entries, portraits of rulers, monstrous births, and representations of various occupations.[15] The prolific quality of this world of representation defies any attempt to offer a succinct catalog. On the other hand such variety is not endless, so rather than regarding these representations as the product of a naive desire to record the life of the age or an attempt to improve communications through mechanical means of reproduction, as has previously been argued,[16] we need to understand their cultural significance for those who produced and acquired them and thus demonstrate the ways these images actively articulated the structure of social relations.

The multitude of subjects represented in woodcut imagery has made it impossible for me to consider the cultural implications of the iconographic repertoire as a whole and still do justice to the problems of interpretation posed by particular themes. I therefore decided to address individual subjects rather than to try to characterize the overall nature of the production. The themes discussed in the following essays—representations of peasants, warriors, and wives—have been chosen for the light they shed on cultural attitudes toward three important social institutions: class, war, and marriage. Understanding these images as cultural "representations" lets us appreciate them as aspects rather than as reflections of social reality. Whereas the notion of representation as mimesis, as determined in part by considerations inherent in the artistic process alone, has tended to ensure its status as a politically neutral activity, analyzing these images as the site of the production of cultural meaning helps us recognize the extent to which they were politically determined.

Recent years have witnessed significant changes in the intellectual climate in which art history is produced. The attitude that tended to shun theoretical issues in the interests of making the discipline a positivistic science has been decisively challenged. Authors such as Svetlana Alpers, Michael Fried, and David Summers, on the one hand, and Michael Baxandall, T. J. Clark, Norman Bryson, Linda Nochlin, and Griselda Pollock on the other have effectively exposed the poverty of a discipline that refused to define and articulate the nature of its own enterprise.[17] Their fresh critical perspectives and innovative interpretive strategies have demonstrated how far the positivistic tradition remains wedded to theoretical models that are unexamined and unproductive. Broadly speaking, one might argue that the former—Alpers, Fried, and Summers—have undertaken the critique of traditional art historical practice from what might be called an "internal" position. They approach works of art as having a self-evident aesthetic status that gives the artistic tradition a coherence and an autonomy that makes analyzing their internal structures more important than analyzing their social and cultural function. For the latter—Baxandall, Clark, Bryson, Nochlin, and Pollock—the artistic tradition is something far less autonomous and self-contained, and the aesthetic status of the work of art is frequently downplayed in favor of understanding its role as a cultural artifact within a social setting. Within the context of such work, this book is more deeply indebted to the latter tradition than to the former. However, it is important to specify the character of the interpretive scheme used in essays that follow in order to define the ways their conclusions have been colored by my theoretical assumptions.

The interpretive strategies used in this book rely heavily on both the theoretical and the historical writings of Erwin Panofsky. However, they also depend on radically different assumptions and have very different aims. Both the similarities and the differences are worth describing. First, I refuse to subscribe to his notion that art history should be dedicated to the analysis and interpretation of great works of art. Although Panofsky was prepared to consider all images, no matter how humble, in the course of his "iconographic" studies, he always treated them as secondary sources used to elucidate works that were securely ensconced in a certain aesthetic canon. While his definition of that canon invoked tradition, or the received opinion of aesthetic judgment current in his day, it also depended, in the treatment of Renaissance works, on the values found in humanist art theory and could thus be said to reflect the artistic values of the social elite of that age.[18] The application of this notion of artistic excellence, however, meant that artistic imagery of the kind discussed in this book, produced beyond the limits of humanist culture, was not deemed worthy of serious art historical attention.

Panofsky's predilection for the art of the Renaissance was undoubtedly a consequence of his allegiance to a resemblance theory that sees representation as the product of the artist's confrontation with nature. For example, in his description of the "preiconographic" level of analysis, Panofsky appears to confuse reality and art by suggesting that our identification of the subject of a painting depends on our capacity to recognize the objects it represents. He makes no distinction between the way we interpret the actions of a man in the street and the way we interpret the subject of a painting.[19] One of the consequences of this view is that he found it necessary to consider landscape and still life incapable of being invested with the kind of meaning the "iconographic" and "iconological" levels of interpretation were intended to elucidate.[20] The most notable contemporary exponent of the resemblance theory, Ernst Gombrich, has argued that despite the degree to which the representational skills of individual artists may have been determined by the artistic conventions reigning in the period when they lived, it was still possible for them to check the representational models they had inherited against their personal perceptual experience.[21] However, the criticism leveled at this view in recent years by such authors as Nelson Goodman, Norman Bryson, and W. J. T. Mitchell would insist that there is no such thing as "universal visual experience" and that representation is an entirely social construct.[22] Rather than see representation as in any way dependent on the artist's experience of the world, this view would deny that direct access to phenomena is possible and insist that the work of representation consists instead in manipulating systems of signs. The work of art's relation to the world it represents would thus no longer depend upon its resemblance to that world but would depend on its capacity to denote it. As Goodman points out, a picture resembles nothing else so much as another picture.[23]

For the social historian of art, one of the most attractive corollaries of adopting a semiotic view of the work of art is that its status as a sign system means it is wholly determined and shaped by the culture in which it has currency. Whereas the resemblance theory maintained that representation was based on a constant and thus ahistorical relation between the artist and the world, a semiotic theory would define representation within the historical horizon in which it occurred. For example, this view has important consequences for our understanding of illusionism. In severing the representation's link with phenomena, a semiotic approach has no special investment or interest in those periods of Western art traditionally privileged because they appeal to what Gombrich would have called our "universal visual experience." Rejecting the very possibility of universal perceptual experience, a semiotic approach would analyze illusionistic works in terms of their "reality effect."[24] In other words, the wealth of references such works make to our perceptual experience would be regarded as a sign system of connotational significance. Adopting a semiotic model of representation is thus a means of escaping the need to address what tradition has deemed "great" works of art.

The question whether it is possible to regard what Panofsky called the study of subject matter or "iconography" as the study of visual sign systems has been discussed by Hubert Damisch and Christine Hasenmueller.[25] While recognizing that many aspects of iconographic investigation approach visual motifs as if they were sign systems, Hasenmueller points out the importance Panofsky ascribed to their relation to literature and documentary evidence. Far from their being autonomous, Panofsky implies that visual motifs depend upon another "master" sign system—namely, the linguistic sign. The recognition that the historical study of visual motifs depends upon their relation to linguistic signs—that is, on the written record of the period when they were produced—does not mean we must abandon our understanding of the work of art as a sign system. On the contrary, it means that our interpretation of the work will depend upon our understanding of the relation between visual and linguistic sign systems for their historical persuasiveness. In the essays that follow I attempt to consider visual themes in light of the way analogous themes were used in the written culture of the sixteenth century. This does not mean images will somehow be "checked" against more reliable forms of information, for the varieties of written documents invoked will all be regarded as cultural "representations." Texts, like images, have been treated as projections of cultural consciousness.

Just as important as adopting a semiotic view of the work of art is recognizing its status as an ideological construct. By ideology, Marx and his followers meant what they called "false consciousness"—systems of thought sponsored and promulgated by the dominant classes as a means of concealing the true nature of class relations. According to this view, ideology offered people a means of rationalizing their existence in such a way that they remained unaware how far their economic welfare and social experience were dictated by the class that controlled the means of production. However, in describing the work of art as an ideological construct, I wish to invoke not this traditional definition of ideology, but rather the one first formulated by the French Marxist Louis Althusser.[26] According to Althusser, ideology is to be equated with systems of social signification. In other words, ideology is defined as cultural semiotics. On this view the word ideology is not meant to suggest an opposition between false consciousness and true consciousness, for insofar as consciousness its itself manifested in sign systems, it is ideologically determined. To put it another way, all consciousness and all systems of thought are ideological.

If ideology is equated with cultural sign systems and sign systems are regarded as projections of consciousness that are intended to make the world of phenomena intelligible, then it follows that all aspects of social life are ideologically meaningful. The importance of this point cannot be overstressed, for it is the means by which Marxist cultural criticism can escape the limitations of the "base/superstructure" model of society imposed on it by Marx himself. According to Marx, society was divided into a "base," which was thought to contain the means of production and the organization of labor, and a "superstructure" that consisted of all forms of cultural activity including religion, philosophy, and ideology. If ideology is identified with cultural sign systems generally, then it is present at all levels of society and the base/superstructure distinction is dissolved.[27] In characterizing the work of art as ideological, therefore, there is no suggestion that it may be said to reflect or transmit events taking place at some other, more fundamental level of society. Finally, by viewing the work of art as a structure of ideological sign systems, I assign it an active role in defining and manipulating class relations.

One of the implications of accepting a semiotic and an ideological definition of the work of art is that what Panofsky called iconological interpretation must be radically revised. Instead of regarding the work as a "symbolic form," or as a means by which a Kantian theory of knowledge would suggest that the structure of the human mind coincides with the structure of the phenomenal world to produce knowledge,[28] this approach treats the work as a sign system whose significance cannot be regarded as univocal. Rather than attempting to determine the meaning of the work in a way that implies that the intention behind its production can ever be fully known, this analysis must be regarded as a "reading" of the possible meanings such sign systems may once have been intended to produce. However, recognizing that works of art are ideological sign systems that are never univocal but are merely suggestive structures active in the creation of meaning does not imply that they are not susceptible to interpretaton. In fact it is precisely because the sign is not univocal that interpretation is necessary.

Norman Bryson has suggested that while it is possible to distinguish between efforts to interpret the significance of sign systems within the historical horizon in which they operated (to attempt to determine their "original meaning") and efforts to interpret the significance of those sign systems within the context of our own times (to afford an account of their "subsequent interpretation"), such a distinction is not a necessary one: "If one chooses to separate 'original meaning' from 'subsequent interpretation,' this is because one's historical horizon, forms of life, and institutions of interpretation conjoin one to do so; if we choose to dissolve the distinction 'original meaning' and 'subsequent interpretation,' it will be for the same reason. What we do and will do when we interpret is a matter, in other words, entirely in the domain of *pragmatics*."[29] The extent to which original meaning and subsequent interpretation can be distinguished will undoubtedly be determined by our understanding of the present. Hayden White has described the historian's position in the following terms: "Since the historian claims no way of knowing uniquely his own, this implies a willingness on the part of the contemporary historian to come to terms with the techniques of analysis and representation which *modern* science and *modern* art have offered for understanding the operations of consciousness and social progress. In short, the historian can claim a voice in contemporary cultural dialogue only insofar as he takes seriously the kind of question that the art and science of *his own time* demand that he ask of the materials he has chosen to study."[30] It will become clear that while the chapters that follow are informed by an intense appreciation of the way the historical horizon in which the work of art is situated defines its nature, and though they insist on the extent to which human consciousness is the product of historical circumstance, they are also written with an awareness that they themselves constitute a cultural representation that has been profoundly determined by the interests and attitudes of the culture to which their author belongs. Among the most evident of these contemporary values is the recognition that notions of class and gender must be invoked if we are to render the past relevant and meaningful not only to the cultural situation we find ourselves in today but to the one we may occupy in the future.

I

Nuremberg in the Sixteenth Century

The following account of the economic and social circumstances reigning in Nuremberg during the first half of the sixteenth century, together with a description of the city's political organization, religious establishment, and other important cultural institutions, is in no sense comprehensive. The history of Nuremberg in this period has been told many times, from varying perspectives.[1] This limited and selective sketch is intended only as a guide to the circumstances in which the images discussed in this book were produced.

Nuremberg was one of the largest cities in Germany at the end of the Middle Ages, being inhabited by between 40,000 and 50,000 people in the period 1500–1550.[2] Unlike that of neighboring Augsburg, the financial capital of southern Germany, Nuremberg's economy depended on its merchants and its manufacturing industries. Neither the size of the city nor its economic power can be regarded as an indication of the wealth of its inhabitants. Although the great merchant families, in whose hands the political power of the city was concentrated, lived like princes and identified themselves with the landed aristocracy, they constituted only a tiny fraction of the total population. More than half the inhabitants were artisans who lived a more or less precarious existence, continually threatened by unemployment and inflation.[3] It has been calculated that while the wages of unskilled workers doubled and those of artisan apprentices tripled during the course of the sixteenth century, living costs rose by an average of 400 to 600 percent during the same period.[4] Many artisans must have lived close to the poverty line, for during periods of scarcity, when the price of food rose above their purchasing power, the city council was forced to intervene with daily distributions of free bread, the *Herrenbrot*. In 1540–41, 13,000 people were regularly fed by these means, implying that close to a quarter of the city's population had difficulty supporting themselves.[5]

The political organization of Nuremberg in the early modern period was established following the Artisans' Revolt of 1348–49.[6] The defeat of the artisans led to a form of government that placed political power firmly in the hands of the patriciate. The city council, for example, consisted of forty-two men, of whom thirty-four belonged to the families of the patriciate and eight were commoners chosen from among the trades. The commoners functioned as witnesses rather than as active members, and their positions, which tended to become hereditary, were of no political significance. Of the thirty-four patricians on the council, twenty-six constituted an inner council composed of thirteen senior mayors and thirteen junior mayors. Within this exclusive group, power was further concentrated in the hands of a group of seven elders, all senior mayors. While there was, to be sure, a larger council consisting of two hundred members, these men were elected by members of the inner council. The larger body seems to have served only as a forum where controversial issues could be discussed or as an appropriate setting for announcing the decisions of the inner council.

In the aftermath of the Artisans' Revolt, the artisan class was deprived of all forms of political expression. Artisans were forbidden by the council to form guilds, and all aspects of their occupational lives were supervised and regulated. The council forbade any form of occupational association that implied group action, a regulation that was strictly enforced,[7] and it determined everything from the length of apprenticeships to the quality and price of the goods sold in the marketplace. The council's ordinances were enforced by a special court, one of whose judges, the *Pfänder*, had the full-time duty of supervising the operations of the marketplace. In addition, master artisans from each craft were made responsible for the actions of their fellows and were expected to inform the *Pfänder* of any infractions that came to their notice.[8] The autonomy of the artisan class was further threatened by the introduction of a capitalist organization of labor. Wealthy artisans banded together to finance the production of their fellows so as to control the prices demanded for their wares.[9] By extending loans or fixing prices, they established a monopolistic control over certain crafts. Since the new arrangements tended to keep prices artificially low, many artisans suffered a gradual erosion of their standard of living.

The power of the council and thus of the merchant patriciate made itself felt in all aspects of the city's life. Long before the Reformation, the council had begun curtailing the power of the church by intervening in ecclesiastical matters so that it gradually usurped the authority of the bishop of Bamberg, within whose see the city lay.[10] In doing so it acted like the governments of other leading German cities in the late Middle Ages, whose actions reveal a tendency for municipal authorities to take greater and greater responsibility for the spiritual welfare of their citizens.[11] The Reformation proved to be the means of completing this process. Unlike Augsburg, for example, in which a Catholic patriciate fought a prolonged holding action against the demands of a reformed artisanate, in Nuremberg the council led the introduction of Lutheran worship. Utilizing the power they had already won to appoint preachers to the city's leading churches, the council named Lutherans to these positions. In 1524 they stage-managed a "disputation" between representatives of the Catholic and Lutheran parties, organized so as to ensure that the latter won the day. This event was the pretext for the adoption of a whole series of decisive measures that effectively made the Lutheran faith the official religion of the city.[12] The Catholic clergy was forbidden to preach, the mass was replaced with a Lutheran service, the feast days were abolished, and a Lutheran seminary was founded. Shortly thereafter the monasteries were dissolved and their property was confiscated.

Of great importance in the council's assumption of responsibility for religious matters was Luther's teaching on temporal authority. Luther's early writings, composed during the period of his own revolt against Rome, claimed that the Christian—that is, the reformed convert—lived in two worlds, one controlled by the secular authorities and the other by God.[13] In the course of time this view, which envisioned a potential conflict of allegiances, was drastically revised. When Luther was charged with having instigated the Peasants' War of 1525 through his appeal to the conscience of the individual, he denied the charge by identifying himself with the social hierarchy and calling for a bloody suppression of the revolt. Later, with the success of the Reformation, he supported the newly constituted reformed authorities, both territorial princes and city councils, in their claims to control both the temporal and the spiritual lives of their people. According to this later view, the temporal and spiritual spheres no longer existed in a state of tension, so the latter could be supervised and administered by the former. In Nuremberg, the secretary to the town council, Lazarus Spengler, an early Lutheran convert and author of numerous Lutheran pamphlets, insisted on the council's power to regulate the religious life of the city.[14] Spengler's attitude led him on several occasions into confrontations with the city's Lutheran ministers, most notably Andreas Osiander. Whereas Osiander argued that the council should act as a secular extension of the spiritual authority of the Lutheran ministers, Spengler consistently maintained that religious affairs were within the jurisdiction of the secular authorities.[15]

Another aspect of the cultural life of the city that bore the stamp of the patriciate's power was the annual carnival procession or *Schembartlauf*.[16] This procession is first recorded in 1449, when it took place in association with a much older tradition, the butchers' dance. The latter, documented as early as 1397, was regarded in the early sixteenth century as having been instituted after the suppression of the Artisans' Revolt. According to the *Schembartbücher*, illustrated chronicles that record the events of each procession year by year, the butchers' dance was a privilege awarded them by a grateful council for their loyalty during the period of unrest. In the course of time the importance of the butchers' dance steadily diminished, whereas that of the procession, which was gradually taken over by members of the patriciate, grew steadily. The number of patrician participants, already half of the total by 1449, increased rapidly thereafter.[17] One of the consequences of the participation of the patriciate was that the costumes of those taking part became more elaborate and luxurious.

The patrician element seems to have been responsible for introducing the *Hölle* or "hells." These hells, which were a constant feature of the processions after 1475, were floats that were pulled through the streets on runners before being ceremonially burned in front of the town hall. The themes represented on the floats varied from year to year. They were often drawn from the subject matter of aristocratic culture—such well-known literary topoi as the garden of love or the storming of the castle of love. They also represented moralizing themes that made use of the court fool, a figure popular among the educated classes of German cities ever since the publication of Sebastian Brant's *Ship of Fools* in Basel in 1494. The floats also illustrated subjects that were accessible to literate and illiterate alike, such as old women being fired from cannons or eaten by devils, and child-eating monsters. Hans Ulrich Roller has suggested that the elaborate pageantry of the *Schembartlauf* in the late fifteenth and early sixteenth centuries was a way the patriciate could display its economic power as well as the imaginative vitality of its culture.[18] What began as an insignificant accompaniment to an artisanal celebration, the butchers' dance, was transformed into a celebration of the values of the city's dominant classes.

The *Schembartlauf* came to an end in 1524 when the town council imposed Lutheran values on the social life of the city. Its association with carnival meant it was regarded as a worthless form of popular entertainment that the orthodox faith had been benighted enough to tolerate. It was revived only once, in 1539, and it resulted in such a scandal that it was permanently abolished thereafter. The subject burned in the "hell" that year represented a ship occupied by fools and devils, in whose midst stood a clearly recognizable per-

sonification of the Lutheran minister Andreas Osiander carrying a large key
in one hand and a backgammon game in the other.[19] The key was a reference
to the debate over absolution in which Osiander had been embroiled with the
city council. Osiander had attacked the Lutheran ministers' practice of dis-
pensing general absolution of sins to their assembled congregations, insisting
that since a minister had the authority to grant or withhold absolution as he
saw fit, it was proper that it should be granted only individually. The key held
by the figure in the hell thus symbolized Osiander's claim to be able to release
mortals from the chains of sin. Osiander's claim, which would have significantly enhanced the power of the clergy, was vigorously opposed by Lazarus
Spengler and the city council. As in an earlier battle in which Osiander had
claimed the power to excommunicate sinners, the council won the day.

The contest of wills between Osiander and the council was well known to
the population as a whole on account of the former's persistence in preaching
about the matter despite the council's repeated instructions that he refrain.[20]
Osiander's satirization in the *Schembartlauf* is yet another indication of patrician control of this institution. Not only were participants often related to
council members, but on this occasion a member of the council, Jakob Muffel, was actually one of their number.[21] Needless to say, the public humiliation
of Osiander and the ensuing riot in which the mob attacked his house could
not be overlooked. Muffel was forced to resign from the council, and the
Schembartlauf was consigned once again to oblivion.

In the late Middle Ages Nuremberg was renowned for its carnival plays.[22]
These plays were sponsored and performed by artisans and artisan apprentices, though the participation of members of the patriciate is occasionally
recorded. They began as revues performed by a limited number of actors in
inns or in the street. Their subject matter often dealt with the life of the
peasantry, and they were filled with obscene and scatological humor. These
coarse peasant satires may be traced to chivalric literature of the High Middle
Ages, in which the figure of the peasant had been used both to mock the
mannered conventions of courtly society and also to uphold them by contrast
with the manners of a class for which they had no meaning.[23] The importance
of peasant satire for Nuremberg's artisans has been much debated. It has been
argued, for example, that the disguise afforded by peasant costume let artisans
temporarily transgress the rigidly prescribed rules of urban conduct laid down
by the council.[24] By masking their transgression in the clothing of those who
were traditionally excluded from the circle of civilized society, they also asserted the superiority of their own urban culture to that of the surrounding
countryside.[25] Although the carnival plays were not banned when carnival was

abolished, their character changed significantly during the course of the sixteenth century. In the hands of the Lutheran playwright Hans Sachs, the plays were toned down and altered by adding moralizing conclusions that left no doubt in the spectators' minds as to the instruction they were meant to draw from the outrageous behavior they had seen.

The political realities of the social life of Nuremberg—that is, the dictatorship of the patriciate—found expression at every level of culture. Even such an institution as the carnival play, so easily mistaken for a manifestation of popular sentiment, not only took its form from sources in chivalric literature but confirmed a sense of urban identity that depended on the leadership of the patriciate. In permitting artisans momentary escape from the iron morality imposed on city life through the council's manipulation of a religious ethic, the plays also asserted the moral validity of the status quo. In this manner the power of the patriciate was successfully propagated and extended to all aspects of the cultural life of the city's inhabitants, regardless of their social class.

With regard to its external policy, Nuremberg's status as an imperial free city made it a political entity with almost complete autonomy. During the Middle Ages the city had freed itself of its feudal obligations to the territorial princes who controlled the surrounding countryside by placing itself under the direct protection of the emperor. This arrangement was of advantage to both sides, for while the city obtained the right to arrange its own fate, the emperor gained a source of capital whose support he could count on in times of need. The economic growth of Nuremberg at the end of the Middle Ages made it a leader among the imperial free cities. Since the beginning of the fourteenth century it had had the honor of hosting the first imperial diet (meeting of the representatives of the estates, or political entities that made up the Holy Roman Empire) of each reign. In 1423 the emperor Sigismund had transferred the imperial regalia, together with a collection of saints' relics, from Prague to Nuremberg. These relics played an important role in the life of the city before the Reformation, being exhibited at an annual fair known as the *Heiltumsmesse* or "reliquary fair."[26] The council commissioned Albrecht Dürer to paint portraits of the emperors Charlemagne and Sigismund to be exhibited on such occasions.[27] The event thus became a way the city could celebrate publicly its identification with the imperial cause. In the sixteenth century the city became the seat of the imperial law courts as well as of a short-lived imperial council that Maximilian I instituted in an attempt to centralize the administration of the empire.[28]

Nuremberg's relations with the emperor underwent severe strain with the coming of the Reformation. As we have seen, the city council rapidly opted for the reformed side while Charles V became the champion of those estates that had remained Catholic. Despite these differences, Nuremberg worked hard to maintain its special relationship.[29] Indeed, its support for the emperor frequently separated it from the rest of the reformed cities and territories and identified it with the Catholic camp. It refused, for example, to join the confederation of reformed estates formed to oppose Charles V at Schmalkalden in 1530.[30] At the Diet of Augsburg in the same year, the city flouted the reformed strategy of withholding financial support for the emperor's war against the Turks until he granted a degree of religious liberty.[31] Similarly at the Diet of Regensburg in 1532, when the empire was threatened once again with a Turkish invasion, the city broke the resolve of the other imperial free cities by being the first of the reformed estates to vote a subsidy.[32] In the years that followed, Nuremberg pursued its pro-imperial policy in isolation. In 1535 the city joined an alliance of Catholic princes and cities under the leadership of Ferdinand of Austria, brother of Charles V; in 1537 it again refused to join the Schmalkaldic League as the latter prepared to make war on the emperor; and in 1541, at another Diet of Regensburg, it was once more the only reformed estate to vote the emperor a subsidy for his war against the Turks.[33] Thus, during the period that concerns us, the Reformation and its aftermath, the city's identification with the imperial cause was part of its communal identity.

The council's identification with the emperor could only have been enhanced by the spread of humanist culture among the upper classes.[34] Deeply impressed with the revival of letters that had taken place in Italy during the Renaissance as part of a project to revive and surpass the glories of ancient civilization, German humanists were eager to lay claim to the same heritage. The emperor figured prominently in this enterprise, for it was through him and the Holy Roman Empire founded by Charlemagne that they too could claim to be true descendants of the ancient Romans.[35] A curious form of historical geography was to become the focal point of this nationalism. Aeneas Sylvius Piccolomini, bishop of Siena and later pope Pius II, was for some time bishop of Ermland in East Prussia. In 1448, after his return to Italy, he composed a description of Germany that was in part modeled on the recently rediscovered manuscript of a Roman account of that country and its inhabitants by Tacitus.[36] Piccolomini's text, which was published in Germany only in 1496 but had circulated earlier in manuscript form, proved the inspiration for a number of works by German humanists in praise not only of the landscape but of the people and history of their native country. Hartmann Schedel made extensive use of Piccolomini's work in composing the text of the *Nurem-*

berg Chronicle of 1493, one of the most lavishly produced and illustrated early printed books published in Nuremberg.[37] In 1495 Conrad Celtis, who had been crowned poet laureate of the empire in Nuremberg by Frederick III in 1487, composed a poem about the city that was meant to serve as the model for a much more ambitious work, the *Germania illustrata*, that he never completed.[38] In the earlier poem Celtis claimed that Nuremberg lay at the heart of the empire, close to a source from which four rivers flowed, a location that was obviously intended as an analogy with the landscape of Paradise. The origins of Nuremberg's culture were traced to the wisdom of the Druids, who allegedly came to Germany after they were expelled from Gaul by Tiberius. German learning thus preceded that of the monks of the orthodox church who came later. In this manner Celtis wove together his resentment of Italian claims to cultural superiority with his anticlericalism to produce a myth that satisfied his romantic nationalism.

The internal and external politics of Nuremberg during the Reformation appear to present a paradox. On the one hand the city council introduced and supported the Lutheran faith as a means of securing its control over all aspects of its citizens' lives; on the other hand it actively supported the activities of the emperor, the most powerful representative of Catholicism in Germany. As we have seen, these interests regularly came in conflict and caused the council considerable embarrassment. One way to understand this unresolved conflict is in light of Luther's theory of "two worlds." Having accepted the right to regulate the religious life of its citizenry on the principle that spiritual considerations should bow to secular authority, the council seems to have viewed its relations with the emperor in the same way. Lazarus Spengler, for example, consistently argued that the reformed estates had no right to take up arms against the emperor because the emperor was a divinely instituted authority against whom there was no appeal. Spengler expressly equates the status of the council before the emperor with that of the citizen before the council.[39] Just as the council insisted that its own subjects acknowledge its authority in all matters material and spiritual, so it bowed before the authority of the emperor. As we shall see, this profound dualism about the "right" and the "real," between the moral and the politically expedient, is also a characteristic of some of the images that will concern us.

2

The Media: Woodcuts and Broadsheets

The woodcuts and broadsheets discussed in this book belong to artistic traditions created during the course of the fifteenth century. Considering the nature of these traditions will afford us insight into their social status and function during the Reformation. One of the primary functions of fifteenth-century woodcuts was to supply cheap versions of widely venerated devotional images for those who could not afford their painted or sculpted equivalents. Early woodcuts often reproduced more famous images from other media that had become known for their miraculous properties, including those that were the objects of pilgrimages, or images of relics that were subject to special veneration.[1] One aspect of the devotional function of such images was the magical power worshipers attributed to them. This accounts, for the popularity of images of Saint Christopher, for example, since the mere sight of his image was thought to protect one from sudden death.[2] Another aspect was that they were intimately tied to the trade in indulgences. Subjects such as the "holy face" of Christ or Christ as "man of sorrows" were printed together with short prayers and promises that specified the number of years in purgatory to be forgiven worshipers who recited them.[3]

The association of single-leaf woodcuts with popular devotion was still common in the early sixteenth century. Albrecht Dürer drew a distinction between them and his artistically more ambitious work in other media. In 1505, for example, he made a number of devotional images that he later referred to as *schlechtes Holzwerk*, "simple" or "modest" woodcuts.[4] These prints appear to have been consciously designed to fit the preexisting character of devotional woodcuts. They consisted of simple figures rendered mainly in outline, devoid of the complex modeling in light and shade that characterized the rest of his figural work in this period. Their simplicity contrasts strikingly, for example, with his woodcut illustrations for the *Life of the Virgin*, a luxury printed book he was working on at the same time. The latter are filled with anatomical ideals and spatial constructs borrowed from the theory and practice of the Italian Renaissance.

Another function of early woodcuts was their use as illustrations for printed books. Woodcuts were associated with the new art of printing from the time of its invention in the mid-fifteenth century. Indeed, they played an important role in one of the forerunners of the printed book, the "block book," in which the text was carved into the same wooden block as the image. In addition, they had often been stuck into manuscripts as a cheap substitute for illumination.[5] The similarity of the processes of printing from a woodblock and printing from type meant that the woodcut was a natural ally of the new invention. Both are relief prints that can be produced in presses exerting relatively little pressure. By the early sixteenth century the centers of woodcut production were no longer the monastic communities that had first promoted the mass production of devotional images, but printers who commissioned illustrations from local artists. Woodcut production in Nuremberg appears to have followed the same development from monastery or convent to secular printer's workshop as the rest of Germany. The earliest woodcuts produced in the city are devotional images dating from the first half of the fifteenth century that can be associated with the Dominican convent of Saint Catherine.[6] Following the establishment of the first printing presses after 1470, woodcut production passed into the hands of the printers, who acted as entrepreneurs and commissioned illustrations from local artists. In 1493 Anton Koberger, Nuremberg's leading printer, ordered woodcut designs from the city's most prominent artists, Michael Wolgemut and Wilhelm Pleydenwurff, for the illustrations of the *Nuremberg Chronicle*, by the humanist scholar Hartmann Schedel, which appeared in 1493.[7] The drawings supplied by these artists, along with some by Albrecht Dürer, who was an assistant in Wolgemut's workshop at the time, would have been cut into the blocks by professional block cutters.

The association of woodcuts with printing took a variety of forms. By the early sixteenth century it appears that certain block cutters or *Formschneider* had broken away from the printing workshops to become printers who specialized in broadsheets that combined images and texts on a single sheet.[8] Another group involved in the specialized production of broadsheets were the "sheet colorers" or *Briefmaler*. The *Briefmaler*, who appear to have had their origins in manuscript illumination, thus became autonomous printers of the same kind as the *Formschneider*.[9] These entrepreneurs commissioned texts and drawings that they would then have rendered into type and cut into blocks to be printed together on single sheets. It is hard to generalize about the subject matter of the production of these broadsheet manufacturers. Their prints illustrated many secular subjects in addition to religious ones. Among the former were many moralizing themes. It is thought, for example, that the chapters of Sebastian Brant's *Ship of Fools*, which appeared in Basel in 1494 and made use of the notion of folly to criticize moral failings of all kinds, were originally distributed in broadsheet form.[10] Other popular secular themes were the dance of death, reports of executions, and alleged eyewitness accounts of celestial apparitions and misshapen births.[11] The last were frequently used to make moralizing statements about God's anger over the state of human affairs as well as predictions about the future.

Early in the sixteenth century woodcuts found a new function when they were used in the creation of humanist propaganda for the emperor Maximilian I. These publications were of truly gigantic proportions. The *Triumphal Arch*, produced between 1515 and 1518, is composed of 174 woodcuts that, when arranged into a composition resembling a Roman triumphal arch, stands nearly four meters high.[12] The *Triumphal Procession*, executed in 1516–19 but not published until 1526, is made up of 137 woodcuts and measures fifty-four meters long.[13] The text for the *Triumphal Arch* was composed by Maximilian himself and the court historian Johannes Stabius. This text was then illustrated, first in miniatures by Jörg Kolderer and then with woodcuts by Albrecht Dürer and others. The program of the *Arch* was much modified in its production by Dürer's humanist friend the patrician Willibald Pirkheimer. In 1512 Pirkheimer had translated the *Hieroglyphica* of Horus Apollo. Though this was actually a Roman work that essayed an interpretation of the hieroglyphs, early humanists regarded it as the key to Egyptian texts.[14] As a consequence these fascinating symbols, which were regarded as a dimension of the learning of antiquity, were incorporated in the design. The text of the *Triumphal Procession*, on the other hand, was dictated by Maximilian himself and merely edited by Stabius. This was once again rendered in miniatures by Jörg Kolderer and Albrecht Altdorfer before being transformed into woodcut designs by Hans Burgkmair, Albrecht Altdorfer, and Albrecht Dürer and his workshop. While working on the *Triumphal Procession* in 1516–18, Dürer and Pirkheimer developed the design and program for a third project, the so-called *Large Triumphal Wagon*, published in 1522.[15]

Maximilian conceived of the *Arch* and the *Procession* as a memorial to himself. Fascinated with the new technology of printing, he added this medium to the more durable materials of painting and sculpture in which he also had his accomplishments recorded for posterity. When he died in 1519, only the

Arch had been published. According to an inventory taken at his death, seven hundred impressions had been taken from the blocks.[16] Some indication of what Maximilian had intended to do with them can be gleaned from the way his heir, Ferdinand of Austria, dealt with this and the other projects upon their completion. Ferdinand regarded them as similar to the self-aggrandizing quasi-chivalric romances Maximilian had composed in his honor; he had them printed in limited editions of three hundred impressions and distributed to the leading nobles and imperial officials throughout the empire.[17] When some impressions of the *Procession* appeared on the open market in the territory controlled by the city of Nuremberg, their sale was considered illegal, and the city council apologized to the emperor for the incident. Maximilian's "giant" woodcuts were thus intended for an upper-class audience rather than for the public as a whole. In casting Maximilian in the guise of a latter-day Roman emperor, such prints were calculated to appeal to the nationalist sentiment that animated the humanist movement in Germany—a movement that found some of its strongest adherents among the upper classes.

The sturdy quality of the woodblock undoubtedly contributed to its adoption for the illustration of early printed books. Unlike the copper plates used for engraving, whose incised lines tended to wear down after printing a few hundred impressions, woodblocks could be counted on to produce thousands of copies before suffering significant damage. Editions of early printed books illustrated with woodcuts are estimated to have averaged between a thousand and fifteen hundred copies.[18] The same woodcuts, moreover, are known to have had a life that far exceeded their original purpose. They were in fact one of the more valuable possessions of early printers, who used them to illustrate books of widely differing content and sold them to others for use in different cities or even foreign countries.[19] Whether editions of woodcuts and broadsheets approximated the size of those of early printed books is difficult to ascertain. Authors working on broadsheets have suggested that these were issued in editions of approximately a thousand copies.[20] The size of the original editions of either woodcuts or broadsheets cannot be calculated from the numbers in which they survive in present-day collections; their rate of destruction must have been rapid. While both were pinned to the interiors of homes and inns as a form of decoration, entertainment, and instruction,[21] broadsheets were also passed from hand to hand or read aloud before small groups.[22] Their survival thus depended on the fragility of the paper, the effect of sunlight on ink, and the speed with which their topical significance lost interest.

The cost of early woodcuts and broadsheets depended largely on the cost of paper. Paper first began to be produced in western Europe in the fourteenth century, and at the end of the Middle Ages it was still available only in relatively small quantities. The invention of printing created an enormous increase in the demand for paper, a demand that could not be satisfied. As a consequence paper accounted for somewhat more than half the cost of the average early printed book.[23] But the price of paper, and therefore of books, fell dramatically during the course of the sixteenth century. According to Rolf Engelsing the cost of books sold at the Frankfurt book fair between 1470 and 1513 fell 40 percent.[24] Little is known about the prices at which the woodcuts and broadsheets discussed here changed hands. The most reliable estimates are those of Bruno Weber, who has calculated that in the sixteenth century the average price of an illustrated broadsheet varied between four and eight pfennig.[25] We can form some conception of the significance of such a price by comparing it with the price of other basic items that figured in the cost of living. According to Weber, in 1522 two pfennig would have bought six eggs or three herrings, or one sausage or half a liter of cider, at a time when a master mason earned twenty-eight pfennig and his assistant twenty-four pfennig a day. While the relation between expenditures and income was doubtless mediated through the complex filters of social and cultural values, one might tentatively conclude that these prints were within the purchasing power not only of the upper middle classes, wealthy merchants, and professionals, but of master artisans and other artisans as well.

With the exception of the prints used in the imperial propaganda of Maximilian I, which were treated by both the donor and the recipients as valuable gifts, woodcuts and broadsheets are not known to have formed part of early print collections.[26] It appears that they were not considered collectible items, in the sense of possessing any aesthetic value, until late in the sixteenth century. The earliest known collection of woodcuts is the collection of broadsheets formed by a prominent Zurich pastor called Jakob Wik. Wik specialized in reports of celestial apparitions and other extraordinary natural events that were widely regarded as eschatological signs.[27] Like other early print collections, these works were assembled for the information they alleged to convey rather than as examples of valued artistic form.

If woodcuts and broadsheets were therefore within the purchasing power of a cross section of the population, how can we determine what groups or classes might have been interested in acquiring them? Some guidance might be afforded by the notion of literacy. Since broadsheets consisted of both image and text, we must suppose that those who bought them were literate enough to use the latter to elucidate the former. It has been estimated that at the beginning of the sixteenth century only 5 percent of the total population of Germany was literate. In the cities and towns, however, this proportion was considerably higher, probably about a third of the inhabitants.[28] To the number of those who could read themselves must be added those who listened to texts read aloud by others. Natalie Davis, Robert Scribner, and Rolf Engelsing have all emphasized the role of communal reading in the dissemination of texts.[29] In an age of religious turmoil, in which differing and conflicting worldviews competed, there must have been a burning curiosity on the part of literate and illiterate alike about the information being communicated by means of the printing press. The increase in literacy during the years of the Reformation was, in fact, enormous. Engelsing has compared it to similar increases that took place in eighteenth-century France and twentieth-century Russia as a consequence of the French and Russian revolutions.[30] Thus, in addition to those occupational groups that were traditionally able to read, such as merchants and professionals, a variety of other occupations would in all likelihood have become interested in the products of the printing press as a means of access to the religious ideas that were transforming their society. Literacy thus is of little help in determining what groups or classes may have been interested in the broadsheets beyond the suggestion that they would have been more accessible to those who had traditionally been literate than to those who had not. On the other hand, the very expansion of literacy taking place in these years made these broadsheets available to a larger and larger audience.

The association of broadsheets and woodcuts with the book publishing industry meant that the city council included *Formschneider* and *Briefmaler* in its censorship regulations.[31] According to the ordinances enacted in 1513, all publishers were required to swear an oath of loyalty and obedience to the city council once a year; forbidden to issue any text or image that might cause injury to private individuals, groups of citizens, the clergy, or any secular authority; and required to present a list of all works purchased at fairs to the council's appointed censor before offering them for sale.[32] After the outbreak of the Reformation these ordinances were frequently repeated and strengthened. In 1523 the *Formschneider* were summoned before the council, where they were warned against the publication of scandalous broadsheets and forbidden to publish anything without the council's permission.[33] In 1527 both *Formschneider* and *Briefmaler* were required to enter their names in the council's book of trades, just as book publishers were, and ordered once more not to publish anything without permission. In addition, they were ordered to appear before the authorities once a year, with their apprentices, to swear an oath of loyalty and obedience.[34]

The policy of the council in enacting this legislation may be inferred from the personality of the first censor. This post was filled until 1528 by Lazarus Spengler, secretary to the city council. As we saw earlier, Spengler was an architect of the Reformation of Nuremberg, a man who had claimed for the council the ultimate responsibility in ecclesiastical matters. The only limits Spengler recognized on the council's authority to determine the fate of its citizens arose when that authority conflicted with the higher authority of the emperor. In adopting the Reformation the city had placed in grave jeopardy its relationship with the emperor, who continued to support the Catholic cause. Despite the gains made by wresting control of spiritual concerns from the Catholic church, the interests of the patriciate would be undone should the emperor's displeasure turn to violence. It was therefore important that the council attempt to ensure that its inhabitants give him no further cause for annoyance.

The passage of the censorship ordinances, however, seems to have been more important than their enforcement. While Spengler and the Lutheran ministers who succeeded him in the censor's role sporadically sought to restrain the city's presses—together of course with the *Formschneider* and *Briefmaler*—from their more outrageous attacks on the papacy and the Catholic church, this policy was honored more in the breach than in the observance. Not only were the works of Martin Luther and other reformers openly published and sold, but the city was flooded with anti-Catholic broadsheets.[35] Examples of the type of broadsheets that escaped the censor's notice were *The Roman Clergy's Procession into Hell* of 1524 (fig. 2.1) and *The Fall of the Papacy* of about the same time (fig. 2.2), for which Hans Sachs provided texts and Sebald Beham illustrations. The text of the former identified the orthodox clergy with the Babylonian captors of the children of Israel, and the latter proclaimed the pope's downfall despite the combined effort of the clergy and the secular princes to sustain him.[36] Another typical example is the virulently antipapal *The Seven-Headed Papal Beast* of about 1530 (fig. 2.3), illustrated by an anonymous artist and accompanied by a text by Hans Sachs. The image represents the pope as a seven-headed monster sitting on a chest used to collect the proceeds from the sale of indulgences, placed before a cross with the symbols of the Passion. In the text Sachs identifies the beast with the seven-headed dragon of the Apocalypse. As Scribner has pointed out, the image plays off earlier devotional woodcuts of instruments of Christ's Passion that were associated with the indulgence trade. An inscription hanging from the cross reads, "A sack full of indulgence may be obtained for money."[37]

None of this was lost on Charles V, however, whose informants kept him abreast of developments in the city. In 1524 he wrote the council an angry letter in which he complained bitterly that it tolerated the sale of Luther's works as well as the public preaching of his views.[38] One of the few examples of the council's determination to avoid offending Catholic sentiment was its confiscation of the illustrated pamphlet *A Wonderful Prophecy concerning the*

2.1. Sebald Beham, *The Roman Clergy's Procession into Hell*, woodcut. (Photo, Nuremberg, Germanisches Nationalmuseum.)

2.2. Sebald Beham, *The Fall of the Papacy*, woodcut. (Photo, Berlin, Staatsbibliothek Preussischer Kulturbesitz.)

Papacy, published by the *Briefmaler* Hans Guldenmund in 1527. This pamphlet was provided with a text by Nuremberg's leading Lutheran theologian Andreas Osiander as well as with short verses by the city's best-known poet and playwright, Hans Sachs. The text, which purported to explain the significance of thirteenth-century wall paintings allegedly discovered in the Carthusian monastery as a prophecy of the defeat of the Antichrist pope at the hands of Martin Luther, was illustrated by Erhard Schön.[39] The ambivalence of the council's position, however, is indicated by the fact that while it sharply rebuked Osiander, Sachs, and Guldenmund for their involvement in this affair, it eventually returned the woodblocks to Guldenmund and allowed him to

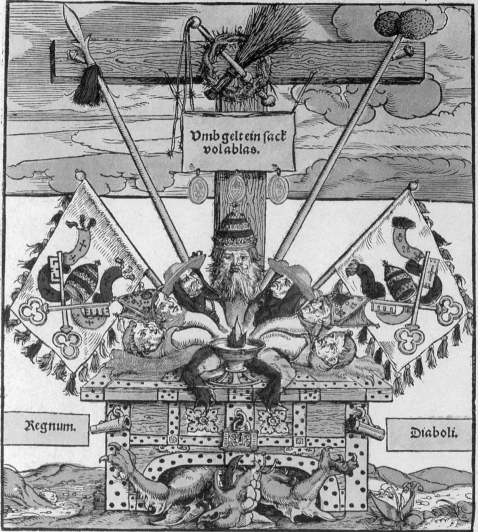

Umb gelt ein sack vol ablas.

Regnum.   Diaboli.

Schawet an das siben hewtig tier
Ganz eben der gstalt vnd manier
Wie Johannes gesehen hat
Ein tier an des meres gestat
Das hat siben vngleicher haubt
Eben wie diß pabstier gelaubt
Die waren all gekrönt bedewt
Die blatten der gaistlichen lewt
Das thier das het auch zehen horen
Deüt der gastlig gwalt vñ rumoren
Das thier trüg Gottes lesterung

Bedeüt jr verfürische zung
Das thier was aim pardel gleich
Bedeüt des Bapst mordische reich
Das auch hinricht durch tiranney
Alles was jm entgegen sey
Auch so hat das thier peren füß
Deüt das das Euangeli süß
Ist von dem bastuim vndertretten
Verschart/verdecket vñ zerknetten
Das thier het auch ains löwen mund
Bedeüt deß bapstum weiten schlund

Den doch gar nie erfüllen thetten
Aples/pallium noch annatten
Bann/opfer/peicht/stifft zü Gotsdienst
Land vnd leüt Künigreich rent vñ zinst
Das es alles hat in sich verschlunden
Das thier entpfieng ain tödlich wunden
Deüt das Doctor Martin hat gschriben
Das bapstum tödlich wund gehieben
Mit dem otten des Herren mund
Gott geb das es gar gee zü grund.
                              Amen.

2.3. Anonymous, *The Seven-Headed Papal Beast,* woodcut. (Photo, Berlin, Kupferstichkabinett, Staatliche Museen Preussischer Kulturbesitz.)

publish the illustrations on condition that he withhold the text. In addition, Guldenmund was voted twelve guilders to offset his losses.[40]

The status and function of single-leaf woodcuts and broadsheets during the first half of the sixteenth century was probably determined mostly by their association with the production of illustrated books. As the need for devotional images waned under the influence of the Reformation, *Formschneider* and *Briefmaler* vigorously exploited the technological capacity to combine images with texts. The reading skills vast numbers of people acquired in the heat of the doctrinal debate must have continued to shape the lives of those who had devoted time and energy to developing them. Indeed, the rudimentary literacy required to understand much of this production indicates that the entrepreneurs who commissioned both woodcuts and texts recognized and catered to the limitations of their audience. The expectations created during the Reformation, when broadsheets must have been regarded with lively interest as a major source of information on religious matters, were built upon by marketing a vast array of provocative themes dealing with all kinds of religious and secular issues.

THE ARTISTS

The preceding analysis of the medium of single-leaf woodcuts and broadsheets has implications for our understanding of the role of the artists engaged in their production. These implications are particularly important in the case of Sebald and Barthel Beham, who were responsible for many of the images discussed below. An important monograph by Herbert Zschelletschky has argued that the Beham brothers held radical religious views that led them to adopt an adversarial attitude toward the Lutheran patriciate of Nuremberg and that this attitude is discernible in many of their works, which are to be understood as attacks on the values of the dominant classes.[41] These views, the book claims, are especially evident in their production during the period of the Peasants' War of 1525. According to Zschelletschky, the Behams sympathized with the peasants, and this sympathy can be seen in their artistic creations. Although chapter 3, "Festive Peasants and Social Order," deals with specific aspects of these claims, the following pages examine the broader implications of this attempt to link biography and art.

Sebald and Barthel Beham were born in Nuremberg in 1500 and 1502.[42] While nothing is known of their early life, their work was so deeply influenced by that of Albrecht Dürer that it has been assumed their artistic training took place in his workshop. An important event in their lives, one on which Zschelletschky rests his case, was their arrest and imprisonment in January 1525, at the height of the Peasants' War, for having expressed radical views regarding the Bible and the sacraments. During their interrogation they said they did not believe in observing the religious rituals, including the sacraments of baptism and the mass, that had been preserved as part of the Lutheran faith. Furthermore they doubted the veracity of the Christian narrative, since they did not regard the Scriptures as sacred. Finally they said they recognized no authority other than God's.[43] The Lutheran ministers who reviewed their case concluded that their views were heretical and that since they showed no signs of repentance they should be expelled from the city.

How are we to understand these responses? What sort of religious convictions, if any, do they betray and did they constitute a challenge to the secular authority of the council? Zschelletschky argued that these views must be understood in terms of the revolutionary teaching of Thomas Münzer, who advocated overthrowing the social hierarchy in order to establish a society governed by the law of God, and that they represent an expression of the artists' sympathy for the peasant's cause in the Peasants' War of 1525.[44] Although it is uncertain whether Münzer visited Nuremberg at this time, Zschelletschky followed Georg Baring, who proposed that Münzer not only visited the city but lived secretly in the house of the schoolmaster Hans Denck, who was arrested at the same time as the Beham brothers.[45] Zschelletschky was thus able to suggest that the Behams came into direct contact with Münzer's revolutionary ideas. Disregarding the conjectural quality of their alleged meeting with Münzer, Zschelletschky equated the opinions of the Beham brothers with those of the radical preacher, asserting that they not only questioned the authority of the city council but actually plotted armed insurrection.

Zschelletschky's interpretation has been questioned by Günter Vogler.[46] Vogler also regards Hans Denck's views as crucial to understanding those of the artists, but he insists that they have little to do with the ideas of Thomas Münzer. According to J. J. Kiwiet, Denck's views were characterized by a mystical quality that identifies him with an important current of reformed thought known as spiritualism.[47] This attitude, which tended to place spiritual enlightenment above the external observance of religious ritual, is familiar to art historians as the faith of such figures as Abraham Ortelius and Christopher Plantin, with whom Pieter Brueghel is known to have associated.[48] Denck, who had been arrested because Sebald Beham mentioned he had discussed the mass with him, was an educated man, and unlike the artists he was asked to write a declaration of faith.[49] In this document Denck claimed to be guided by an inborn inner light that permitted him to find his way through a world of sin. He regarded the Scriptures as contradictory and useless unless read in accordance with this inner light. Because there was still so much darkness in him, he did not pretend to understand much of them. Whoever was not prepared to wait for God's enlightenment in such matters, thinking the Scriptures afforded the believer access to the truth, made a mockery of their meaning. Much the same attitude informs his views about the sacraments. Baptism is an external washing that has nothing to do with the inner life of the spirit and is unnecessary for salvation. The bread and wine of the eucharist are regarded as an allegory of the virtues of love and faith. Denck argued that it was possible to live without the former but not without the latter.

According to Vogler, it is likely that the Beham brothers shared Denck's spiritualist views.[50] Such an attitude would enable us to understand their denial of the validity of the sacraments as well as their rejection of the divine authority of Scripture, which is also the clue to their denial of the historical existence of Christ. Finally, it is possible that their failure to acknowledge the authority of the city council is not so much an expression of a revolutionary attitude as an affirmation of the primacy of their faith in the inner light. In fact it is only if we approach the Beham brothers' testimony in the light of the spiritualist position adopted by Denck that it is possible to understand why they were not more severely punished for their transgression. While there is no doubt the artists held radical religious views that challenged those of the Lutheran faith, which the council had adopted as the official religion of the city, it is clear that these could not have had the social implications Zschelletschky attributed to them.

Whereas Denck, whose position as schoolmaster of Saint Sebald's, one of the city's principal churches, made him an influential figure in the religious life of the community, was banished for life, the Beham brothers' expulsion was relatively short. Forced to leave Nuremberg in January 1525, they were allowed to return in November of the same year. Temporary expulsion was not the sort of punishment the council meted out to those it perceived as its enemies, especially during 1524 and 1525, when the Peasants' War had thoroughly alarmed the patriciate about the danger of popular unrest within the city walls. In 1524 two artisans who had attended peasant meetings in the countryside were ordered to leave the city forever.[51] In the same year, another pair of artisans who had spoken out against the council and its right to levy taxes were beheaded in the marketplace.[52] While the heretical views of the Behams would certainly have been regarded as manifestations of not only religious but civil disobedience, had they plotted armed insurrection as Zschelletschky has claimed, there is little doubt they would have been executed. Far from being implicated in a call for social change, the Beham brothers' views seem entirely compatible with the mystical ideas of Hans Denck.

Interpreting the religious and social views of the Beham brothers in 1525 is less important for our understanding of their art than is assessing the role such views played in their subsequent careers. The Behams did not remain in Nuremberg long after their return. Barthel left the city permanently in 1527 to become court painter to the Catholic dukes Wilhelm and Ludwig of Bavaria in Munich. In doing so he sought the patronage of rulers who were engaged in Counter-Reformation policy aimed at reimposing religious orthodoxy on a population that had been much affected by Lutheran ideas. Sebald also left Nuremberg temporarily in 1527 to work at Ingolstadt, a Catholic city, where he found employment illustrating books by Luther's archenemy the theologian Johann Eck. That the brothers could live and work as easily in a Catholic environment as in a reformed one implies that their personal religious convictions were irrelevant to their artistic production.

Sebald returned to Nuremberg in 1528 but was expelled again in the same year after being falsely accused of pirating Albrecht Dürer's ideas for a manual on the ideal proportions of the horse.[53] After an even briefer exile than in 1525, Sebald returned to Nuremberg before exchanging reformed for orthodox patrons once again in 1530, when he returned to Ingolstadt and illustrated another work by Eck. He then traveled to Munich, where the counts of Bavaria commissioned him to do a giant woodcut recording the celebrations held to celebrate the entry of the emperor Charles V into the city. The following year, 1531, he worked for Cardinal Albrecht of Brandenburg at either Aschaffenburg or Mainz, contributing miniatures to two prayerbooks and decorating a tabletop.[54] In working for Albrecht, Sebald associated with a figure who was intimately identified with some of what the reformers regarded as the worst spiritual abuses of the Catholic church. Albrecht had acquired the right to hold three bishoprics at the same time by paying Pope Leo X an enormous sum, which he financed by obtaining a loan from the Fugger family banking house of Augsburg.[55] When the pope permitted Albrecht to repay this loan by keeping half the proceeds raised by the sale of a special letter of indulgence, Luther condemned the transaction as a flagrant example of the venality of the orthodox church. Albrecht was also renowned for his massive collection of saints' relics (containing forty-two complete bodies and 8,133 particles), which depended on the worship of saints—a practice expressly repudiated by Martin Luther.

A review of the biographical information on the Beham brothers indicates that, far from being principled revolutionaries who sought to express their opposition to the Lutheran patriciate of Nuremberg out of a commitment to radical religious and social ideas, they were artisans who made a living wherever they could. Like his brother Barthel, who died in 1540, Sebald ended his days in a Catholic culture. In 1535 he left Nuremberg for good and settled in Frankfurt. Although Frankfurt was a Lutheran city at that time, it was occupied by imperial forces after the defeat of the Lutheran confederation in the Schmalkaldic War of 1546. The Proclamation of the Interim, the uneasy compromise between the faiths agreed upon in 1548, meant that the city's churches reverted to Catholic worship sometime before Sebald's death in 1550.

The Beham brothers, whose work was decisively influenced by that of Albrecht Dürer, appear to have shared his interest in the new subject matter as well as in the artistic vocabulary of the Italian Renaissance, together with his exalted view of the artist as an intellectual innovator rather than a routine craftsman. Patricia Emison has shown that their work in the media of engraving and etching is filled with mythological subjects and themes drawn from ancient history,[56] and Jayney Levy has described their willingness to experiment with both the form and content of the humanist tradition in a way that betrays a self-awareness of their role as creative inventors.[57] Their experimentation, however, must be viewed as contained within the limits of the culture of which the new vocabulary formed a part. To suggest that they could have turned their newly won control of the artistic language of humanism against the Nuremberg patriciate, as Zschelletschky asserts,[58] is to propose that they were willing to alienate themselves from the very class on which their livelihood depended. Zschelletschky's interpretation of the imprisonment of the Beham brothers in 1525 as a manifestation of their revolutionary views has perpetuated a romantic myth of the artists as autonomous creators who stamped their art with their personal beliefs regardless of the political and social circumstances in which they operated. Such a conception of their role is completely at variance with what we know of their place in the productive process.

With regard to the media of woodcuts and broadsheets—which they, like Dürer, must have regarded as *schlechtes Holzwerk*, or simple woodcuts meant for a popular audience[59]—the possibility of social criticism is reduced even further. In working for print publishers, the *Formschneider* and *Briefmaler*, they produced designs on commission for a public art form that had nothing to do with the assertion of personal artistic identity. Far from their being a vehicle by which the artist could either assert his or her unique artistic personality or express personal political ideas, the print publishers treated woodcuts as components in the mechanized production of cultural commodities. All that was required was that their images illustrate in a relatively legible manner the texts they were associated with. Although it is possible that these publishers were receptive to suggestions from the artists, such proposals would have had more to do with the anticipated audience—with the prints' marketability—than with the artists' personal opinions. In view of the severity with which the ruling elite had defended itself against threats to its authority during the period of the Peasants' War, the Beham brothers' use of woodcuts and broadsheets to question this class's values cannot be demonstrated without insisting that the status of the work of art has more to do with personal artistic expression than with the construction of social meaning.

3

Festive Peasants and Social Order

Among the secular subjects that became popular in the graphic media of engraving and woodcut shortly after their introduction into German art in the mid-fifteenth century is the figure of the peasant.[1] During the Middle Ages, peasants had appeared as staffage in Christian iconography—for example, in paintings of Christ's birth or of his Passion. They were also found in the illustrations of political treatises, histories, and agricultural handbooks, but they were most conspicuously present as a class in cycles of the months as represented in sculpture, tapestries, or illuminated manuscripts.[2] Beginning in the mid-fifteenth century, engravers were responsible for inventing a whole series of new images in which peasants played a leading role. Among these subjects whose cultural significance has still to be satisfactorily explained and whose popularity is not at present properly understood are some in which the peasant is represented as either dancing or drunkenly carousing.[3] Here I will focus on the analysis and interpretation of representations of festive peasants by Albrecht Dürer's Nuremberg followers. Within that context I will concentrate particularly on a woodcut by Sebald Beham known as the *Large Peasant Holiday* (fig. 3.1), executed in 1535.[4] Although this is by no means the earliest work of its type, it is associated with a sudden proliferation of images of carousing peasants that makes questions about their popularity and social function particulary intriguing.

The *Large Peasant Holiday* has often been interpreted as a fresh depiction of everyday life in which the artist's talent is displayed in his ability to convey the celebrants' boisterous vitality. In this and similar works the artist's approach to the peasants is regarded as sympathetic, and the image is thought to illustrate important changes in social attitudes toward this class brought about by the Peasants' War of 1525. According to Renate Maria Radbruch and Gustav Radbruch, for example: "The style of this art is naturalistic, not

3.1. Sebald Beham, *Large Peasant Holiday*, woodcut. (Photo, London, British Library.)

caricatural; its object is the representation of a robust, brutal, and obscene reality, without disgust for uncorrupted nature, without criticism or satire or moralization, but rather with a taste for the natural, the coarse, and perhaps the indecent. The peasantry had achieved at least one thing as a consequence of the Peasants' War—they could finally be seen as they really were."[5] Similar sentiments have been expressed by Herbert Zschelletschky: "These prints give the impression not of being the product of a laborious studio process, but rather of being fresh reproductions of a directly experienced reality recorded in sketches made in a sketchbook of Nuremberg's surrounding countryside."[6] According to Zschelletschky the historical significance of Beham's *Large Peasant Holiday* lies in its asserting the importance of the peasantry for society as a whole: "In his conception of the class existence of the peasant we

may see a reflection of the . . . Great German Peasants' War, which first brought the peasants as a class to the consciousness of all other classes."[7]

It is only in the older literature that one occasionally encounters a very different interpretation of these prints. Adolf Bartels, for example, wrote: "The artists of the period, who all belonged to a middle-class background . . . continually betray a satirical intention . . . to depict the arrogance and boorishness of the peasants as drastically as possible in order to enhance the position of the middle class."[8] For Bartels, therefore, the representation of peasants such as those in Beham's *Large Peasant Holiday* would be a satire rather than an unmediated reflection of reality; the image before us would reflect the imaginative application of malice to the characterization of the peasant as a visual subject. Another writer who viewed the type of peasant subject the

Beham brothers favored as expressing a negative attitude toward the peasantry was Kurt Uhrig: "Satires of peasant figures dominate following the crushing of the Peasants' War. . . . Everything dealing with the mockery and disdain of the peasants, which was still lively in the literature of a bygone age, was not taken up and represented in the visual arts, and the figure of the greedy, drunken, stupid, vulgar, boorish, and quarrelsome peasant was depicted with extrordinary freshness and vivacity by the fully conscious power of a newly aspiring young artistic movement."[9]

We are thus faced with two distinct and conflicting attitudes toward the interpretation of this woodcut. On the one hand there is a tradition that insists upon the "transparency" of Beham's imagery, claiming that what we see corresponds with what once actually existed. On the other hand there are those who in arguing the "opacity" of this image assert that it represents a comment upon social circumstances rather than a reflection of the circumstances themselves. These differing opinions in turn depend upon distinct interpretations of the significance of the Peasants' War of 1525. Those who believe in the transparency of peasant imagery suggest that the war permitted the expression of a favorable attitude toward the peasants as a class; those who insist on their opacity believe that the Peasants' War was responsible for a negative artistic image of the peasant.

This chapter evaluates these conflicting interpretations to establish, first, the extent to which images such as Beham's *Large Peasant Holiday* depend upon preexistent iconographic traditions as opposed to nature studies and whether there are correspondences between Beham's artistic imagery and that employed in the literary and dramatic traditions of his day. Second, it sketches the ways religious and social attitudes toward the German peasantry were affected by the Peasants' War and shows how they bear upon our understanding of the subject of Beham's print.

Before we embark upon a detailed analysis of the visual sources of Beham's composition, it will be useful to describe briefly the components of the scene before us. At first sight the surface of the woodcut impresses us as rich and varied, replete with incidents that have not been subordinated to any one particular event. In a landscape whose horizon is dominated by a castle, we are offered a view of the outskirts of a village filled with animated peasant figures. It is reasonable to assume that the scene represents a holiday, not only because any form of work is conspicuously absent but because the flag that waves from the church in the background indicates the celebration of a church festival.[10]

A wedding is taking place before the church door. This was the traditional location of such ceremonies throughout the Middle Ages, a custom still shared by many Protestants and Catholics in the sixteenth century.[11] In Nuremberg, however, a city ordinance of 1525, drawn up in consultation with the city's Lutheran preachers, established that marriages would no longer be celebrated outside the church, but would take place before the altar.[12] To a Nuremberg audience, therefore, that the marriage ritual in Beham's print is taking place in front of the church may very well have suggested that this was a Catholic ceremony. The sculpture of the Virgin and Child that adorns the doorway also suggests the orthodox faith. Luther was the most tolerant of the reformers on the issue of religious images, being prepared to permit their continued existence and manufacture on condition that they were not worshiped.[13] Devotional images of the type to which this sculpture belongs, however, were regarded as the least desirable because they served no instructional function. In Nuremberg such images were occasionally removed or covered in the years following 1525, on the grounds that they led superstitious worshipers into idolatry.[14]

The most interesting event on the left of the composition is undoubtedly the group constituted by the dentist, his patient, and his assistant. While the dentist operates on the unsuspecting peasant, the assistant surreptitiously robs the patient's purse.[15] The incident is given added pictorial prominence by the fact that it is being witnessed by the lovers on the bench on the left.

At the center of the scene is a table around which a number of people have gathered to drink. A couple behind the table embrace one another, and the man standing behind them raises his hand as if to express surprise. If one of the consequences of drink is desire, then another is manifested by the man who vomits in the immediate foreground. The location of this repugnant event at the center of the composition means the spectator cannot overlook it; rather, one's attention is drawn to it.

In the center before the doorway is a man whose costume identifies him as a priest, being respectfully offered a glass of wine by the man on his right.[16] Three additional figures are not dressed in peasant clothing—those standing at the extreme left and the extreme right of the table, as well as the man sitting to the right of the priest. All may be identified as *Landsknechte*, mercenary soldiers usually drawn from the lower order of society including the peasantry.

On the right there takes place a spirited row dance in which couples follow each other around in a circle. The most active couple, with the male partner lifting the female in the air, wear garlands. The woman wears a chaplet of

leaves around her head, and the man has one stuck in his hatband. Garlands were associated with marriage festivities, suggesting a thematic connection between the foreground festivities and the church ritual taking place in the background.[17] The couple dancing on the extreme right are not in peasant costume. Like the man at the center of the table, the man is dressed in priest's garb, while his companion wears the clothes of the urban middle class.

In the background a test of skill is taking place; a barefoot man leaps over upturned sword blades while balancing a glass on his head. Fierce fighting has broken out behind the bowling green, and the game of ninepins is about to be interrupted. Peasants have drawn large swords while their women

struggle to keep them from murdering one another. One man has taken advantage of the confusion to steal the cock from the top of the pole. Finally, in
the distance we can discern a horse race, a women's footrace, and some children wrestling.

The subject of the peasant holiday was not new to Sebald Beham when he
worked on the *Large Peasant Holiday*. Shortly before 1535 he had executed a
copy of a work by his brother Barthel on much the same theme.[18] Although
only the left side of Sebald's copy survives, the appearance of the whole may
be determined by Barthel's original composition (fig. 3.2).[19] Comparing this
woodcut with the *Large Peasant Holiday* (fig. 3.1) reveals that Sebald studied

3.3. Sebald Beham, *Church Anniversary Holiday at Mögelsdorf*, woodcut. (Photo, Gotha, Schlossmuseum.)

his brother's composition very closely and preserved its elements while reworking them into a spatially more coherent and artistically more accomplished whole. The row dance, the table set before the inn (whose company includes a priest), the game of ninepins, the sword contest, the brawl, even the women's footrace in the distance are common to both works. Specific formal borrowings are found in the disposition of figures in the fight scene as well as in the sword contest. In the former, the actions of the leading combatants, together with the body and the gruesome severed hand lying at their feet, are identical in both works; in the latter, the direction of the figures has merely been reversed.

The comparison establishes beyond doubt that Sebald Beham's woodcut of

1535 cannot be regarded as the product of direct observation from nature. One the contrary, it is clear that it is precisely the kind of studio work Zschelletschky was anxious to discount. While Barthel's earlier work demonstrates that Sebald's print can in no sense be considered a "mirror" of reality, it offers us no insight into the significance of the image for the age, beyond establishing that the subject of the peasant holiday must have enjoyed unusual popularity in sixteenth-century Nuremberg.

Greater insight into the historical significance of these peasant holiday scenes is afforded by a woodcut known as the *Church Anniversary Holiday at Mögelsdorf* (fig. 3.3).[20] Like the print just discussed, this work exists in two versions—an original by Barthel and a copy by Sebald. Both versions are

Der Nasen tantz zu Gümpelsbrunn bis Sonntag:

Eins tags vil kurtzweyl ich vernam
Vnd auff ein Pawren kirchtag kam
In ein dorff Gümpels prunn genant
Da ich vil voller Pawren fandt
Schreyend all stedel vol gesessen
Da war ein trincken vnd essen
Die Mayd in die Sackpfeyssen sungen
Die Pawren knecht lüffen vnd rungen
Warffen ein einander auff den semper
Das manchem kracht im leib der gemper
Eins teyls spulten in die Leckuchen
Noch mer kurtzweyl thet ich suchen
Vnd kam zu einem Hanen tantz
Da machtens wunderlich kramantz
Mit gnippen gnappen/vnd verdiecn
Das man in thet waiß wo hin sehen
Offt einer an den andern hust
Das er sich gleich vmb dieen must
Tratten einander mit den stheffeln
Ich dacht es wirde sich noch ach die steffeln
Ein hader bey dem trug vnd trag
Ich gieng vnd scharte den kugelplatz
Da hieng ein rotes Hoßbruch bey
Da sertzten sie offt zwen an drey
Ich gedachte mir ob disem kegels

Werden sie noch einander slegeln
Ich gieng furbaß auff einen plan
Sach da vil alter Pawren stan
Mitten darauff an einer stangen
Sach ich drey schöner kleynat hangen
Ein Nasenfüter büch/vnd krantz
Da sagt man mir ein Nasentantz
Wurde auff dem plan noch disen abent
Die größten drey naßn wurn begabent
Die größte naß gewun den krantz
Vnd wurde ein Küng am Nasentantz
Die ander gewun das Nasenfüter
Die drit die büch gar wolgemüter
Verzog ich da in meinen sinnen
Groißlich ein kleynat zu gewinnen
Wurde ich anders ein Küng gar
Re ich verzog ein viertel dar
Kamen zwen Pfeiffer mit Schalmayen
Die pliessen auff zum Nasen rayen
Her drungen Pawren vnd ir Basen
Vnzal/mit also grossen nasen
Lang dick/vnd krum henckt vnd pucklet
Murret muncket pieyt pflumsche/vnd hucklet
Fincket hacket knoret vnd knollet
Die eckicht viereckicht/vnd dickollet

Gleissent vnd rot küpffen vnd högret
Volengerling wimeret vnd knögret
So vnfug das ich auff den tag
Tantzens vnd kleynat gar verwag
In dem die Pfeyffer beyd auff pfiffen
Einander sie zum nasen griffen
Zogen einander an den rayen
Vnd sprungen her nach den schalmayen
Bey zweintzig person man vnd frawen
Daran ich meine lust thet schawen
Ich dacht wie wost ich jr so vil
Die all recht weren zu dem spil
Die wunschet ich all zu mir dar
Vnd als der tantz am besten war
Do erhub sich ein grosses schlagen
Am kugelplatz die wurden jagen
Einander her in dem gedöß
Wurd ein gelauff vnd groß gestöß
All liessen sie am rayen faren
Vnd auch von leder zucken waren
Do ward der Nasentantz zertrent
Jedoch der Scherg kam an dem ende
Vnd schrey der Richter vnd mein herren
Verkunden euch nahmen vnd ferren
Weyl der Nasentantz ist zerstrewt

Sol man nicht weyter tantzen herre
Biß Suntag wöllens in an stellen
Ob einer hat ein güten gsellen
Vnd der auch wol benaset wer
Den mag er mit jm bringen her
Sey Burger Pawr arm oder reich
Dem wirde man messen eben gleich
Mit zirckel daßhart vnd dreyangel
Das er sey vnklaghafft vnd mangel
Wem dem ein kleynat thut geburen
Der mags on einred mit jm füren
Also der kirchtag nam ein ende
Eylende ich wider heimwartz wende
Hab das beyd jungen vnd alten
Im besten wöllen nicht verhalten
Weyl der Nasentantz ist angestelt
Ob etwer einer daran wölle
Der mach sich auff biß morgen frü
So kumbt er eben noch darzu
Gen Gümpels prunn an Nasentantz
Vnd ob er da erlangt den krantz
Vnd wurde zu Nasen Küng erwelt
Allen grossen Nasen fürgestelt
Der funde vil dießund jenset des bachs
Vil Hoffgesindes/spricht Hans Sachs.

accompanied by verses written by Hans Sachs, Nuremberg's leading poet. The text of the poem determines the subject of the image. The first verse reads:

One day I went to a *Kirchweih*
At Mögelsdorf, where I saw
The peasants carousing
At a large inn.[21]

A *Kirchweih*, or church anniversary holiday, commemorated the founding of a particular church.[22] It was therefore a special holiday shared by members of a single congregation.

The identification of this scene of drinking and dancing peasants as a church anniversary festival suggests that similar prints by Barthel and Sebald Beham may also illustrate such celebrations. If so, then works like this characterize the commemoration of a religious event as an opportunity for riotous carousing. Sachs's attitude toward the goings-on is manifest, for example, in the third verse, where he describes the activities at the table:

The wine was knocked back so hastily
That many of them fell under the bench.
They also raised a great clamor of farting and spitting,
Shouting, screaming, singing, and crying.[23]

In addition the peasants are given ridiculous names, and their actions and comments are characterized as coarse and indecent. According to the thirteenth verse:

The donkey miller from Potenstain,
Who was the greatest drinker at the table,
Sprang about with Elsie the farmer's wife,
And squeezed her so close to him that she choked.[24]

Sachs's verses therefore characterize the peasants as greedy and drunken, gross and uncouth, as well as suggestive and obscene.

The association of church anniversary holidays with carousing peasants is also found in a broadsheet entitled *The Nose Dance at Fools' Town,* dated 1534, which was illustrated by Sebald Beham and provided with verses by Hans Sachs (fig. 3.4).[25] The scene includes many of the incidents found in Sebald's *Large Peasant Holiday* of 1535; dancing, eating and drinking, a merchant's stall, a bowling green, and a violent brawl. Once again the text affords us valuable information concerning the subject:

One day I found much enjoyment
In going to a peasant *Kirchweih*

At a village called Fools' Town.
There I found many greedy peasants
All full to the gills,
Eating and drinking and shouting.
The maids sang to the bagpipe music
While the youths ran and sprang about,
Throwing each other down on their backsides
So that many were badly hurt.[26]

Tiring of this entertainment, the poet decides to look for amusement elsewhere. He proceeds to the green in the foreground, where he is told that a
"nose dance" is about to begin. The prizes suspended from the pole are for
the largest noses entered in the competition. The largest will win a garland,
the second a nose sock, and the third a pair of underpants. Soon the pipers
begin to play, and we are told:

Peasants and their relatives came running up,
An enormous multitude all provided with long noses
Long, fat, and bent, droopy and pocked,
Crooked, snotty, broad, plump, and spotty,
Pointed, broken, knotty, and lumpy,
Triangular, rectangular, and round,
Glistening and red, coppery and bent,
Wormy, woody, and knotty.
So awful was this exhibition that
I completely forgot about that day,
About the dancing and the prizes.
When the pipers both played up
They [the dancers] grabbed each other by the nose
And pulled one another into the ring.[27]

Clearly Sachs does not describe a contemporary folk dance but rather portrays
an allegorical one that he has placed within the setting of the church anniversary holiday. Similarly, his comments upon the dancers cannot be interpreted
as directed at the peasantry, since his figures represent a type rather than a
class. The type he has in mind is, of course, the fool; and the allegory depends
upon the notion of Folly. Not only is the location of the celebration defined as
Fools' Town, but to pull someone by the nose was a well-known expression
meaning to decieve or make a fool out of someone.[28] These figures therefore,
who are said to pull each other by the nose, deceive one another.

It is important for our understanding of the subject of the *Kirchweih*, to
which the *Large Peasant Holiday* of 1535 appears to belong, that Sachs found
it a fitting setting for his allegorical dance of Folly. The ridiculous leaping of

his long-noxed dancers, he suggests, is perfectly at home amid the frantic goings-on with which he chooses to characterize the celebration of church anniversary holidays.

Having described the "nose dance," Sachs continues:

And when the dance was at its best
A frightful fight broke out
On the bowling green, where
They were busy chasing one another about.
    In the uproar
One was stabbed and the other ran away,
So that all the people left the dance.[29]

The fight therefore must be considered just another of the lurid incidents that enliven his account of the *Kirchweih*.

The prominence of dancing in these representations of church anniversary holidays is remarkable. Its usefulness in characterizing the peasantry as wild and unruly undoubtedly derives from the moral opprobrium in which dancing was held by religious and civil authorities alike. Not only were sermons and devotional treatises continually directed at what was regarded as a vice, but in Nuremberg, city ordinances also regulated it.[30] While all dancing was suspect, certain types particularly attracted the ire of moralists. These were uninhibited dances in which the female partner was lifted off the ground and either tossed in the air or whirled around. Such dancing seems to have particularly exercised Sebastian Brant, who in his *Ship of Fools* included the following comments in the chapter "On Dancing" (fig. 3.5):

There's naught more evil here on earth
Than giddy dancing gayly done
At kermess, first mass, where the fun
Is shared by priests and laity.
Where cowls can flap in zephyr's breeze
They swing their partners in the breeze
Till girls' bare legs high up one sees.[31]

The woodcut illustrating this chapter shows a number of couples dancing around the Golden Calf, dressed in fool's costume that is symbolic of their idolatrous worship of sensual pleasure. A male figure on the left of the composition has thrown his companion up in the air, thus raising her skirt. Their action bears a striking resemblance to the movements of a couple in the right foreground of Beham's work.

The dance performed in Sebald Beham's *Large Peasant Holiday* (fig. 3.1), as well as the composition by Barthel Beham on which it is based (fig. 3.2), is a "cock dance." The choice of this dance appears to be far from accidental, for it was endowed with suggestive connotations by its very name. As in English, the word *Hahn* or "cock" was used to refer to the male sexual member.[32] This dance was used in Nuremberg carnival plays of the late fifteenth century as part of a satirical form of humor based on the figure of the peasant. In the play entitled *The Old Cock Dance*, peasants compete for a cock and a pair of men's underpants.[33] The humor depends on the boastful way the peasants describe their dancing abilities before demonstrating them. The movements and gestures used in these displays must have offered many opportunities to heighten the comic impact of the play. Two of the peasants quarrel over whether a peasant girl has lost her virginity to one of them, and in the violent struggle that ensues one is mortally wounded. The play thus not only satirizes the nature of peasant dancing but suggests that peasants are amoral and violent as well. Another carnival play called *The Short Cock Dance* is openly suggestive.[34] Each of the male dancers in turn expresses his desire to make love

3.5. Albrecht Dürer, *Dance around the Golden Calf,* woodcut illustration to Sebastian Brant, *The Ship of Fools* (Basel, 1494), chapter 61, "On Dancing." (Photo, *Das Narrenschiff,* ed. Hans Koegler [Basel, 1913].)

to his partner. Far from being shocked by the comic double entendres in which these propositions are phrased, the peasant women accept them enthusiastically.

Confirmation of this reading of Beham's choice of a cock dance, as well as the use of vigorous dance postures and graceless gestures in characterizing it as a comment upon the nature of peasant dancing, is offered by the way dancers from other social classes are depicted by Nuremberg artists working at the same time. Cycles of aristocratic dancers were just as popular as those of peasants, and they constitute a counterpart to such subjects as the *Church Anniversary Holiday at Mögelsdorf.* An example, perhaps the earliest cycle of its kind, is the woodcut series by Georg Pencz and Hans Schäufelein that was published in Nuremberg between 1531 and 1535.[35] Part of the anonymous inscription above the figures of the leaders of this procession reads, "Let us lead the procession slowly / as is the custom of the nobility" (fig. 3.6).[36] The dancers who follow proceed at a measured and stately pace, their movements controlled and graceful. The inscriptions above the couples represent an exchange of courtly pleasantries that contrasts sharply with the suggestive banter of the couples in the peasant holiday scenes. A very similar poem published without illustrations, entitled *The Burgher's Dance,* was written by Hans Sachs in 1559. The poem begins with the following lines, "Let us lead the procession in an elegant manner / As is fitting for the burghers' class."[37]

Peasant and aristocratic dancing are contrasted in two engravings dating from the late sixteenth century by Johann Theodor de Bry,[38] whose format and scale indicate they were meant to be pendants. The inscription below the aristocratic dancers, whose movements are depicted as mannered and deliberate, reads: "Here is modesty, here honesty of character, here courtly persuasion, and charm, and noble restraint shines forth. What wonder if gods follow goddesses of their own accord?" That beneath the peasant dancers, who are represented in violent motion, whirling their partners around so that their feet leave the ground and contorting their bodies in grotesque dance steps as limbs flail about with abandon, reads: "As far as the court is from the sheepfold, so is the courtier from the peasants. This bawdy round dance will soon teach you that. But thus do the different sorts of life manifest themselves."[39]

The conclusion that the iconography of the peasant dance represents a satiric form of humor that depends upon a negative attitude toward the peasants as a social class is reinforced by an engraving by the Antwerp artist Frans Huys, dating from the middle of the sixteenth century (fig. 3.7).[40] The composition represents the interior of a shop, where a man and a woman holding

3.6. Hans Schäuffelein, *Dance Leaders and Torchbearers,* woodcut. (Photo, Berlin, Staatliche Museen Preussischer Kulturbesitz, Kupferstichkabinett.)

lutes confront each other. The text beneath the image communicates their conversation: "Master John Bad Head, will you string my lute? I will do so Dame Long Nose, but leave me in peace, because I must keep it for Mother Mule who also wants her lute fixed."[41] The print depends for its meaning on the sexual symbolism of the lute in the sixteenth century. It was used in literature, drama, and song to refer to a woman's sex.[42] The print thus represents a sexual allegory in which several women approach a man for his sexual services. In the background of this suggestive scene, attached to the wall above the mantelpiece, is a frieze of dancing peasants, copies of two engraved series executed by Sebald Beham in 1537 and in 1546–47.[43] The presence of the

MEESTER IAN SLECHT HOOT, WILT MIIN LVIITE VERSNAREN· ICK EN SAL VROV LANGNVESE, LAET MII ONGEQVELT.
WANT ICK MOETSE, VOOR MODDER MVIILKEN BEWAREN · DIE HADDE HAER LVIITE, OOCK SEER GEERNE GESTELT.

3.7. Frans Huys, *The Lute Maker's Shop*, engraving. (Photo, Amsterdam, Rijksprentenkabinet.)

peasants on the wall of what appears to be a peasant interior suggests that this social class is to be associated with sexual misconduct.

It is no accident that the representation of different styles of dancing was used as a vehicle for social comment. The Nuremberg Dance Statute of 1521, which established what families could attend dances in the city hall, also defined what families could have members elected to the city council.[44] These forty-five families constituted an oligarchy that retained its hold on political power in the city until the eighteenth century. The clear distinction drawn in both the visual and the literary imagery of the period between the way the aristocracy danced and the way the peasants danced, in which control and restraint are played off against uninhibited sensual enjoyment, represents a structural opposition with social and moral implications. These representations of the different classes function as two sides of the same coin, each defining the other. The manners of the patriciate, which are still presented in terms of an ideal of chivalry, are opposed to a vision of the peasantry as a class without a code of social conduct. Both were convenient fictions whose existence was required for the efficient function of a hierarchically organized society.

There is one aspect of Sebald Beham's *Large Peasant Holiday* that cannot be found in the representations of the *Kirchweih* developed by his brother

Barthel. This is the figural group of the dentist, his assistant, and his patient on the left-hand side of the composition. This amusing, if slightly sinister, incident is borrowed directly from an engraving by the Dutch artist Lucas van Leyden dated 1523 (fig. 3.8).[45] Lucas's composition was copied on the woodblock as it appeared in the print, so the image was reversed in the printing process. Other differences between the two works are relatively minor. Although there is no text in this case that can be used to decipher the meaning of the image, the composition contains within itself a comment on its ostensible subject. Instead of seeking his patient's welfare and thus fulfilling his role as healer, the dentist takes advantage of his privileged position to rob him. The point of Lucas's print depends upon the contrast between appearance and actuality, between the ideal and the real. That the dupe of the piece should be a peasant is undoubtedly a major component of the joke. An appreciation of the print's humor depends upon a certain alienation from the suf-

3.8. Lucas van Leyden, *The Dentist*, engraving. (Photo, New York, Metropolitan Museum of Art.)

3.9. Leonhard Beck, *The Dentist*, woodcut. (Coburg, Kunstsammlungen Veste Coburg.)

fering of the person being deceived. The spectator's privileged position enables him or her to laugh at the patient's discomfiture from a safe and superior distance. Because the image insists on a lack of identification between viewer and patient, it is possible for us to regard him as simple, naive, and even stupid for allowing himself to be trapped in such circumstances. The incident's characterization of the peasant as gullible contributes to our overall conception of his class already partly defined by the peasant dance. It informs us that not only are peasants a rude lot, but they are not particularly intelligent either.

A woodcut of about 1521 by the Augsburg artist Leonhard Beck appears to be another caricature of the dental profession (fig. 3.9).[46] The figure and expression of the tooth puller, who triumphantly waves the extracted tooth at his audience to publicize his success—along with the striking advertisement for the effectiveness of his parasite cure, as well as the entire drawing's rather tenuous grip on reality, which reminds one of the simplifications typical of cartoon art—suggest that this is an attempt not to record an event but to offer a humorous image of a comic type. Certainly Hans Sachs understood this image as caricature according to the satirical verse he is thought to have added

ISB

Aspice quàm suaueis quærat sibi turba leueisque Rustica delicias, celebrans Encænia Baccho. Nulla Sacerdoti reuerentia, nulla Dynastæ, Cum quouis jugiter potius sua Gretula saltat.
Pictura:um omnium, imprimis verò chalcographicarum, admiratori vero, sincero, et excoptando Stephano les Pre-
rano, festum hoc rusticanum (vt, et sogdenter socuit huius delicias) ab, examie iste Sebaldo Bohemo olim derg-
natum, nunc verò compendiosè iari incisum, lubentissime deducit Ioan. Theodorus Bryeus
calcator ac diuulgator.

3.10. Johann Theodor de Bry, *Peasant Holiday*, engraving. (Photo, New York, New York Public Library.)

in 1569.[47] The negative attitude toward dentists evinced by these prints finds a counterpart in the figure of the doctor or dentist on the German stage in this period. In the Nuremberg *Fastnachtspiele* or carnival plays of the fifteenth century, as well as in Hans Sachs's contribution to this genre in the sixteenth century, the doctor is consistently presented as a quack and a charlatan who makes a living by taking advantage of gullible peasants.[48]

An analysis of Sebald Beham's *Large Peasant Holiday* in terms of iconographic precedents has proved fruitful for understanding the meaning originally associated with his image of the peasant celebration. Equally illuminating is the way his composition was interpreted by subsequent artists. Toward the end of the sixteenth century Johann Theodor de Bry executed a very close engraved copy in reverse, which is provided with the following Latin inscription (fig. 3.10):

Look at the way the rustic crowd
Seeks sweet and transient delights
While celebrating the foundation feast of Bacchus.
They reverence neither priests nor rulers,
For their [the mob's] Gretchen dances with whoever she pleases.[49]

In Beham's composition Johann de Bry found the means to formulate a negative comment about peasant mores. The celebrating peasants are accused of heeding neither spiritual nor temporal authority when they are determined to get drunk. In 1559 a Flemish artist called Pieter van der Borcht executed an engraving that is clearly indebted to Beham's work or to a Netherlandish copy (fig. 3.11).[50] Far from being a slavish repetition of the original, it is an imagi-

54

native reworking of its themes. The number of figures, for example, is multiplied so that it seems that we look upon a sea of peasant exuberance and excess. The dancing is more frantic, the drinking more uninhibited, the fighting more murderous, yet we can still make out the underlying forms of Beham's composition. The print is accompanied by the following inscription:

Drunkards rejoice in such feasts,
Arguing and fighting and drinking themselves as drunk as beasts.
Therefore let the peasants hold their feasts
And go to the church festivals,
Whether they be men or women.[51]

Pieter Brueghel executed a similar print in the same year, the *Fair at Hoboken*, that bears a text almost identical to the one cited above.[52] Brueghel and van der Borcht therefore found Beham's imagery a means of commenting upon villagers' abuse of church holidays. By the mere addition of a text they made his composition the vehicle for a moralizing comment upon a contemporary

3.11. Pieter van der Borcht, *Peasant Holiday*, engraving. (Photo, Rotterdam, Boymans-van Beuningen Museum.)

Ein neuwer Spruch/ wie die Geystlicheit vnd etlich Handtwercker vber den Luther clagen.

Der geitzig clagt auß falschem můt/
Seit jm abget an Eer vnd Gůt.
Er zürnet/ Dobet/ vnde Wůt/
Jn dürstet nach des grechten plůt.

Die warheit ist Got vnd sein wort/
Das pleibt ewiglich vnzerstort.
Wie ser der Gotloß auch rumort/
Gott bschützt sein diener hie vnd dort.

Der Grecht sagt die Gotlich warheit/
Wie hart man jn veruolgt/ verleit.
hofft er in Gott doch alle zeit/
Pleibt bstendig in der grechtigkeit.

H. B. 26

<table>
<tr><td>

Die clag der Gotlosen.

Hör vnser clag du strenger Richter/
Vnd sey vnser zwitracht ein schlichter.
Eh wir die hend selb legen an/
Martin Luther den schedlich man/
Der hatt geschriben vnd gelert/
Vnd schir das gäz Tütsch land verkert.
Mit schmehen/ lestern/ nach vnd weit/
Die Erwirdige Gaistlichait.
Von jren Pfrůnden/ Rent vnd Zinst/
Vnd verwürfft auch jren Gotzdinst.
Der Vätter gepot/ vnd aufftzen/
Haßt er vnütz/ vnd menschen gschwer/
helt nichts von Aplaß vnd Fegfewr/
Die Meß kum auch kain Sel zu stewr/
All Kirchen Pew/ zir/ vnd geschmuck/
Veracht er gar/ er ist nit cluck.
Des clagen die Prelaten ser/
Pfaffen/ Münch/ Stationirer/
Glockengiesser vnd Organisten/
Goltschlager vnd Jlluministen/
Tädtmaler/ Goltschmit vñ Bildschnitzer/
Ratschmit/ Glaßmaler/ seydensitzer/
Stainmetzen/ Zimerleut Schreiner/
Paternoster/ Kertzen macher/
Die Permenter/ Singer vnd Schreyber/
Fischer/ Zopffnun vnd Pfaffen Weyber/
Den allen ist Luther ein gschwer/
Von dir wirt ein Vrteil begert.
Sunst werde wir weiter Appelliern/
Vnd dem Luther die Piend recht schirn/
Müß Prümen/ oder Reuociern.

</td><td>

Antwort D. Martini.

Actuũ .1.

O da erkenner aller hertzen/
Hör mein antwort des ist kein schertzen.
Die schreyen fast ich thů sie jrren/
Vnd wöllen doch mit Disputirn.
Sonder mich mit worten schicken/
Jn thůt we das ich thu auffdeckn.
Jr grossen geytz vnd Simoney/
Jr falsch Gotzdinst vnd Gleissnerey.
Jr Bannen/ Auffsetz vnd gepot/
Vor aller welt zu schand vnd spott.
Mit deinem wort/ das ich denn ler/
Nun jn abget an gut vnd Eer.
So kunden sy dein wort nit leiden/
Darüb mich schelten/ hassen vnd neiden.
Wenn ich hett geschriben vnd gelert/
Das jr nit Reich vnd het gemert.
So wer kein besser auff gestandn/
Jn langer zeit in Teutschen Landn.
Diß ist auch die vrsach ich sag/
Das gegen mir auch stent in clag.
Der Hantwerck leut ein grosse zal/
Den auch abgeet in disem val.
Seyt diß Abgötterey entnimpt/
Also seynd vber mich ergrimt.

3. Regů. 18.

Von erst des Baals Tempel knecht/
Den jr jarmarck thut nimmer recht.
Vnd Demetrius der werckman/
Dem sein handtwerck zu ruck wil gan.

Actuũ. 19.

her durch dein wort wirt das ich thů schreibn/
Jr di sen soll mich nitt abtreibn/
Bey deinem vrteil will ich pleiben.

</td><td>

Das Vrteil Christi.

Joãnis. 5.

Das mein gericht das ist gerecht/
Nů merck vermaints gaistlichs gschlecht.
Was ich euch selb beuolhen han/
Das jr in die gantz welt solt gan.

Mar. vltio.

Predigen aller Creatur/
Das Euangeli rain vnd pur/
Dasselbig hant jr gar veracht/
Vnd vil newer Gotzdinst auff pracht.
Der ich doch kein geheissen hab/
Vnd verkaufft jst vmb gelt vnd gab.

Mathei. 15.

Mit Vigil/ Jartäg vnd Selmessen/
Den witwen jr die hewser fressen/
Vnd verspert auch das Himelreich/

Math. 23.

Jr seyt den Doten grebern gleich/
Vñ schlacht zu dot auch mein Propheten/
Der gleich die Pharisee theten.
Also veruolgt jr die warhait/
Die euch teglichen wirt geseit.

Luce. 13.

Vnd so jr euch nit pessern wert/
Jr vnkaũ ion. Darumb so kert.
Von ewrm falschen widerstreit/
Dergleichen jr handtwercks leyt.
Die jr mein wort veracht mit dütz/
Von wegen ewrß aygen nutz.

Mathei. 6.

Vnd hört doch in den worten mein/
Das jr nit sole sorgfeltig sein.
Vmb zeitlich gůt/ gleich wie die Haydn/
Sö der sucht das Reich gots mit freudn.
Das zeitlich wirt euch wol zufalln/
Sunst wert jr in der hellen qualln/
Das ist mein vrteil zu euch alln.

</td></tr>
</table>

Hans Sachs Schuster.

practice. In light of the subsequent interpretation of Sebald Beham's *Large Peasant Holiday,* it is clear that his work was susceptible to interpretation as a negative vision of peasant life, one that could be used to formulate moralizing comments about peasants' behavior.

Having analyzed the pictorial structure of Beham's work in terms of the iconographic tradition it was based on as well as the one it in turn inspired, it is time to ask whether the appearance of this theme at this particular time had special significance. Before his work on the theme of the peasant holiday, Sebald Beham had represented the peasant in a variety of guises corresponding to iconographic types established by late fifteenth-century engravers. These themes include depictions of peasants carrying produce to market as well as dancing or making merry.[53] Although these subjects were rendered in engravings and etchings on a very small scale, with the coming of the Reformation Sebald not only developed different characterizations of the peasant but depicted them in the large-scale format offered by the woodcut medium. In 1525, for example, he provided an illustration for a broadsheet with a text by Hans Sachs entitled *Luther and the Artisans* (fig. 3.12).[54] The poem is an outspoken defense of Martin Luther against the criticism of the Catholic church. The voice of the "godless" complains that Luther has attacked the clergy by writing against the rental of church lands, the practice of tithing, and the sale of indulgences. Furthermore, in advocating that churches be swept clean of images and other decorations he has deprived of their livelihood a number of craftsmen such as bell casters, organ makers, goldsmiths, miniaturists, painters, sculptors, masons, and carpenters. In the poem Luther answers that the clergy are upset because he has uncovered their avarice and simony, their false worship and their hypocrisy, for all the world to see. Christ's judgment is cast in favor of Luther and against the clergy, who are criticized for neglecting their responsibilities. Their mission is to spread God's word, not to institute rituals by which to make money. He instructs both the clergy and the craftsmen to give up their complaints, forget about their material concerns, and seek the kingdom of God.

When we turn to Beham's illustration we realize that he has envisioned the debate in somewhat different terms. The "godless" led by a priest and a nun consist of members of the trades dependent on religious commissions as described in the poem. These are a painter clutching a stick and a brush, a bell caster, and a fisherman. Luther confronts his accusers, pointing to the Scripture as his source of inspiration. Whereas the poem says nothing about his having a retinue, Beham has provided him with a group of workmen who support him. Very prominently placed in this group, in fact leading the procession, is a peasant with a threshing flail over his shoulder.

In selecting the figure of the peasant as the counterpart to the artisans whose livelihoods were threatened by Luther's preaching, Beham followed a pattern established in the broadsheet literature of the early years of the Reformation, which made the peasant a symbol of the common man or the personification of the audience at which the reformed message was directed.[55] This usage may be seen, for example, in one of the most popular reformed pamphlets, the anonymous "John Hoe" tract, which first appeared in Strasbourg in 1521 and rapidly went through ten editions.[56] The anonymous woodcut that adorns the front page (fig. 3.13) shows "John Hoe," characterized in the text as a vigorous defender of Luther, as a peasant carrying a hoe over his shoulder.

Beham's use of the figure of the peasant in the woodcut *Luther and the Artisans* therefore coincides with a widespread tendency for both reformed writers and artists to characterize the common man of Lutheran theology as a peasant. In view of his sympathy for this idea, how are we to account for Beham's repeated treatment of the peasant *Kirchweih* subject, in which, as we have seen, spectators are asked not to identify but to distance themselves, not to sympathize with but to condemn the image of the peasant represented? Although the processes underlying this transformation are too complex to be entirely understood, there are important religious and social changes resulting from the Peasants' War, some of which offer us a glimpse of the mechanism through which this change in attitude was effected.

Luther's first reaction to the Peasants' War was his *Admonition to Peace: A Reply to the Twelve Articles of the Peasants in Swabia,* published in Wittenberg in 1525.[57] In this treatise he attempted to be evenhanded, sharing the blame for the insurrection between the peasants and their feudal lords. While acknowledging that he thought the peasants had been oppressed and sympathizing with their desire for religious liberty, Luther ultimately accused them of revolt against the divinely instituted order of society. As the conflict grew in scale and Luther's appeals to the peasants went unheeded, he became increasingly anxious lest the destruction of the existing social order also threaten the success of the new faith. Luther wished to see his religious reforms enacted within the context of a hierarchically organized secular society rather than having to insist that they be instituted in a theocracy. As a consequence his attacks on the revolt became increasingly violent. In a treatise entitled *Against the Robbing Murdering Hordes of Peasants,* published in Wittenberg in

3.13. Anonymous, *John Hoe*, woodcut, frontispiece to the anonymous pamphlet *Karsthans* (Strasbourg, 1521). (Photo, Basel, University Library.)

1525, he wrote: "Furthermore, anyone who can be proved to be a seditious person is an outlaw before God and emperor; and whoever is the first to put him to death does right and well. . . . Therefore let everyone who can, smite, slay and stab, secretly or openly, remembering that nothing can be more poisonous, hurtful or devilish than a rebel."[58]

The end of the Peasants' War coincided with the disappearance of popular pamphlets and broadsheets addressed to the common man, together with the heroic peasants that had illustrated them. The defeat of the revolutionary wing of the Reformation, along with Lutheran hostility to the radical social demands of the peasant movement, ensured that the image of the peasant vanished from popular literature.[59]

The consequence of Luther's insistence on maintaining the existing order of society is reflected in the social teaching of his followers. A significant example is the Lutheran transformation of a traditional myth concerning the origins of the social orders into a powerful new didactic tool for teaching the basic tenets of the reformed faith. This story, known as the "unequal children of Eve," was already in existence in the fifteenth century. It appeared, for example, in the popular *Eclogues* of the Italian poet Baptista Mantuanus, which was first published in Mantua in 1498 and had had three German editions by 1512.[60] In the form originally taken up by German writers and dramatists, this story consisted of the following tale. After Adam and Eve had been expelled from the Garden of Eden and had reared a large family, they were visited by God. Eve hurriedly washed some of her children to make them presentable to meet the Lord. Not having time to wash them all, she hid the rest about the house, pushing some of them into the stove. God was delighted to see those children who were presented to him, and he rewarded them by making one a king, another a duke, a third a judge, and so forth. Seeing that things were going so well, Eve decided to get the rest of the children out of hiding. They appeared before God looking dirty and disheveled, and he then proceeded to make one a peasant and the others artisans of various kinds. When Eve asked him to explain this unequal treatment of children who shared a common parentage, God answered that in order for society to function it was necessary to have representatives of all the occupations.

In 1539 Philipp Melanchthon wrote a letter to a colleague in which he transformed this tale into a vehicle for promulgating the Lutheran faith.[61] According to his version of the story, God used his visit to ascertain whether the children of Adam and Eve had been properly instructed in the faith. He first questioned Abel and the other obedient and dutiful children, eliciting a Lutheran definition of the function of prayer followed by a discussion of the Ten Commandments and the articles of the faith. On becoming aware that the disobedient and troublesome children, whose leader was Cain, had been hidden from him, God insisted on questioning them, discovering to his horror that they knew nothing and cared less. He then proceeded to reward Abel by making him a king and punished Cain by making him a slave.

Among several Lutheran playwrights who subsequently used Melanchthon's version of the story in their writing was Hans Sachs, who dealt with the theme on four occasions.[62] Whereas in three of them he was content to use the tale to justify the current organization of society, in his most elaborate play he developed Melanchthon's version as a kind of Lutheran catechism. The occupations with which the good are rewarded are listed as king, prince, ruler, scholar, and pastor. Those to which the wicked are condemned are peasant, shepherd, bathhouse attendant, woodcutter, broom binder, day worker, executioner, soldier, and shoemaker (Sachs's original occupation!).

By the second half of the sixteenth century the dialogue between God and the children of Eve had been incorporated into Lutheran catechisms, the questions and answers being regarded as an effective dramatic vehicle for stating the basic tenets of the faith.[63] In some of these works the opposition between Abel and Cain is characterized as a Lutheran Catholic one in which Abel is identified with Lutheranism and Cain with Catholicism.

In view of this tradition, it is clear that Lutheran social teaching was intimately associated with the preservation of the social order and that it cannot be regarded as responsible for developing a recognition of the social value of the peasant class, as some have suggested. The Lutheran reaction to the Peasants' War was to seek greater identification with the secular authority and to reject as wild-eyed radicals those who believed Christian justice might be implemented in the temporal world. As a consequence it was only natural that the peasants should be viewed with suspicion and hostility by those who felt the very existence of the new faith had been threatened by their impetuous rebellion.

The popularity of the story of the unequal children of Eve as a specifically Lutheran form of instruction became a feature of German literature only after the publication of Melanchthon's letter in 1540. Its popularity therefore postdates by some years the Beham brothers' interest in the peasant *Kirchweih* theme. The point of discussing this tradition in this context is not to suggest that one form of cultural preoccupation with peasants influenced the other, but merely to illustrate the parallel that exists between the evaluation of the same social class in two distinct cultural representations belonging to the same period.

If I am right in believing that Sebald Beham offers us a negative vision of the peasantry, one that expresses a hostility felt toward this class by the dominant Lutheran culture of Nuremberg, it is fair to ask why his comment should have taken this particular form. Why did he choose the subject of the peasant church anniversary celebration?

The multitude of feast days observed by the church in the late Middle Ages had elicited a number of calls for reform during the fifteenth century. Nicholas of Clémanges, Nicholas of Cusa, and Pierre d'Ailly had all written against both the number of official holidays and their abuse. A proposal for reform was formulated at the Council of Constance, but it was not until the Council of Basel that a reform measure was incorporated in the official resolutions of the meeting.[64]

Needless to say, the indignity to which supposedly spiritual observations were subjected as a consequence of popular delight in secular entertainment and sensual excess was deeply disturbing to Martin Luther. Luther attacked the institution of the church holiday as early as 1520 in his epistle *To the Christian Nobility of the German Nation:* "All festivals should be abolished and Sunday alone retained. If it be desired however, to retain the festivals of Our Lady and of the major Saints, they should be transferred to Sunday, or observed only by an early morning mass after which all the rest of the day should be a working day. Here is the reason: since the feast days are abused by drinking, gambling, loafing and all manner of sin, we anger God more on holidays than we do on other days. Things are so topsy-turvy that holidays are not holy but working days are."[65]

Included in his general condemnation of religious holidays is special reference to church anniversary celebrations: "Above all, we ought to abolish church anniversary celebrations outright, since they have become nothing but taverns, fairs and gambling places and only increase the dishonoring of God and foster the soul's damnation."[66]

Luther's objection to the celebration of church holidays stemmed not only from outrage at the way spiritual institutions were profaned, but from the profound dichotomy he felt existed between the spiritual life and life in the world. In a sermon of 1527 he made a distinction between the "inner church anniversary" and the "outer church anniversary"—the former taking place within the soul of the believer and the latter in the external world: "When there is a church anniversary in this temple [that is, the inner temple], no one rings bells or clashes cymbals, no one plays the organ or blows the bagpipes and no one places flags on the tower, for this is a hidden temple."[67] Ritual festivities of any kind could not therefore be regarded as an adequate reflection of the subjective experience of the event commemorated; instead, they could only serve to profane it.

Urbanus Rhegius, one of Luther's followers, went so far as to dedicate a special sermon to the problem of the *Kirchweih* that was published in 1522.[68] Another reformed author who passed comment on such festivals was Sebastian Franck, who included the following comments in his *Weltbuch:* "Then there follows the holy church anniversary holiday, when there is a great feasting among both laymen and priests who are invited from far and wide. The peasants usually invite their priest down to the inn together with his cook or housekeeper (since he dares not take a wife). Sometimes the priest gets drunk so that the peasants have to lead him home. Other times the priest holds the peasant's head when he has to throw up."[69]

Practical measures against the celebration of religious holidays were taken by reformed communities at the earliest possible date. In Nuremberg, a city ordinance of 1525 abolished most of the church holidays long before the formal constitution of Lutheran worship was promulgated there in 1533.[70]

Reformed concern with the celebration of church anniversary holidays in the early years of the Reformation constitutes an evident parallel to the representation of this subject in the graphic work of the Beham brothers. The coincidence of these traditions is so suggestive that it is important to analyze the pictorial means by which this visual statement was made. How exactly were these ideas portrayed, and what are we to conclude from the means selected?

In the almost complete absence of visual precedents for the iconography of the peasant festival before the work of the Beham brothers, it is necessary to examine peasant imagery in other dimensions of cultural life to determine whether it casts any light upon the subject.[71] The peasant was one of the standard literary characters of late medieval German literature and drama.[72] The type was developed in the context of chivalric poetry and used as a vehicle for parodying courtly ideals of behavior. The particular genius of this genre is that its humor acted as a double-edged sword. While mocking aristocratic cultural institutions such as love service, tournaments, and feasts, it also offered the reader or listener a vicious satire of the uncouth manners and obscene sexual conduct attributed to the peasantry. The classic statement of this tradition is the Basel jurist Heinrich Wittenwiler's poem *The Ring*, written at the beginning of the fifteenth century.[73] This poem, which recounts the story of a peasant wedding, contains many aspects of the peasant theme exploited by later writers. It describes the bride and groom Betsy Wagglebottom and Berty Dripnose as paragons of ugliness. The description of their manners is doubly amusing as a satire not only of their vulgarity but of the chivalric ideals they attempt to ape. The wedding feast is a wild and barbaric affair in which the peasants' eating and drinking is characterized as senselessly immoderate, the dance that follows is lewd and indecent. Finally the poem ends with a battle scene in which the inhabitants of one village take on those of another over some imagined slight.

The figure of the peasant as the vehicle for expressing vulgar sentiments and portraying scandalous behavior became a favorite of the Nuremberg carnival plays that flourished in the second half of the fifteenth century. When these plays involved peasant subjects, they were performed by artisans dressed in peasant costume who would give their simple performances in the tavern and in the street.[74] Plays in which peasant figures appeared were invariably the most foul mouthed and obscene of the carnival play repertoire. They most often deal with ugliness and deformity, lapses in manners, and scatological and sexually offensive behavior. Recent critical opinion has tended to characterize this humor as serving a double function.[75] It is thought that artisans adopted peasant costume as a way to indulge in scandalous and provocative behavior that was otherwise proscribed by the rules with which the Nuremberg authorities regulated urban life. Although the peasant was regarded as a representative of a lower social class, despised by urban dwellers as morally inferior, appropriating his cultural stereotype enabled artisans to step outside the stifling moral climate of the city and vent their frustrations during a brief but officially sanctioned period of license.

In the carnival plays of the post-Reformation era, the figure of the obscene peasant plays a less important role. In the hands of Hans Sachs the obscenity is qualified, and the plays are provided with edifying moralizing conclusions that compromise the provocative intensity of this comic type.[76] This change in the character of the stage figure of the peasant took place in the context of the suppression of carnival. Not only was the carnival of the elite—the *Schembartlauf*—abolished in 1524, but the popular masking and merrymaking that accompanied it were also discouraged.[77] Typical of the reformed attitude toward the celebration of carnival is the following comment by Sebastian Franck. In a critical description of Catholic festivals he writes:

Then comes the carnival, the Bacchanalia of the Roman church. Many entertainments characterize this feast. Spectacles, such as jousts, tournaments, dances, and carnival plays. People dress up in costume and run about the city like fools and madmen playing whatever pranks and games they can think up. Whoever can think of something foolish to do is master. On such occasions one sees outlandish outfits and strange disguises; women wear men's clothing and men adopt women's dresses. As a result shame, good discipline, honor, and piety are rarely found at this Christian festival where (to the contrary) much foolishness takes place.[78]

The heightened moral content of the carnival plays, together with the critique of the principle of inversion inherent in the suppression of carnival, must have made it more difficult for artisans to find within the negative stereotype of the peasant a cultural space for the temporary violation of the moral code.

If we turn to the peasant holiday scenes of the Beham brothers in the light of the peasant humor of the carnival plays, certain correspondences become apparent. First, the peasant figures of both Barthel and Sebald possess a curiously depersonalized air. Far from representing particular individuals, the Beham peasants seem to repeat basic types, using different gestures and clothing as the principal means of differentiating them. Both men and women are short and stocky, the men characterized by strong features remarkable for their ugliness. Second, many of the incidents represented in the *Large Peasant Holiday* resonate with echoes of the literary and dramatic traditions. The excessive drinking, the exuberant dancing, the senseless violence, were all classic constituents of the peasant wedding poems exemplified by Wittenwiler's *Ring,* while the suggestive actions of the dancers and the revolting image of the prominently placed vomiting man were common elements of the raucous humor of the *Fastnachtspiele.*

The Beham brothers thus transformed a cultural stereotype associated with social satire and obscene humor into a visual vehicle for the expression of class ridicule. From our twentieth-century perspective as inhabitants of a culture whose values have taught us not to laugh at those less fortunate than ourselves, not to disdain poverty or notice deformities, not to enjoy vulgar and obscene forms of language, we may find it difficult to appreciate a brand of humor that invites us to do just these things. We are asked, that is, to laugh at the credulous victim of the unscrupulous dentist, to find amusing the plight of the drunkard who vomits in the foreground, to regard the clodhopping dancers as ridiculous. Laughter is certainly present in Sebald's print, just as it was in Sachs's wry description of his "amusement" and "entertainment" at the sights afforded him at the church anniversary festival described in *The Nose Dance at Fools' Town.* However, it is a purposive laughter, the laughter of ridicule, laughter that depended on satirizing a particular social class.

The social implications of the image of festive peasants developed by the Beham brothers must have been differently perceived by different portions of their audience. It was perhaps the upper classes, merchants, and professionals that were most likely to buy "giant" woodcuts such as Sebald Beham's *Large Peasant Holiday* or Barthel Beham's *Church Anniversary Festival at Mögelsdorf.* If we assume for the sake of argument that each section of a "giant" woodcut was sold for the price of a single-leaf woodcut—approximately five pfennig, then the former, which is made up of four sheets, would have cost twenty pfennig and the latter, composed of six, thirty pfennig. Such an expenditure would have constituted a considerable outlay for members of the artisan class, equaling or exceeding a full day's wage. While there is little indication of the way such monumental prints were displayed, it is clear that they are better appreciated when hung vertically, so the whole composition can be taken in at a glance, rather than stored in boxes and examined horizontally one at a time. Some indication that they were displayed vertically is found in what is known of the way Dürer's "giant" woodcuts were exhibited. His design for the *Large Triumphal Carriage of Maximilian I*, published as a woodcut in 1522, was painted by his followers on one of the walls of the council chamber in Nuremberg's town hall.[79] Furthermore, an early nineteenth-century description of the castle at Nuremberg mentions that an impression of the gigantic *Triumphal Arch of Maximilian I* had been attached to boards—presumably so it could be displayed vertically.[80] Since the breadth of these compositions exceeds their height, Horst Appuhm has suggested that they were used in middle- and upper-class interiors to decorate the wall space between the top of the wood paneling and the ceiling.[81] In such a location the ridiculous antics of the dancing peasants would have constituted a striking contrast to the ideals of refinement and elegance that inspired upper-class life. It is analogous in some ways to the practice of the Burgundian aristocracy, who commissioned tapestries of working or dancing peasants for their princely surroundings.[82] Indeed, in some of these tapestries the verbal exchanges between music-making shepherds and shepherdesses, which were woven into the fabric, function as a form of suggestive humor in much the same way as the brief texts that accompany the images in the prints.[83] Members of the upper classes must thus have looked at these prints as a source of amusement and as a gratifying confirmation of the superior quality of their own class identity.

Should artisans have invested in such prints, they too would have been amused by the grotesque capering of their country cousins,[84] but it is likely that they also viewed these prints with a certain ambivalence. On the one hand artisans would have taken pride in their status as members of an urban community whose social identity was elaborately defined by the ordinances of the town council. On the other hand they may have longed for the less restricted and regimented lives so many of them had forsaken in favor of earning a better living in the city. These feelings must have been especially nostalgic at a time when the traditionally outrageous figure of the stage peasant was being cleaned up in the interests of an ever more restrictive code of moral conduct.

4

Mercenary Warriors and the "Rod of God"

Soldiers occupy a prominent place among the most popular secular subjects in German prints of the sixteenth century. Whether presented singly or in groups, in images accompanied by texts or not, their animated forms, vigorous gestures, and striking costumes are a familiar aspect of the graphic art of this period. Despite their number and variety, these images, which have attracted historians as well as students of the history of costume, have received little attention from historians of art.[1] The scholarship relating to them has been largely restricted to attribution and dating, so that questions concerning their significance for the people who bought and sold them, their relation to the historical moment when they were produced, and the nature of the social values they were associated with have never been raised.

The image of the soldier was first introduced into the iconographic repertoire of the graphic arts by Flemish and South German artists of the late fifteenth century.[2] At the beginning of the sixteenth century it played an important role in the work of Swiss and South German artists such as Niklaus Manuel Deutsch, Urs Graf, Hans Holbein the Younger, Albrecht Altdorfer, Albrecht Dürer, and Hans Baldung Grien.[3] This chapter will focus on representations of soldiers produced in Nuremberg in the 1530s, for it is in this context that the theme reached the height of its popularity. I will concentrate here on an analysis of a woodcut by Erhard Schön known as *A Column of Mercenaries*, dated about 1532 (fig. 4.1).[4] This woodcut was printed with texts by Hans Sachs that define the various military ranks represented, describing their duties and praising the way they are performed. The composition of this image is derived from a section of one of the most remarkable commissions of Maximilian I, the "giant" woodcut known as the *Triumphal Procession of Maximilian I*, executed by a team of artists that included some of the outstanding figures of the day, such as Albrecht Dürer, Hans Burgkmair, and Albrecht

4.1. Erhard Schön, *A Column of Mercenaries*, woodcut. (Photo, Braunschweig, Anton Ulrich Museum.)

Altdorfer (fig. 4.2).[5] The *Triumphal Procession*, modeled on the revival of the iconography of the Roman imperial triumph by Italian artists in the course of the fifteenth century, was specifically intended to spread the fame of Maximilian as Holy Roman Emperor.[6] But unlike most of the works patterned on this model, which were used to glorify the power of a specific monarch, no

ruler is represented in Schön's print.[7] In view of the absence of the central idea this imagery was originally constructed to celebrate, how do we interpret Schön's image? What does this elaborate structure of pictorial signs signify?

The focal point of Schön's composition is the ensign or standardbearer. Rivaled only by the figure of the mounted captain at the head of the column, who shares the distinction of being accompanied by bodyguards, the ensign's central position, together with the scale of the flag that swirls behind him, draws attention to his presence. The flag itself, decorated with the cross of Saint Andrew and the flint and sparks of the duchy of Burgundy, is the imperial flag Maximilian adopted after his marriage to Mary of Burgundy.[8] This marriage, which dramatically increased the territory under Maximilian's direct control, marked the transformation of the house of Habsburg from a princely family of Austrian and South German importance to a dynasty destined to play a major part in European history. The flag therefore serves to establish that these soldiers are in imperial service. In the absence of the emperor himself, the prominence of the flag suggests that the whole panoply of

4.2. Leonhard Beck and Hans Schäuffelein, *Marching Mercenaries,* woodcut, detail from the *Triumphal Procession of Maximilian I.* (Photo, Stanley Appelbaum, *The Triumph of Maximilian* [New York, 1964], pl. 126.)

signs constituting the image should be understood as a glorification of imperial military strength.

Who are these soldiers, and why are they presented in this heroic light? The text above the mounted captain informs us he is recruiting *Landsknechte* or mercenaries to lead into battle.[9] The rise of the mercenary as the primary instrument of warfare is a development of the late Middle Ages, associated with the gradual replacement of a social system based on feudal obligations with one organized around the principle of monetary exchange. By the sixteenth century armies owed their existence not so much to a network of feudal allegiances as to the investment of capital. Armies no longer consisted of the nobility and their retainers but were made up of hired mercenaries. These changes were accompanied by new means of making war. Whereas battles had once been dominated by the clash of the mounted aristocracy, hand-to-hand combat by foot soldiers became all-important. Mercenaries were organized into densely packed phalanxes that attacked one another frontally with spears and halberds. Since victory depended on the cut and thrust of hand-held weapons, battles were often decided by sheer weight of numbers.

Hans Sachs's texts not only inform us of the rank and function of the soldiers represented but praise the way they carry out their duties. For example, the text above the ensign reads:

I have been appointed standard-bearer,
Chosen from the noisy ranks.
Whoever sees the flag flying
Believes that his side can still win
And is thus encouraged to carry on the battle
And to fight with all his might.
Therefore I wave my flag
Since it is worth my life and limbs.
I will not retreat a step;
Because of this I must be given triple pay by a powerful lord
Who goes to war for honor and renown.[10]

The military status of the ensign in armies of this period lent itself to this type of heroizing. The basic German infantry unit, which consisted of three hundred to four hundred men, was known as a *Fendlein* or "flag" of soldiers. Soldiers chosen to bear the standard were paid five or six times the ordinary rate and were provided with bodyguards and substitutes to take their place should they fall in battle.[11] The figure in Schön's woodcut therefore represents an idealized image of a member of a military elite.

The striking costumes worn by the mercenaries depicted in Schön's marching column seem to have been neither damaged nor sullied by the rigors of military life. These gaudy, eye-catching garments with their intricate slit patterns were by no means common in German society of the sixteenth century. This style of clothing, which echoes northern Italian fashions of the late fifteenth century, was popular in aristocratic and wealthy burgher circles in southern Germany between 1500 and 1520.[12] This may be seen for example, in Lucas Cranach the Elder's portrait of Duke Henry the Pious of Saxony in Dresden, dated about 1514 (fig. 4.3).[13] Whereas the fashion for slit clothing was a passing whim among the upper classes, it was appropriated by the mercenaries, and they retained it long after it had been abandoned by other social groups. A short-lived aristocratic fashion thus became a lasting identifying characteristic of the military profession. In adopting aristocratic fashion, the mercenaries seem consciously to have sought to identify themselves with a class that had traditionally monopolized the making of war. Although most of the officers in mercenary armies appear to have had links with the aristocracy even if they were not themselves noble, the bulk of these armies comprised impoverished urban dwellers and peasants.[14] The adoption of aristocratic fashion by all ranks therefore suggests that the new military profession born of the capitalist organization of warfare sought to identify with the chivalric traditions that had animated the ideology of war in a bygone age.

The heroic characterization of the mercenary found in Schön's *Column of Mercenaries* is a feature of many representations of soldiers produced in Nuremberg in the 1530s. The *Briefmaler* Hans Guldenmund and Niklas Meldemann competed to bring out cycles of single standing mercenaries in heroic attitudes accompanied by flattering texts. These series, which were illustrated by Erhard Schön and Sebald Beham, tend to represent only those soldiers whose specialized duties entitled them to higher than average pay. The series illustrated by Schön includes an ordnance master, a recruiting officer, a field doctor, a sergeant major, a squad leader, and the chief of military police, while Beham's series depicts an ensign, a drummer, a piper, a sergeant major (fig. 4.4), the master of the watch, the provisions master, and the leader of the musketeers, among other ranks.[15] A number of the texts allude to service in the military campaigns of Maximilian I and Charles V so that, as in the case of *A Column of Mercenaries*, the figures are identified with the imperial cause.

In attempting to assess the meaning these sympathetic representations of the mercenary profession had for sixteenth-century Nuremberg culture, we must ascertain how mercenaries were regarded by their contemporaries. The figure of the mercenary as a personification of imperial power was used, for example,

4.3. Lucas Cranach the Elder, *Duke Henry the Pious of Saxony,* Dresden, Staatliche Kunstsammlungen. (Photo, Dresden, Staatliche Kunstsammlungen.)

in the nationalist literature of the German humanists. The fighting ability of the German people, a quality they discovered in reading a newly found and recently published Roman work, the *Germania* of Tacitus, was much stressed in their support of Maximilian's projected crusade against the Turks.[16] In a play by the humanist Jakob Locher (a pupil of Sebastian Brant, one of Maximilian's most enthusiastic supporters) dated 1502, which called on the Christian kings of Europe to support Maximilian's plans for a crusade against the Turks, the kings of France, England, and Hungary, are joined by an allegorical personification of the *Landsknechte* in pledging themselves to service in the war.[17] In a somewhat earlier play by the same author, which also advocated a campaign against the Turks, the last act is illustrated with a woodcut representing a group of mercenaries surrounding the idealized figure of a standard-bearer whose flag bears a cross and the imperial eagle (fig. 4.5).[18]

The mercenary was frequently invoked in pro-imperial songs, particularly

4.4. Sebald Beham, *Sergeant Major,* woodcut. (Photo, Max Geisberg, *The German Single-Leaf Woodcut, 1500–1550,* 4 vols., trans. Walter Strauss [New York, 1974], vol. 1, cat. no. 278.)

4.5. Anonymous, *Standard-Bearer with Mercenaries*, woodcut, illustration to Jakob Locher, *Spectaculum de Thurcorum Rege et Sultano rege Babiloniae more Tragico effigiatum in Romani Regis honorem* (Strasbourg, 1497). (Photo, Wolfenbüttel, Herzog August Bibliothek.)

those dealing with events in the campaigns undertaken by Maximilian I and Charles V in Italy. In these songs the *Landsknecht* personifies imperial power while the Swiss *Reislaufer*, who was usually in the employ of the French, represents the cause of Francis I. Recent scholarship has tended to characterize these "historical folksongs" (which were published as broadsheets), more as a means of expressing a particular attitude toward events—a means, that is, of molding public opinion—than as a means of communication.[19] Typical of this genre is a song that celebrates the imperial victory at the battle of Pavia when the French king was taken prisoner. Aside from a brief description of the course of events, the song is principally concerned to assert the superiority of the *Landsknechte* over their enemies the Swiss. The song, which appeared as a broadsheet, was illustrated with a woodcut by Sebald Beham representing a mercenary (fig. 4.6).[20] The mercenary also appears as a personification of imperial power in songs composed in response to the Turkish invasions of 1529. Hans Sachs wrote a song entitled *In Praise of the Worthy Mercenaries at*

Vienna that was published together with a woodcut by Hans Vogtherr the Elder representing two mercenaries.[21] The song begins:

Wake up heart, mind, and imagination;
Help me praise the good mercenaries
For their chivalrous deeds
Which they performed in Austria,
At Vienna, within the city.

Sachs's discussion of the political and religious problems of his day often reveals a deep concern for the fate of the empire as well as awe and respect for

4.6. Sebald Beham, *Mercenary,* woodcut, illustration to Hans von Würzburg's broadsheet *Ain schönes Lied von der schlacht vor Pavia geschehen* (n.p., n.d.), Berlin, Staatsbibliothek, Ve 2701. (Photo, Gustav Könnecke, *Bilderatlas zur Geschichte der deutschen Nationallitteratur* [Marburg, 1895], p. 125.)

the emperor himself.[22] In 1529 he contributed texts for a series of fifteen images of Turkish warriors together with the atrocities they were alleged to have committed during the siege of Vienna.[23] These woodcuts by Sebald Beham, Erhard Schön, and Niklas Stör were marketed by the Nuremberg *Briefmaler* Hans Guldenmund. The images were clearly intended to inflame public opinion against the Turks. Sachs's texts either describe the functions of the troops, lament the fate of the captives, or attempt to move the viewer's emotions by describing the inhumanity of the invaders. In Erhard Schön's woodcut *Turkish Rider with Two Christian Captives* (fig. 4.7), for example, the text voices the captives' complaint.[24] They tell how the Turks have killed their children, stolen their sheep and cattle, and set fire to their houses. They themselves are condemned to slavery, being forced to pull plows and fed nothing but barley, as if they were horses. Their lament closes with a plea that death

4.7. Erhard Schön, *Turkish Rider with Christian Captives*, woodcut. (Photo, Geisberg, *Woodcut*, vol. 4, cat. no. 1241.)

may release them from the hand of the "gruesome Turk." In the same year
Sachs provided Guldenmund with a hundred-verse poem describing the siege
of Vienna to accompany a view of that event he had commissioned from Erhard Schön.[25] Even though its publication was delayed because Guldenmund's competitor Meldemann obtained a one-year copyright from the council for another map of Vienna he had commissioned from Sebald Beham, this
project must also have served to dramatize the plight of the empire in the eyes
of a Nuremberg audience.

The identification of the mercenary with the imperial cause was evidently
common enough for the image of a standard-bearer to be used as the frontispiece of pamphlets urging support for the war against the Turks. Hans Busteter's war manual addressed to the mayor and city council of Augsburg during the Turkish emergency of 1532 has a frontispiece by Hans Schäuffelein
representing an ensign with other soldiers (fig. 4.8).[26] The same woodcut was

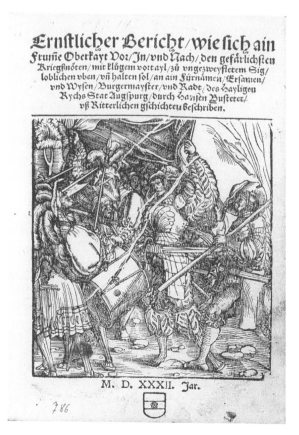

4.8. Hans Schäuffelein, *Standard-Bearer with Mercenaries*, woodcut, frontispiece to Hans Busteter, *Erstlicher Bericht, wie sich ain frume Oberkayt . . .* (Augsburg, 1532). (Photo, Nuremberg, Germanisches Nationalmuseum.)

used later during the Turkish invasion of 1542 to illustrate a popular anonymous pamphlet entitled *An Attack on the Gruesome, Bloodthirsty Tyranny of the Turks.*[27]

In view of the way the image of the mercenary was used to further the imperial cause in literature and song, it seems likely that the *Column of Mercenaries* served a similar purpose. What meaning did an expression of pro-imperial sentiment have for the Nuremberg audience for which this print was designed? As we have seen earlier, one of the characteristics of Nuremberg's policy during the sixteenth century was its pro-imperial stance. There is indeed some evidence that the city council made an effort to use the visual arts in support of this policy. The only graphic art commissioned by the civic authorities during the first half of the sixteenth century was a large-scale map of the Turkish siege of Vienna (fig. 4.9).[28] In 1529 the *Briefmaler* Niklas Meldemann was granted permission to prepare a view of the siege and promised an exclusive copyright on his work for one year. The person delegated to advance him fifty florins to cover his expenses was none other than Lazarus Spengler, secretary to the council and the man who had been instrumental in shaping Nuremberg's policy of nonresistance to the emperor.[29] The map, which measures two-and-a-half by almost three feet, was executed by Sebald Beham based on a drawing done on the spot by an artist Meldemann hired. It offers a bird's-eye view of the city and the surrounding landscape taken from the top of Saint Stephen's cathedral, which is represented in the center of the composition. The striking view of the city encircled by a landscape filled with scenes of Turkish violence must have served to dramatize the plight of what the cathedral characterizes as a bastion of the Christian faith. It is significant that an early nineteenth-century description of the imperial castle in Nuremberg mentions a map of Vienna that had been mounted on canvas.[30] It is possible that this map was an impression of the one executed by Sebald Beham and that it had been presented to the emperor by the city council.

The praise of the imperial mercenary that characterizes Schön's *Column of Mercenaries* coincides not only with the traditional use of this figure to express pro-imperial sentiment but with the pro-imperial policies pursued by the Nuremberg city council during a period of national emergency. The council had consistently voted funds for military resistance to the Turks and in 1529 and 1532 had even raised troops.[31] Some aspects of Sachs's text for this print may have had something to do with this effort. The text above the ordinary soldiers that bring up the rear of the column informs us that they are about to go into battle, but that once it is over, every preparation has been made for their comfort:

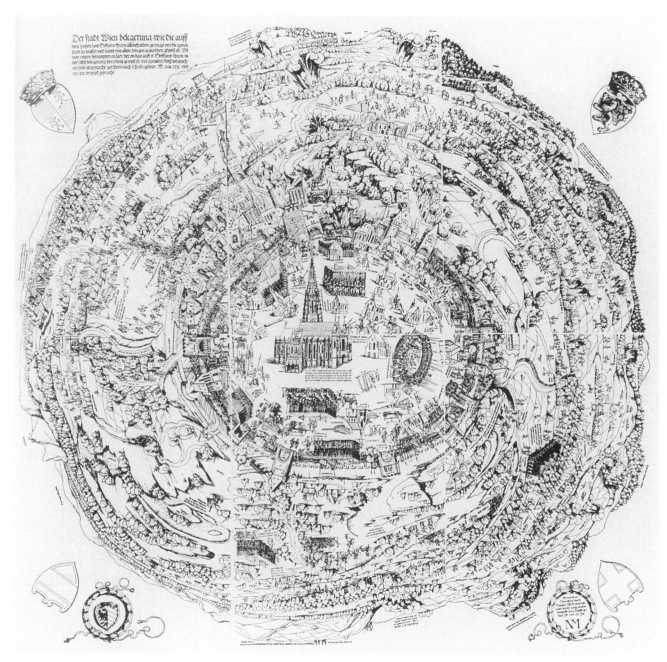

4.9. Sebald Beham, *The Siege of Vienna*, woodcut. (Photo, Berlin, Staatliche Museen Preussischer Kulturbesitz, Kupferstichkabinett.)

4.10. Erhard Schön, *The Baggage Train with Death*, woodcut. (Photo, Berlin, Staatliche Museen Preussischer Kulturbesitz, Kupferstichkabinett.)

Here we follow with cheerful spirits;
Early this morning the scouts went off
To prepare a camp for us tonight.
As soon as we have beaten the enemy
We will stay there overnight.
The wagons will be drawn in a circle,
And the master of the watch and the quartermaster
Are waiting for the army there.[32]

The text goes on to describe how tents have been pitched and provisions laid on; a surgeon will take care of the wounded, and the paymaster will distribute a bonus if they are victorious. The deliberate effort to play down the dangers and discomforts of the military life, and to characterize it as profitable and praiseworthy, suggests that Sachs's text may well have been connected, if only indirectly, with one of the council's recruitment drives.

A Column of Mercenaries (fig. 4.1) finds a striking contrast in a woodcut published at exactly the same time (1532) entitled *The Baggage Train with Death* (fig. 4.10),[33] for which Erhard Schön provided the image and Hans Sachs a text that has unfortunately been lost. Curiously enough, the visual inspiration for this work was also the *Triumphal Procession of Maximilian I*. This time, however, the reference is not to the ranks of marching soldiers but to the baggage train that brings up the rear of the procession (fig. 4.11).[34] In spite of

the missing text, we can gain some idea of the significance of this work by analyzing the pictorial traditions to which it is related. In contrast to the disciplined, hierarchically ordered ranks represented in *A Column of Mercenaries*, this shapeless crowd of soldiers and camp followers ambles along in an unstructured and disorderly fashion. They are accompanied by a couple of horse-drawn wagons that carry provisions and munitions. Bringing up the rear are a group of Turkish and mercenary prisoners and an allegorical figure of Death flanked by two skeletal companions, one of whom wears elements of mercenary costume and the other items of Turkish dress. One of the foci of the composition is the figure of the ensign. Unlike his counterpart in *A Column of Mercenaries* (fig. 4.1), he is not represented in heroic isolation, for an attractive young woman holds his arm. The contrast suggests that a very different view of mercenary life is being represented. Camp followers were the subject of literary and visual satire in this period, as may be seen in the woodcut attributed to Martin Weygel and executed in Nuremberg about 1560, entitled *The Mercenary's Whore* (fig. 4.12).[35] The text that accompanies the image reads:

If you're not into gluttony and boozing
I don't want to follow you for long.
If I stay near you for any length of time
I'll certainly let you have the "French disease."

4.11. Albrecht Altdorfer, *Baggage Train*, woodcut, detail from the *Triumphal Procession of Maximilian I*. (Photo, Appelbaum, *Triumph of Maximilian*, pls. 132–37.)

You'll wish you had stayed at home
And had never set forth.

It is perhaps no accident that the whore is looking over her shoulder as if addressing the cock that sits on the bundle she carries on her back. It will be noticed that in *The Baggage Train with Death* cocks are prominently placed at various points in the composition. The cock sitting on the wagon to the left stands in the middle of a wreath (fig. 4.10), suggesting that it cannot be regarded as an incidental detail added to heighten the work's naturalism but rather serves a symbolic function. The cock was a well-known symbol of lust in this period,[36] one that had also been used to assert the need for male authority in allegories of marriage. This may be seen, for example, in a woodcut by Hans Vogtherr the Younger that was published about 1545 (fig. 4.13).

I am called a proud cock
Who knows how to keep his hens in order
So that they will do my will.
I keep watch vigilantly and call them often.
I turn around a lot and take good care of them.
Whatever man does not do the same
Is a hen, not a cock,
And will not be able to wear the pants.[37]

The function of the cock in this composition therefore is analogous to the pair of pants displayed on the flag borne by the ensign of the baggage train in the *Triumphal Procession of Maximilian I* (fig. 4.11). It comments on the relation-

ship between the soldiers and the camp followers, suggesting that one aspect of the mercenary's character was his aggressive sexuality.

The camel and the Turkish prisoners identify the campaign these soldiers have been engaged in as part of the effort to defend the empire against the Turkish invasion of 1529.[38] Interestingly enough the captured Turks are not alone in their imprisonment, for they are followed by a pair of mercenaries who have fallen foul of military justice. The equation of mercenaries and Turks is further emphasized by the companions of Death, whose clothing identifies them as personifications of the two antagonists. By erasing the differences between the Turk and the mercenary, the figure of Death denies the heroic qualities ascribed to the mercenary in such works as *A Column of Mercenaries*. In this setting, the imperial cause appears no worthier than that of the foe.

The idea of using the figure of the mercenary in allegories of death was not a new one. The soldier was, for example, part of the iconographic tradition of the Dance of Death in the fifteenth and sixteenth centuries.[39] An anonymous woodcut dated 1504 (fig. 4.14)[40] explores the implications of death for the mercenary profession:

However bold and strong and tall you may be
And however many men have suffered your violence,
You must nevertheless give in to me.
I have long denounced your pride.
Your halberd no longer has the power to cut;

83

Die Landsknechts hür.

Wan nit wer das fressen vñ sauffen
Ja ich wolt dir nit lang nach lauffen.
Solt ich vmb sanfft lang naby trabñ
Liesz dich wol die frantzhosen haben.
Wolt wol dahaymen sein belyben
Vnd wolt das nien haben tryben.

4.12. Martin Weygel, *The Merce-nary's Whore*, woodcut. (Photo, Nuremberg, Germanisches Na-tionalmuseum.)

4.13. Hans Vogtherr the Younger, *Allegory of Marriage*, woodcut. (Photo Geisberg, *Woodcut*, vol. 4, cat. no. 1471.)

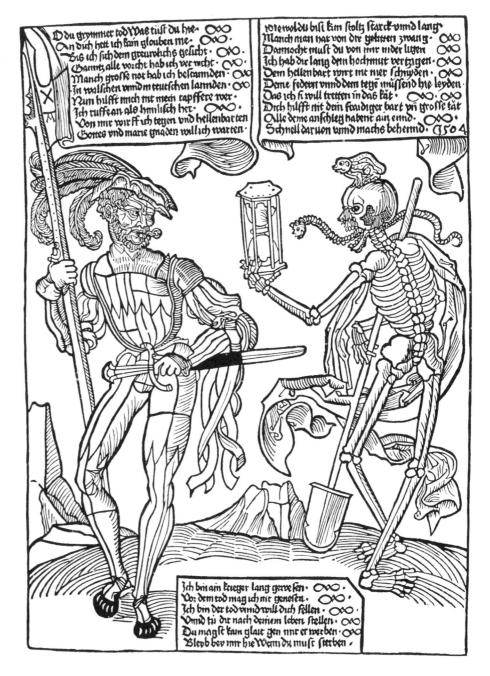

4.14. Anonymous, *Death and the Mercenary,* woodcut. (Photo, Berlin, Staatliche Museen Preussischer Kulturbesitz, Kupferstichkabinett.)

Your feathers and your dagger must fall,
Since I intend throwing them into the grave.
Your fashionable beard and great deeds
Will not help you now;
All your battles have come to an end.
Quickly, away from here and be smart about it.

The soldier replies:

Oh, grim death, what are you doing here?
I did not believe you existed any more
Until I saw your gruesome face.
I had eliminated all fear.
Many great trials have I withstood

4.15. Urs Graf, *Two Mercenaries,
Whore, and Death*, woodcut.
(Photo, Berlin, Staatliche Museen
Preussischer Kulturbesitz, Kup-
ferstichkabinett.)

Procinctu tali gens ferrea militiae
Pergit, Equis, Scortis, Plaustris & cincta Camelis.

Vastatura domos, Vrbes & florida regna
Infelix certe numerus, furumq; maniplis:
N. 30.

Cui ne perdendi & periundi occasio desit,
Mors Comes à tergo trahitúr truce lurida falce.
Ieremias Wolff excudit Aug. Vind.

4.16. Johann Theodor de Bry, *Baggage Train with Death*, engraving. (Photo, London, British Library.)

On Italian and on German soil;
However, my brave weapons are no use to me now.
I shall call upon my heavenly lord
And throw away my dagger and my halberd
To wait upon the grace of God and Mary.

Closer to the ideas contained in *The Baggage Train with Death*, however, is a woodcut executed by Urs Graf in 1524 (fig. 4.15).[41] In this composition the proverbial enemies of sixteenth-century warfare, the Swiss *Reislaufer* and the German *Landsknecht*, are represented at peace with one another. The Swiss mercenary is identified by his long spear and by the slit crosses that appear on his chest, arm, and shin, while his German counterpart is identified by his two-handed sword and the diagonal cross of Saint Andrew on the apronlike garment that hangs before his thighs.[42] The reason for their coexistence is the allegorical figure of Death in the tree behind them, who looks out of the composition at the viewer while pointing at an hourglass. The differences between the antagonists have disappeared in the face of a deeper reality that threatens them both with extinction. The aggressive masculinity of the youthful mercenaries, emphasized by their flamboyant costumes, the violence associated with their weapons, and the pert expression and suggestive pose of the camp follower to the left of the tree, is mocked by the assertion of their mortality.

Another work that throws light on the original meaning of *The Baggage Train with Death* is an engraved copy produced toward the end of the sixteenth century by Johann Theodor de Bry (fig. 4.16).[43] This engraving is accompanied by a Latin text that reads:

Armed in this way, the pitiless soldiers sally forth
Accompanied by horses, whores, wagons, and camels.
They stand prepared to devastate houses, cities, and flourishing landscapes,

A troop of pernicious thugs and villains,
So that they lose no opportunity of killing others or of destroying themselves,
Death has been added to the end of their train, together with his corpse-creating
     scythe.

The text undoubtedly bears little relation to the lost original by Hans Sachs, which was seventy-four verses long, but it does inform us that the image was interpreted as a representation of the destructiveness of the mercenary profession. The allegorical figure of death is understood as a reference not only to the damage they inflict on others but to the destruction they bring down upon themselves.

The equation of the hostile parties, the mercenaries and the Turks, by means of the personification of Death suggests that Schön's print and Sachs's text gave expression to another and more critical reaction to war against the Turks than that voiced in *A Column of Mercenaries*. The verses that accompanied this print were certainly not Sachs's only criticism of the mercenaries. The poet, who as we have seen was capable of penning a paean in their praise, also made a concerted effort to pillory their moral failings. In the work entitled *Argument between a Housemaid and a Young Man* of 1532, Sachs used a fictive conversation between two young people to criticize youths who imitated mercenary customs and dress.[44] Instead of leading a loose and antisocial existence, drinking, gambling, whoring, swearing, and brawling as mercenaries do, he urges that young people become apprentices and dedicate themselves to the serious and sober task of learning a trade. In his *Comparison of a Mercenary with a Crab*, also published in 1532, Sachs portrays the mercenary's life as filled with hardship and suffering.[45] The mercenary endures cold, wind, and rain and must await the resumption of spring operations in a shelter dug in the ground just as the crab spends the winter buried in the sea bottom. Like the crab, which is always wet because it lives underwater, so the mercenary must always be drunk. In this he resembles a pig, whose greed also prevents it from knowing when it is to be butchered. Like the crab that can grow back the claws it loses, so the mercenary replaces the limbs lost brawling at the camp with iron substitutes. And just as the crab is caught by the fisherman's trap while searching for food, so is the mercenary killed by peasants while pillaging the countryside. Sachs's moralizing conclusion condemns mercenaries for offering their services in any conflict, suggesting that the only legitimate war is one conducted in defense of one's country.

The humor of this last play is echoed in a number of songs that were published as broadsheets in the 1530s. In *The Order of Mercenaries* by the Nuremberg bag and belt maker Jörg Graff of about 1517, the popular comparison of mercenaries to the old orders of chivalry was transformed into an analogy with the religious orders.[46] In this case, the humor depends upon the contrast between the piety of monks and the wild life of wandering soldiers. Two other anonymous songs produced in Nuremberg about 1530 satirize the mercenary's style of life. In the *Mercenary on Stilts* it is their reckless disregard of danger that is mocked.[47] The song is placed in the mouth of a mercenary who presents his chosen fate in utopian terms and whose cheerfulness is unaffected by the loss of an arm, a leg, and finally his life. In the *Mercenary's Customs and Habits*, a similar utopian vision is painted in which robbery and violence are ironically extolled as the way to earn a living.[48] The mercenary finishes his song by saying that since the Turks have invaded Poland he now has a chance to find service and thus a means of paying the innkeeper's bills.

These humorous songs may help us understand a series of images whose texts suggest that the mercenaries depicted in them are to be regarded as far from heroic. The woodcuts by Niklas Stör entitled *Cobbler* and *Tailor* (figs. 4.17 and 4.18),[49] which date from the 1530s, differ from the series of single standing mercenaries of a heroic type (see fig. 4.4) only in being seen from the rear. While their figures and gestures are admirably noble and their costumes stylishly elegant, that they are seen from behind gives them an informal air. Instead of describing their military status and function with reference to imperial service and outstanding accomplishments, the texts reveal the motives that led these men to become mercenaries. The text, in other words, provides the viewer with insight into the image, and the play between the two provides an opportunity for humor. The *Cobbler* says:

May shoemaking go to the Devil;
I've had to suffer too long
Before making a week's wage.
However, things are different over there.
I want to take up something else
And go wandering in a doublet and trousers
To see if I can't earn some money in the war.
I'll leave this place like all the other good fellows.

The *Tailor* answers:

Stay, good fellow, I want to go with you.
What has happened to you is my fate too;
I must sit long hours for little pay
With which I can hardly survive.
Therefore I must take up something else
And start sewing with a hop pole

In the open field to the sound of pipes and drums
And see if I can't earn a little money there.

The contrast between the homely nature of their occupations and their military aspirations, between the tailor's needle and the soldier's hop pole or lance, seems to serve an ironic function. The temptation to enter military service must have been considerable, for mercenaries of even the lowest rank were paid more than many skilled craftsmen.[50] It is possible that such humor may have been good-natured and even sympathetic to the plight of artisans driven by economic circumstances to adopt this type of employment. The ironic intent underlying such images is more obvious in Erhard Schön's woodcut *Ursula and the Cobbler* (fig. 4.19).[51] As in the prints just discussed, the

4.17. Niklas Stör, *Cobbler*, woodcut. (Photo, Geisberg, *Woodcut*, vol. 4, cat. no. 1363.)

4.18. *Niklas Stör, Tailor,* woodcut. (Photo, Nuremberg, Germanisches Nationalmuseum.)

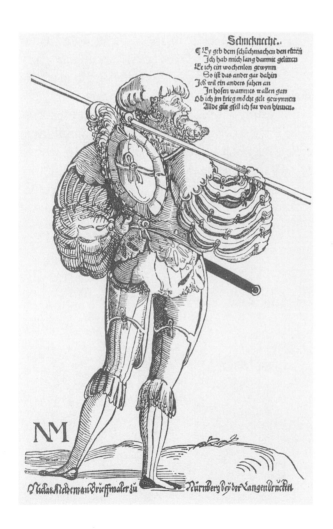

4.19. Erhard Schön, *Ursula and the Cobbler*, woodcut. (Photo, Geisberg, *Woodcut*, vol. 3, cat. no. 1213.)

4.20. Hans Weiditz, *Farmer Ulin and His Wife*, woodcut. (Photo, Gotha, Schlossmuseum.)

cobbler has decided to leave his craft and seek his fortune in the Italian wars, and he invites "little Ursula" to accompany him. Ursula is more than happy to give up her employment as a spinner, even though it means becoming "a cobbler's whore."

Interestingly enough, peasants, who constituted the greater part of the mercenary armies of this period, are rarely referred to in this imagery. The only example that includes them is a particularly gross caricature. Whereas Schön's *Ursula and the Cobbler* represents an elegantly dressed couple in which the mercenary is indistinguishable in appearance and bearing from the heroic genre discussed earlier, Hans Weiditz's woodcut *Farmer Ulin and His Wife* (fig. 4.20)[52] depicts a grotesquely fat soldier with a protruding lower jaw and a large goiter, whose body threatens to burst out of his nondescript clothing.

His companion is equally ugly, having a large hooked nose and an enormous belly. The soldier says:

I am called farmer Wallow from the linden tree
Where can one find a tougher warrior?
I'm well armed with spear and pole,
And my armor hangs about me.

The woman replies:

I carry good wine and a goose along
And stick close to this John.
I also feel his goiter for him
So that he feeds me all the more.

Schramhanns.

¶ Ich pin genent Valtein Schramhanns.
Jn Dennmarck wert ich mich des mans.
Jn dem Wirtzhawß auff dem vmplatz.
Lig ich noch tag vnd nacht im hatz.
Vnd welcher mich vnlustig macht.
Der müß pald liefferen mir ein Schlacht.

4.21. Erhard Schön, *Scarface*, woodcut. (Photo, Geisberg, *Woodcut*, vol. 3, cat. no. 1202.)

Whereas the humor of *Ursula and the Cobbler* depends on the ironic comment passed on the desire for gain, that of *Farmer Ulin and His Wife* rests upon a satire of the sexual relationship uniting the couple. The psychological distance established between the figures and the viewer by means of caricature is confirmed by the coarse and suggestive character attributed to them by the text.

Finally, some of the most sinister characteristics of mercenary behavior in the view of contemporary moralists also proved susceptible to treatment by this type of humor. Erhard Schön's woodcut *Scarface* (fig. 4.21)[53] is indistinguishable from those works that describe the function of particular ranks. Yet the text informs us:

I am called Valentine Scarface.
In Denmark, I thought highly of myself;
I caroused day and night
In the tavern on the campground,
And whoever annoyed me
Promptly had to fight me.

In this case the degree of immorality, drunkenness, and brawling suggests that the humor might be better described as satire than as irony.

Among the information that must be considered in attempting to determine the original function of mercenary imagery is the curious evidence afforded by a painting by the Brunswick Monogrammist, an Antwerp artist active in the 1540s, who depicted a series of mercenary prints on the back wall in one of his tavern scenes (figs. 4.22, 23).[54] This scene, in which prostitution, drinking, and fighting figure prominently, was probably intended to illustrate the consequences of drunkenness.[55] In view of the scene's allegorical nature, it would be unwise to view the mercenary series as merely part of the decor—though it does not seem impossible that such prints were used in this way.[56] On the other hand, that these images are represented as stuck on a wall that is covered with sexual drawings and scribbled obscenities suggests they were thought to belong in what is clearly a den of iniquity. Since one of the prints on the wall depicts a couple—a mercenary with a camp follower—it is possible that the series may have belonged to those that dealt with mercenary life in an ironic manner. If this is the case, irony has been incorporated in what is meant to be a satire on the habits associated with mercenaries.

The criticism of mercenaries found in the work of Hans Sachs, and the part these figures play in humorous songs as well as in the woodcuts just discussed, suggest an unease about their social role, evoking the debate on the legitimacy of war that was of importance in the early years of the Reformation. With the advent of the sixteenth century, the medieval doctrine of the "just war" had been subjected to considerable criticism by those interested in the reform of both the church and society.[57] The most vigorous and influential voice raised against war during the early years of the century was undoubtedly that of Erasmus. In his essay *How Sweet Is War for Those Who Have Not Tried It*, Erasmus launched a sweeping attack on contemporary justifications of war. After listing races, kingdoms, and peoples that mistakenly believe they can wage war on each other, he writes: "Finally a thing which in my opinion is worse than these, Christians fight against men; reluctantly I must add, and this is the very worst of all, Christians fight Christians. And, O blindness of the human mind! no one is astonished, no one is horrified."[58] Needless to say, Erasmus was offended by the very idea of a mercenary: "We recoil in horror from an executioner, because he cuts the throats of condemned criminals, although he is paid by order of the law to do it; but men who have left their

4.22. Brunswick Monogrammist, *Tavern Scene*. (Photo, Berlin, Staatliche Museen Preussischer Kulturbesitz, Gemäldegalerie.)

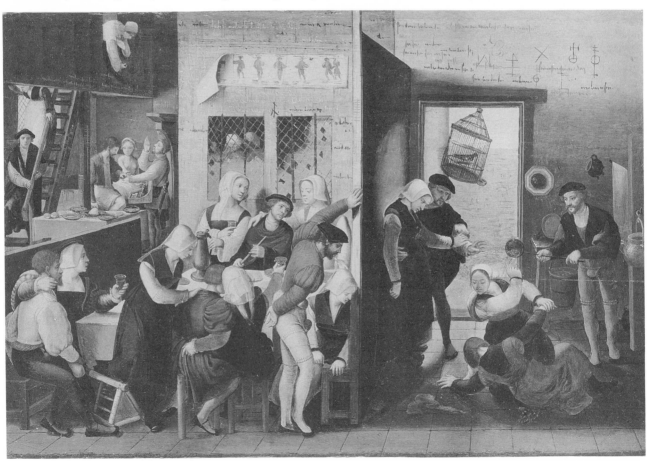

parents, wives and children to rush off to war uncompelled, not for honest wages but asking to be hired for some infamous butchery—when these men go home they are almost more in general favour than if they had never gone away."[59]

Erasmus incorporated similar criticism of this profession in his *Education of the Christian Prince*. Among the considerations the prince should keep in mind before entering war are the following: "Weigh the worries, the expenditures, the trials, the long wearisome preparation. That barbaric flux of men in the last stages of depravity must be got together, and while you wish to appear more generous in favor than the other prince, in addition to paying out money you must coax and humor the mercenary soldiers, who are absolutely the most abject and execrable type of human being."[60]

Erasmus's views were shared by many early reformers, even among the followers of Luther. For example, the Lutheran propagandist Johann Eberlin

4.23. Brunswick Monogrammist, *Tavern Scene*, detail.

von Günzburg included the following remarks in his antipapal pamphlet, *I Am Surprised That There Is No Money in the Land:*

An incalculable amount of money was wasted on the wars of Emperor Maximilian in the Netherlands, Hungary, Italy, against the Venetians, and in France. And in his time a new order of soulless people grew up called the *Landsknechte*. These people, who have no respect for honor or justice, travel to the place where they hope to receive payment and offer their services to the danger of their souls and to the detriment of ordinary honesty and good manners. There they learn and become habituated to all kinds of vice, to abuse, swearing, the use of bad words, oaths, and so forth. Indeed, they also learn whoring, adultery, rape, gluttony, drunkenness, and beastly things, such as stealing, robbing, and murder. These things become their daily bread, and they commit them against poor people who have never harmed them. In short, they are entirely in the power of the devil, who pulls them about wherever he wants.[61]

Martin Luther's early attitude toward the issue of war was much influenced by that of Erasmus. His earliest attacks on the papacy included criticism of the call for a crusade against the Turks. In the ninety-five theses of 1517, Luther condemned Leo X's plan for a crusade, arguing that the Turkish invasion was a sign of God's punishment of mankind, against which no human precaution could or should be taken.[62] Luther's view was severely criticized by his Catholic opponents and was often used to embarrass him as the Turkish menace grew more ominous. As a consequence of the Peasants' War of 1525, which had threatened to identify the Reformation with social revolution, Luther adjusted his views in such a way that they could no longer be regarded as a challenge to secular authority. He changed his position and insisted on the duty of the Christian to obey temporal authority over the demands of the individual conscience.[63] In the *Treatise on Secular Authority* of 1523 and *Whether Soldiers Too Can Be Saved* of 1526, Luther argued that it was the Christian's duty to bear arms if ordered to do so regardless of the cause he was called upon to serve.[64] On the other hand, Luther continued to believe that the Turks represented the "rod of God" (as he put it), or divine retribution for the sins of mankind. This meant that on a spiritual plane, the only way the Turks could be halted was by individual repentance and contrition. The works he composed in response to the Turkish invasion, the treatise *Concerning the War against the Turks* of 1529 and *An Army Sermon against the Turks* of the same year, are largely dedicated to explaining the eschatological significance of the Turkish threat and the need for repentance.[65] The Christian is not to take up arms in the name of Christ but only in the name of the divinely instituted authority—namely, the emperor. Just as the emperor may make war only in defense of his kingdom, so a soldier can go to war only in the service of his ruler. Neither may make war for honor or profit.

Luther's ambivalence regarding armed resistance to the Turks is echoed in the writings of his followers, who tend to stress the need for personal piety over practical defense measures. In 1532 the *Twenty-two Sermons on the Turkish War* by Johannes Brenz, the reformer of Schwäbisch Hall, appeared in Nuremberg together with a preface by Luther.[66] Brenz dwelt at length on the sins that had caused God to express his anger by means of the Turkish menace and the need for his people to change their ways if this punishment was to be averted. The war is thus transformed into a spiritual allegory, a psychomachy or battle between the virtues and the vices, rather than a practical response to a pressing historical situation. When the Turks threatened western Europe once again in 1541, the Nuremberg city council summoned the Lutheran pastors Andreas Osiander and Veit Dietrich to the town hall and asked them to urge the populace to prayer.[67] Both men not only conducted preaching campaigns but published treatises on the way Christians should react to the emergency. In these works, the war is once again used as the occasion to call for spiritual renewal. Both assert that the Turkish threat is God's punishment for, on the one hand, Catholics' failure to give up their benighted ways and, on the other, Protestants' failure to give up their sinful life.[68] The dualism of the Lutheran position thus results in a war that is waged on two fronts, one in the field and the other in human hearts, and success in the former is contingent upon success in the latter.

It was the primacy of the spiritual war over the temporal war in the Lutheran view that permitted the mercenary life itself to be used as an allegory of the Christian response to the Turkish menace. The preface to an anonymous pamphlet published in 1532 titled *A Christian Expedition against the Turks* states that since the Turks have been sent by God as a punishment, there is no prospect of defeating them as long as people continue their sinful ways.[69] According to the author, the text is intended as an "exemplar" of the way an expedition against the enemy should be undertaken. The mercenaries in this expedition include personifications of the virtues that are eager to join the army so as to serve a "colonel" who is identified as God himself and a "captain" who is none other than the emperor Charles V. The virtues—Faith, Love, Loyalty, Charity, Fear of God, Obedience, and Respect—take turns explaining why they are necessary to the life of the army. No victory can ever be obtained unless the mercenaries display the qualities they describe. The emperor then composes a new code of military discipline prescribing stiff penalties for sinful behavior. Some of the recruits, such as Martin Krug (Martin

Jug) and Hans Wildt (Wild John) are appalled by the new regulations and complain that they wanted to join an army, not enter a cloister. Nevertheless, they are persuaded to join the expedition because of the presence of God and the virtues. In a remarkable manifestation of the "two world" theory, the pamphlet ends with a song in praise of the emperor, placed in the mouth of a mercenary who expresses his willingness to fight for the imperial cause. In this manner the duty to obey temporal authority is incorporated within a broader program of spiritual improvement.

A Christian Expedition against the Turks, whose format both echoes and satirizes the frequent calls to arms issued in these years, is not the only work of its kind. Another anonymous work, *The Almighty, Undefeatable Emperor, Advises His Praiseworthy and Trusted Commanders, That They Should Arm Themselves and Make Ready as Soon as Possible Avoiding All Delay* (fig. 4.24),[70] bears a woodcut frontispiece of a standard-bearer between a drummer and a flutist—an image that was, as we have seen, a conventionalized visual means of referring to imperial power. The format of the pamphlet is intended to resemble a code of military discipline. It advises mercenaries who respond to

4.24. Anonymous, *Standard-Bearer between Drummer and Flutist*, woodcut, frontispiece to the anonymous pamphlet *Der Altermechtigste und unüberwindtlichste Keyser, . . .* (n.p., n.d.). (Photo, Wolfenbüttel, Herzog August Bibliothek.)

this call that service is for life and that the reward is eternal. The "almighty emperor" is of course God, and the mercenaries' weapons are described as the belt of truth, the breastplate of justice, the shield of faith, and the boots of the gospel. The transformation of external to internal action is complete. The events of the temporal world pale in the face of the appeal for spiritual renewal. In light of the Lutheran attitude toward the Turkish menace, it seems likely that Schön's *Baggage Train with Death* and the Sachs text that once accompanied it had more than *vanitas* significance. The equation of mercenary and Turk does not merely suggest the omnipresence of death and the need to prepare for the life to come; to a Lutheran audience, it must have evoked an eschatological view of the Turkish threat.

How do we account for the fact that both *A Column of Mercenaries* and *The Baggage Train with Death* were produced by a collaboration of the same artists at approximately the same time and yet project radically different attitudes toward their subject matter? In one the mercenary is the vehicle for an assertion of imperial strength made at a time of national danger, and in the other the mercenary is the means of suggesting that the Turkish invasions constitute a moral rather than a military emergency and that physical force is both inappropriate and inadequate to deal with what should be understood as divine retribution. To the largely Lutheran population of Nuremberg, such a contradiction may have appeared more apparent than real. Luther's "two world" theory made it possible both to respond positively to the emperor's appeal for assistance in organizing a military resistance and to view the Turkish menace as a sign of God's displeasure. Whereas one image addressed the world of temporal events, the other penetrated appearances to address their underlying spiritual significance.

There is little doubt that mercenary imagery also had powerful social implications. *A Column of Mercenaries* with its ranks of elegantly clad officers must have appealed to those in the upper classes who filled such positions and whose ideas about military life were still associated with the chivalric ideal. It is perhaps no accident that one of the surviving impressions of this print, that illustrated in figure 4.1, may once have formed part of a princely collection. Not only would its status as a "giant" woodcut have made it an expensive item, but whoever first owned it went to the trouble and expense of having it colored. It is possible that *A Column of Mercenaries* also appealed to this class because it resembled both the visual format and the literary tenor of the *Triumphal Procession of Maximilian I*. As we have seen, the *Triumphal Procession* had been given to a select group of nobles and imperial officials. Its sale on the open market was prohibited, so that it was unavailable to those who were aware of its existence but had not been fortunate enough to receive a copy in the original distribution. Where these images were used as a form of interior decoration, the figure of the mercenary would have served as a way a household could display the fervor of its allegiance to the emperor. Rather than contrasting with the ideals of the class that occupied the house, like the images of carousing peasants, the mercenaries would have served as symbols of the law and order on which their position in the social hierarchy depended. It is possible that the appeal of the heroic imperial mercenary cut across the social spectrum. Such images represented an assertion of Nuremberg's identity as an imperial free city. It was a means by which all classes could take pride in their urban identity. The city's fate was exalted by its identification with the fate of the nation. To those members of the upper classes, including merchants and professionals, who subscribed to the new humanist culture, these images would have had an additional resonance. Since they regarded the emperor in a nationalistic rather than a feudal light, they would have viewed the image of the heroic imperial mercenary as an attractive sign of the vitality and power of a new civilization. For those artisans who had suffered from the introduction of a capitalist organization of labor, the swashbuckling gestures and splendid costumes would have combined with the decriptions of high pay and plunder to make the mercenary's life appear highly attractive. Such images may well have encouraged them to disregard the miseries of war, thus contributing to their decisions to abandon their trades.

The appeal of the comic or satiric representations of mercenaries is more difficult to assess. For those members of the patriciate who served in the officer corps, the idea that artisans and peasants should engage in war may still have seemed outlandish and faintly ridiculous—a necessary evil but a profanation of the feudal memories and chivalric ideals that still colored their own attitudes. Other members of the upper classes such as merchants and professionals who did not go to war may have found something comic as well as reprehensible in the economic motives that impelled artisans to leave their appointed social station. Artisans on the other hand, must have looked at such images more ambivalently. For those who were doing well—master artisans, for example—the images may have shown the folly of those less successful than themselves, who were seduced into a disorderly and dangerous life by the attractions of higher pay. For the less fortunate, they must have constituted an ironic commentary on their own economic plight.

5

The Battle of the Sexes and the World Upside Down

Illustrated broadsheets produced in Nuremberg during the first half of the sixteenth century dealing with the subject of marriage have received scant attention from art historians. The images have been attributed to various artists and cataloged according to the principles of stylistic connoisseurship, but no attempt has been made to interpret their historical significance as cultural artifacts.[1] Rather than survey the entire genre I will concentrate on one particular example, the *Briefmaler* Albrecht Glockendon's broadsheet titled *There Is No Greater Treasure Here on Earth Than an Obedient Wife Who Covets Honor,* which was published in Nuremberg in 1533 and illustrated with a woodcut by Erhard Schön (fig. 5.1).[2]

Schön's image represents a man pulling a cart, who is urged onward by a woman holding a whip. This pair is watched by another young couple together with a woman dressed in fool's costume and an old man. The ritual substitution of humans for beasts of burden was a traditional means of symbolizing the inversion of the social order in German carnival celebrations in the late Middle Ages. Women of marriageable age who had no suitors, or sometimes old unmarried women, were mocked for their lack of husbands by being forced to pull a plow through or around their villages.[3] Hans Sachs made use of this theme for a broadsheet illustrated by Erhard Schön, dated 1532 (fig. 5.2).[4] In the text that bears the title *The Housemaids Pull the Plow,* Sachs takes the opportunity to moralize against the old carnival custom, saying that instead of rushing into marriage, young people should give it very careful consideration. This carnival practice had been put to revolutionary purposes during the Reformation when monks were forced to pull the plow. In this instance the anticlerical mockery seems to have consisted in equating celibate men with unmarried women who failed to perform their "social duty."[5] In the light of this tradition it is hardly surprising that this form of

5.1. Erhard Schön, *There Is No
Greater Treasure Here on Earth
Than an Obedient Wife Who Covets
Honor*, woodcut, 1533. (Photo,
Gotha, Schlossmuseum.)

ritualized mockery should have been used to invoke the idea of folly. Albrecht
Dürer's woodcut illustrating chapter 47 of Sebastian Brant's *Ship of Fools* (fig.
5.3) represents a man in fool's costume pulling a cart through an open field.
The chapter, titled "On the Road to Salvation," is introduced with lines that
read:

Some men persist in folly's road
And draw a cart with heavy load
The right cart awaits in heaven's abode.[6]

Kein edler schatz ist auff der ert / Dann ein frums weib die ehr begert.

Der arm götze.

Ach weh ach weh mir armen narren
Wie hart zeuch ich in disem karren
Darzu hat mich weybnemen bracht
Ich wolt ich het mirs nie gedacht
So man ist kumen in mein hauß
Zeucht mir schwert / bruch vñ tasche auß
Nacht vnd tag hab ich kein rhu
Vnd kein gürtes wort darzu
Mein trew ist jr nicht angenehm
Meine wort sind jr gar widerzehm
Also geschicht noch manchem man
Der nichtes hatt / waß er kan
Wil doch bey zeyt ein frawen han.

Die fraw spricht.

Ey lieber gesell ists aber war?
Schweyg still ich fall dir in das har /
Wiltu ein schönes frumes frewlein han
Das dir allzeyt ist vnderthan
So bleyb daheym in deinem hauß
Vnd lauff nicht alle lüder auß
Nacket gan vnd haussieren lauffen /
Zunger leyden vnd wasser lauffen
Vnd bleyben bey weyblicher eer
Ist schönen jungen frawen schwer
Wiltu nit arbaiten vnd mich erneren /
So mustu waschen / spülen / vnd keeren /
Vnd must dir lassen dein bad erberen.

Der geselle.

Was sagt jr darzu junckfraw seyn /
Wolt jr auch also sy man seyn
Vnd selber haben in ewr bende
Schwert / bruch / taschen vnd regiment
Mit wort beissen / schnarre vñ schneide
Das künd vnd möcht ich re nicht leide
Solt ich mich mit euch rauffen vñ schlag
Villeycht müst ich in einen wagen gen
Wie diser man im karren leyden
Vnd alle freud vnd kürtzweyl meyden
Sol ich mein freies leben verzeren
Mit spülen / waschen / kochen vnd keren
Ich wolt ehe weybnemen verschweren.

Die junckfraw.

Gesel glaube mir bey meiner ehr
Solches gewales ich nicht beger
Wann jr wöllet nach ehren ringen
So seyd selb man in allen dingen
Vnd wenn jr mich allein gewert
Was einer frawen zugehert
Zu lieb vnd layd noturffte vnd ehren
So wil ich anders nicht begeren
Dann alheyt erwein willen than
Daran solt jr kein zweyffel han
In ewrem dienst wil ich mich yeben
Vnd euch in stäter freundschafft lieben
Wil euch mit keinem wort betrieben.

Die Nerrin.

Hüt dich bey leib du junger knecht
Ich arme nerrin sag dir recht
Man sagt vil gürtes von der Ee
Sy hiesz vil billicher das wehe /
Du müst leyden biß in den todt
Vil angst / sorg / kummer vnd auch not
Das dir kein mensch nicht wenden kan
Findstu doch sunst wol frewlein schan
Die geren thun den willen deyn
Nur vmb ein kendlein mit weyn
Darnach magst du sie faren lan
Vnd ein andere nemen an
Eyn ehweyb müstu ewig han.

Der weiß man.

Gesel ich wil dich bessers leren
Thu dich nicht an ein nerrin keren
Hüt dich allzeyt vor buren list
Du wirst betrogen zu aller frist
Nym dir ein frewlein zu der Ehe
Got geb wie es dir mit jr gehe
So bleyb bey jr in lieb vnd leyt
Vnd biß gedultig alle zeit
Ob dir begegnet kummers vil
Gedenck dir es sey Gottes wil
Ner sie im schweyß deyns angesicht
Wie Got am ersten Genesis spricht
Gedult vnd leyden ist ein port
Durch die wir kumen an das ort
Da die Engel wonung han

Also spricht Albrecht Glockendon.

5.2. Erhard Schön, *The House-maids Pull the Plow,* woodcut, 1532. (Photo, Vienna, Albertina.)

The image of Schön's cart-pulling man, with its references to carnival practice and the idea of folly, suggests that we witness a situation in which the "natural" order has been inverted. The carnival practice of harnessing women or monks to a plow to mock their failure to get married was turned inside out when a man was represented in this position for having done so.

This transformation is comprehensible only in terms of the idea of the "power of women" to which this image also makes reference. During the course of the fifteenth century the image of a man ridden by a woman had been developed as a visual metaphor of the abasement and humiliation to which men were liable as a consequence of their susceptibility to the seductive attraction of women. This may be seen, for example, in an engraving by the Housebook Master representing the legend of Phyllis and Aristotle (fig. 5.4).[7] Illustrations of this thirteenth-century legend, according to which the ancient philosopher was induced to carry a pretty young woman about on his back because of his sexual infatuation with her, formed part of a series of scenes representing the way great men were humiliated as a consequence of the evil power of women.[8] Much the same motif was used to satirize marriages in which the woman had usurped her husband's "natural" position of authority. This idea was also illustrated by the Housebook Master in a satirical coat of arms in which a peasant woman rides on her husband's back while he is forced to hold her distaff (fig. 5.5).[9] In this case, that the image represents a violation

Vil ðünt jnn ðorßeyt ßye beßarren
Vnd zießen vaſt eyn ſchweren karrßen
Dort würt ðer recßt wag naßer faren

võ dẽ weg der ſellikeit

Gott laßt eyn narren nit verſton
Syn wunder/ðie er ßat getßon
Vnd tãglicß ðũt/ðar vmß verðyrßt
Gar mancßer narr/ðer zittlicß ſtyrßt

5.3. Albrecht Dürer, *On the Road
to Salvation*, woodcut illustrating
chapter 47 of Sebastian Brant's
Ship of Fools (Basel, 1494).
(Photo, Hans Koegler, ed., *Das
Narrenschiff* [Basel, 1913].)

of the "natural" sexual hierarchy is made explicit by a peasant standing on his
head in the center of the shield.

In Schön's woodcut (fig. 5.1) the inversion of the established marital order
is also alluded to by the articles in the woman's left hand: a sword, a purse,
and a pair of pants. All three items were used to symbolize male authority in
both the literature and the art of this period. For example, the anonymous
woodcut frontispiece to the Nuremberg playwright Hans Folz's poem *The
Evil Smoke* (fig. 5.6) represents a woman beating her husband after having
deprived him of his purse, his sword, and his pants.[10] The poem recounts a
marital struggle for the right to wear the pants, which—then as now—are
used as a metaphor of authority.[11] The "battle for the pants" was in fact one
of the more popular images used to satirize wifely insubordination.[12] For example, an engraving by Israhel van Meckenem (fig. 5.7) represents a woman
beating her husband with a distaff while the object of their struggle, the man's
pants, lies prominently displayed in the foreground.[13] The demon who abets

the woman's efforts makes clear the moral we are to derive from her behavior. The characterization of a dominating woman as evil is also found in the visual tradition of the battle between the old woman and the devil. This theme, which may have its origins in the medieval Latin proverb "A bad woman is three times worse than the devil,"[14] was a popular one in fifteenth-century art and literature. An anonymous broadsheet published at Augsburg about 1475 (fig. 5.8) shows an old woman beating a number of devils into submission with a spoon.[15] The text makes a point of equating the fate of the devils with that of a man married to an angry wife. Finally, the contents of the barrel the

5.4. Housebook Master, *Phyllis and Aristotle*, engraving. (Photo, Amsterdam Rijksprentenkabinet.)

5.5. Housebook Master, *Coat of Arms with a Peasant Standing on His Head*, engraving. (Photo, Amsterdam Rijksprentenkabinet.)

Eyn liet genant der póß rauch
Jn der flam weis

5.6. Anonymous, *Battle for the Pants,* woodcut frontispiece to Hans Folz's poem *The Evil Smoke.* (Photo, Gustav Könnecke, *Bilderatlas zur Geschichte der deutschen Nationallitteratur* [Marburg, 1895], p. 101.)

5.7. Israhel van Meckenem, *Battle for the Pants,* engraving. (Photo, Berlin, Kupferstichkabinett, Staatliche Museen Preussischer Kulturbesitz.)

man pulls in the cart in Schön's woodcut are a reference to the term *Windelwascher* (diaper washer), a derogatory name for a henpecked husband.[16] The batlike object perched on top of the load was a primitive laundry aid used to beat out the dirt. This object may be identified through a woodcut by Hans Schäuffelein (fig. 5.9) that once illustrated a lost broadsheet by Hans Sachs titled *Ho, Ho, Diaper Washer.*[17]

The text of Glockendon's broadsheet serves both to articulate more fully the theme of female insubordination and to pass judgment on it. The title *There Is No Greater Treasure Here on Earth Than an Obedient Wife Who Covets Honor* is not only a reference to the Old Testament book of Proverbs, "Who can find a virtuous woman, for her price is far above rubies," but a quotation

Ich kam auff ein gewilde wege
Do sach ich zu der selben tzeit
Ein ubel weyb das ist war
Strepten mit des teuffels schar
Es geschach auff ein morgen fru
Die teuffel setzte de ubeln weib zu
Mit mangerley schalckhait
Einer schwur auff seinen eyd
Er wolt grousse ding began
Wolt das ubel weib allein bstan
Sie hpelten gegen einannder
Die teuffel mit prem pancr
Das ubel weib stund allein dort
Vnd sprach greuweliche wort
Wol her ir teuffel alle gemein
Bey de grouß vnd auch klein
Wir wollen an annder peyssen
Zerren grymmen vnd reyssen
Sie zerriß in kurtzer stund
Der teuffel mer dann tausunt
Ir aller meyster der lag tot
Do hub sich angst vnd not
Vber das ubel weib also
We we sie thut vns allen also
Do sprach ein teuffelischer man
Von dem strept sullen wir lan
Vnnd wider in die helle faren
Da muge wir vns wol bewaren
Vnd do sie in die helle komen
Ir einer sprach bey namen
Vñ were wir lenger hie gewese
Vnser kainer wer vor ir genesen

Von der bösen vnseligen dyet
Ir aller syn in das do ryet
Wol vns lieben gesellen mein
Das wir also entrunnen sein
Wann wer mit ubeln weiben
Sein tzeit muß hye vertreyben
Dem wer vil weger der tod
Denn das er kome in solhe not
Ist sie ubel vnnd arg von art
Weim das er ye geboren wart
Ist er traurig so ist sie fro
Wil er denn sunst sie will so
Wil er gen sie wil lauffen
Wil er strelen sie wil rauffen
Wil er traben sie wil tzelten
Wil er kpfeln sie wil schelten
Wil er essen sie wil trincken
Wil er springen sie wil hincken
Wil er denn ligen sie wil sitzen
Wil er auffsten sie wil schwitzen
Wil er denn kalt sie wil heyß
So er sie nart so läst sy ein scheiß
Sy gat tzu einem pfaffen
Also kan sie es geschaffen
Darumb wer ein ubel weyb hab
Der thu sich ir bey tzeit ab
Vnnd füre sie da in die hellen
Zu den teuffelischen gesellen
Das ist von den ubeln weyben
Die tugenthafften leyd vertreyben
Des das ubel weyb nit enkan
Darumb hasset sie yederman

of a well-known sixteenth-century German proverb, "A devoted wife is worth more than her weight in gold." [18] In invoking the notion of the ideal wife, the title thus offers us the opposite of the unruly woman in the image. The text printed above the man pulling the cart reads in part:

Oh woe, oh woe is me, poor fool
How I must work to pull this cart!
And why? Because I took myself a wife.
Would that the thought had never crossed my mind!
A shrewish scold has come into my house;
She has taken my sword, my pants, and my purse.
Night and day I have no peace,
And never a kind word from her. [19]

The woman behind him replies:

Hey, dear boy, what you say is true,
But be quiet or I'll hit you over the head.
If you want a beautiful and pious little wife
Who obeys you at all times,
Then stay at home in your own house
And stop carousing about.
. . . If you will not work to support me,

5.9. Hans Schäuffelein, *Diaper Washer*, woodcut to lost poem *Ho, Ho, Diaper Washer* by Hans Sachs, 1536? (Photo, Coburg, Kupferstichkabinett, Kunstsammlungen Veste Coburg.)

Then you must wash, spin, and draw the cart
And be beaten on your back.

The couple standing to the right of this argumentative pair pass comment on their behavior in the following exchange. The young man asks the woman whether she would treat him as badly if they were to get married. She replies that she would do no such thing:

Boy, believe me on my word of honor,
That I have no desire for such power.
If we have an honest disagreement
You will remain the man in all things.
I only ask you to grant me
Those things that belong to a wife.
That you love, honor, and suffer with me in times of need.
More I shall not demand.

The woman standing behind them, who is dressed in the costume of a court fool, warns the young man against marriage, saying that it will only bring him "much anxiety, uncertainty, worry, and want." She proposes as an alternative that he seek his pleasure with women who will do his will for a bottle of wine. Although the image of the court fool had become identified with sinful behavior of all kinds as a result of the publication of Sebastian Brant's *Ship of Fools*, it is significant that it should first have been used as a way of moralizing against lust.[20] An example of this usage is found in an engraving by the anonymous Master E. S. (fig. 5.10) that represents an allegorical figure of lust being approached by a fool.[21] As a consequence it is fair to conclude that her costume is a comment on the promiscuous way of life she recommends.

The woman's advice is opposed by that of the old man, whose speech brings the text to a close:

Do not listen to this foolish woman.
Beware the wiles of whores,
Who will always deceive you.
Go and take a wife.
God determines how your life together will be,
So stay with her in love and suffering
And always be patient.
And if you should have much worry and care,
Look on it as God's will.
Provide for her by the sweat of your brow
As God commanded in the first book of Genesis.

The figure of an old man as a source of moralizing wisdom is familiar in the art and literature of this period. A visual example is found in Israhel van

Meckenem's allegory *The Hunt for Fidelity* (fig. 5.11).[22] The engraving represents a noblewoman who, while out hunting with falcons and dogs, encounters an old friar. The banderole surrounding her reads: "I set out with birds
and greyhounds / To see if I could find true fidelity." The friar replies:
"Maiden gentle and pure, / You will find that only in God."[23] The old man in
Schön's print is a secular equivalent of Meckenem's friar. The contrast between the woman's commendation of promiscuity and the old man's call for
restraint and self-sacrifice constitutes an opposition of reason and desire in
terms of sexual alterity that affords a symbolic justification for the insistence
on female subordination in marriage.[24]

The broadsheet *There Is No Greater Treasure* is typical of those dealing with
marriage in its preoccupation with the need for male authority. Two comple-
mentary broadsheets with the titles *Doktor Syman* (Doctor Sheman) and *Doktor Kolbman* (Doctor Cudgel), illustrated with woodcuts by Niklas Stör, were
published in Nuremberg about 1530 (figs. 5.12, 5.13).[25] The names *Sieman*
and *Kolbman* occur frequently in German literature of the late fifteenth and

5.10. Master E. S., *Lust and the
Fool*, engraving. (Photo, Dresden
Kupferstichkabinett.)

5.11. Israhel van Meckenem, *The Hunt for Fidelity,* engraving. (Photo, Basel Kunstmuseum.)

sixteenth centuries to refer to overbearing wives and husbands respectively.[26] The woodcut of the *Syman* broadsheet represents an innkeeper greeting two female travelers. The anonymous text informs us that *Syman* is a famous doctor who can analyze urine (which accounts for the beaker in her hand) and operate on kidney stones. Her title was undoubtedly intended to heighten the impression that her claim to power is illegitimate, since women were excluded from the medical profession. The innkeeper is reluctant to afford her hospitality because he has heard bad things about her. However, he is finally persuaded to do so only to discover that as soon as she enters the inn she takes control of his household, steals his money, and drives him into the street. The conclusion warns men to beware of *Doktor Syman*, because once she has entered a house it is very difficult to get rid of her. The corresponding broadsheet is intended as a reply to the one just described. *Docktor Kolbman* is described as the "cure" for disorderly households, one who holds the remedy (a cudgel) in his hand. Needless to say, the innkeeper, who has in the meantime been reduced to a servant, is delighted to let him in so that he can rid him of *Doktor Syman*. At the approach of *Doctor Cudgel*, "Doctor Sheman" beats a hasty retreat through the back door.

Another undated broadsheet illustrated by Barthel Beham showing a bagpipe player riding a horse backward (fig. 5.14)[27] also advocates subordinating wives to husbands by force. Ruth Mellinkoff has shown that riding backward was a form of humiliation used in the Middle Ages to shame criminals and

5.12. Niklas Stör, *Doctor Sheman*, woodcut. (Photo, Gotha, Schloss-museum.)

Docktoꝛ Syman.

¶ Docktoꝛ Symans Legat.
Herꝛ Wirt hie kumen frembde Geſt
Docktoꝛ Syman der erbar vnd veſt
Wil bey euch ſtecken ſeine Pferdt
Im hauß / ſtuben vnd vmb den herdt
Möcht er von euch geweret ſein
So wolt er zu euch zehen ein.
¶ Der Haußwirt.
Dein Herꝛen ich gar nit beger
Wer er noch ſo eyn groſſer Herꝛ
Seyt man jm vil arges nach ſaget
Wie er ſein eygen Wirt auß jaget
So er das bey mir vben wolt
Ich ſein lieber geraten ſolt
Mit wie vil Pferden reyt er eyn
So ſag ich dir den wille mein.
¶ Legat.
Herꝛ wirt ſein vermögen iſt gros
Im volgen etlich hundert Roß
Die werden jm bald kumen zů
Du darffſt nit ſoꝛgen vmb vntů.
¶ Haußwirt.
Behüt mich Gott voꝛ ſeinem kumen
Ich hab gehöꝛt von manchem frumen
Das man jn mit eym pferd vnd knecht
Gar ſelten kan verſehen recht.
Ich ſchweig dã mit vil hundert pferdt
Wie wil Syman ſo gwaltig werden.
¶ Legat.
Meyn lieber wirt haſt nit erfarn
Das die welt ſo in kurtzen Jarn
Zu groſſer verendung iſt kumen
Alſo hat ſich derꝛlich zugenumen
Docktoꝛ Syman in aller welt
Wie wol er nit hat groſſes gelt
So nun doch Docktoꝛ Syman an

Der dir den Bꝛunnen ſchauen kan.
¶ Haußwirt.
Wie / kan dein Herꝛ den Bꝛunnen ſchawẽ
So kömen zů jm man vnd frawen
Wer möcht ſein ein vñ auß gen leyden.
¶ Legat.
Den Harmſtein kan er auch ſchneiden
Das dir die augen vber lauffen
So wurt er dir der kirchey kauffen.
¶ Haußwirt.
So ſchweig ich wil deins herꝛen nicht
Vnd red es hie bey eydes pflicht
Darumb dein Herꝛ hie hat keyn ſtat.
Reyt foꝛthin das dich Gott berat.
¶ Legat.
Herꝛ Wirt ſchlag es nit ab mit eyl
Der ſuch es voꝛ mit jm eyn weyl
Na wo die Jungen Gſellen ſein
Da ſeind ſy frölich bey dein wein
Thond ſer wider mein Herꝛen puchen
Vnd wan ſy jn acht tag verſuchen
Macht er ſy ſo mürb vnd gelenck
Das ſy ſchlieſſen vnthert benck
Darumb ſchlag mein Herꝛen nit auß
Zu herbürgen in deinem hauß.
¶ Haußwirt.
Ach wie hat ſich gewent das ſpil
Das dein Herꝛ Docktoꝛ Symanwil
Sein herbürg wil hieinen hon
Bey mir armen betrübten man
Doch wan er mich lies Herꝛ im h auß
Wolt ich jn gleich nit treyben auß.
¶ Legat.
Regieren magſt zu aller friſt
Wan Syman in dem bade iſt
Zu marckt oder zu kirchen auß

Die weyl ſo biſt du Herꝛ im hauß.
¶ Haußwirt.
O ich armer elender man
Kumbt heind zu mir Docktoꝛ Syman
Nun mag es ye nit anderſt ſein
So ſeyt zu frid vnd ziecht herein
Bald Docktoꝛ Syman kam inß hauß
Da ward des mannes herſchung auß
Da thet Syman nach ſeinem will
Der gute Man muſt ſchweigen ſtill
Vñ doꝛfft kein woꝛt dar wider murren
Syman der in dem hauß vmſchnurret
Mit meiſterſchafft in alle ecken
Der man wolt jn in harniſch ſchꝛecken
Da thet jm Syman wol auß ſcheren
Vnd ward jm ſeinen Seckel lehren
Das jm kein pfening blyb darin
Der man nam jm in ſeinen ſin
Vnd meind Syman zu dieyben auß
Da yagt jn Syman aus dem haus
Bald ward dem ſchertz der boden auß
¶ Beſchluß.
Darumb jr menner ſchaut dar zů
Vnd rath wie man den dingen thů
Das wir den Syman dieyben auß
Dan wo er eynwurtzt in ein Hauß
Da man jn gar kaum kan vertreyben
Da wil er ſtetigs meyſter bleyben
Der Scheffer zu der Newen Sat
Sein Röſſlein aus geboten hat
Zu geben eynem yeden Man
Der den ſyman vertreyben kan
Vnd ſelb in ſeinem Haus Regiert
Nit weis ich wem das pferdlein wirt.

Gedruckt zu Nürnberg durch
Hanns Wandereiſen.

5.13. Niklas Stör, *Doctor Cudgel*, woodcut. (Photo, Gotha, Schlossmuseum.)

Doctor Kolbman.

Wo Doctor Kolbman wont im hauß / Da ist alles Regiment auß

Das Doctor Syman thůt treyben / Wiewol er solchs hart ist meyden

Vnd ymer hofft im sol gelingen / Auff das letzt so wil jm zerrinnen

All sein witz/kunst vnd finantzen / hilfft nicht/er můß sich doch selb wantzen

Doctor Kolbmans Legat.
Glück zů lieber herr Wirt glück zů
Den abent spat vnde auch frů.

Der Haußwirt.
Des hab danck lieber freunde mein
Vnd solts mir auch Got wilkum sein
Was ist die bit vnd dein begeren
Sage an/villeycht ich geweren
Möchte dich nach dē willen dein
Hie/da oder im hauße mein.

Doctor Kolbmans Legat.
Herr Wirt ich byn zu euch gesand
Von meinē herrn/der da zuhand
Kompt hernach zu roß vnd begert
Bey euch zůstellen seine pferd
Darüb so gebt mir zů verstan
Das ich mich mach gar bald auff ban
Vnd thů was kunde meinem herren
Der kompt schnel/vnd ist nicht ferren
Auff das er solchs erfar vnd wiß
Drumb ich da bin zubegeren diß.

Der Haußwirt.
Lieber freunde nun merck mich eben
Bald ich dir zůuerstehen geben
Wil nach deiner bit vnd begeren
Noch eyns des thů du mich geweren
Vnd zeyg mir an zu diser frist
Wie mechtig vnd gewaltig ist
Dein herr/der da bald wirt komen
Als ich von dir hab vernomen
Deßgleychen auch den namen sein
Ob ich erkēt den herren dein.

Doctor Kolbmans Legat
Herr Wirt ich thů jn nicht nennen
Villeicht jr jn möcht erkennen
So er zu euch wurd eyntreyten
Darüb so sagt mir bey zeyten
Ob er bey euch möcht herberg hon
Wenn er ist gar ein tapffer man
All sein thun ist so gewaltig
Auch regirt er manigfaltig
Wo er hinkompt zu diser frist
Drumb er wol anzůnemen ist
Wo Doctor Syman thůt regieren
Vnd mit seiner bracht jubilieren
Vber das gantze haußgesinde
Auch darzů man vberwinde
Das er můß thun nach seinē willen
Mit einē wort kan er jn stillen

Das er jm můß sein vnterthan
Vnd helt jn für ein göckelman
Treybt mit jm solches affenspil
Das er leben můß wie er wil
Vnd dråt jm gar bald ein nasen
Darzů er jm thůt verglasen
Die augen mit seiner list so gschwind
Das er zůsehend darob erblindt
Noch vil mehr/die jetz nicht wil
Die doch gehörn zů disen spil
Erzelen/vnd hie zeygen an
Allen gwalt von Doctor Syman
Den er treybt/wo er thůt regieren
Vnd mit aller macht gubernieren
Darüb so besynnt euch eben
Ob jr nun wölt herberg geben
Meim herrn/der euch wol helffen kan
Auch so jr jm thůt zeygen an
Ewern beschwerde vnd vberlaß
So euch widerfert on alle maß
Von doctor Syman zůgewende
Mit der artzney in seiner hende.

Der Haußwirt.
Lieber freunde so vernym mich rechte
Ich byn meins haus ein armer knechte
Mein gewalt ist mir genomen
durch eyn/der zů mir ist komen
Newlich in mein gar kleynes hauß
Do er kam/mein herschen war auß
Drumb so darff ich mich nit vnterstan
An sein willen dein herrn nemen an

doctor Kolbmans Legat.
Nun merck ich wol lieber herr Wirt
das auch in eweim hauß regirt
Doctor Syman mit grosser gwalt
darumb so verneimpt mich gar bald
Vnd euch nicht lang thut besynnen
Sonder meim herren zu vergynnen
In ewr hauß/der euch gar wol kan
Erretten vor doctor Syman.

Der Haußwirt.
Ey lieber freundt wenn ich das weß
Das es wer der erbar vnd vest
doctor Kolbman/auff den ich allzeyt
Verhofft/darüb so gee / vnd nit beyt
die herberg sey jm zůgesagt
Denn ich wirt also wol geplagt
In meym hauß von doctor Syman
Tag vnde nacht ich kein rhů han

Mit pochen/beyssen/ vmbschnurren
Vil böser wort/wider murren
Mit schüffel spüln/teren vnd kochen
Nicht ein gut wort die gantze wochen
Das ich möchte von jm haben
Am narren sayl můß ich traben
Vnd also ziehen in dē pflug
Das wasser tragen in dē krug
Ein das hauß vnd in die kuchen
Noch werd für vnd für jr puchen
Gegen mir also vil armen
darumb so last euchs erbarmen
Herr Kolbman/vnd ziehet herein
Ein werder gast solt jr mir sein.

Herr doctor Kolbman.
Ey lieber Wirt nun merck mich eben
Ein guten rath ich dir wil geben
Dem soltu folgen allezeyt
Ich sey dir nahent oder weyt
Seyd du mich hast genomen an
So wil ich dir on argen wan
Verschaffen frid vnd eynigkeyt
Gescheh dir was/es wer mir leyt
dann es muß sein vnterthan
Auch allezeyt doctor Syman
Der vberal so mechtig ist
Wo ich nicht wone zu diser frist
Doctor Kolbman/der edl vnd vest
Mit meinē scepter der aller best
Welches ich für in seiner hande
damit ich offt dickmals verpanc
doctor Symans widerpellen
der sich nicht dargegen darff stellet
Als wer es jm gar widerzem
Sonst ist die recht artzney nem
damit ich stil das groß prallen
Welchs da geet auß seiner schnallen
daraus denn folgt vil vngemach
darüb höret zu was er sprach
Als ich zum Wirt einziehen thet
Wie bald er das vernumen het
Vnd trolte sich zur thür hinden auß
Wolt nicht erwarten mein im hauß
dann er mich so fast wol erkent
Wie ich zerstör sein regiment
Damit sein herschen hat ein ende.

Mit trewen rath ich Doctor Syman
Das er allzeyt flieche Doctor Kolbman

113

other wrongdoers.[28] In France and England this form of punishment was also used for the public humiliation of men who had been beaten by their wives.[29] In Germany such a custom was recorded at Darmstadt and elsewhere in the sixteenth century.[30] According to the anonymous text printed with the image, the hunchbacked rider identifies himself as "The Shepherd from Newtown." "The Shepherd from Newtown" was also the name of a popular fifteenth- and sixteenth-century German dance that had been singled out for comment by moralists, possibly because of the way the men hugged their partners.[31] The rider's name, therefore, must have conjured up images of sexual license in the mind of the sixteenth-century viewer. According to the text, the shepherd confesses to having liked women too much. He advises other men not to do the same or they will find that women become thorns in their sides (literally "eyes"). The consequence of his own infatuation is that he must ride his horse backward. He advises men that if their wives answer them back, they should beat them soundly or throw them to the ground. If they follow his advice they

5.15. Barthel Beham, *The Nine Hides of an Angry Wife*, woodcut. (Photo, Gotha, Schlossmuseum.)

will find that, just as he tamed his horse with beatings and spurs, so will their wives become obedient.

In contrast to the allegorical images of female insubordination just discussed, the illustrations to many of the marriage broadsheets are conspicuous for their "naturalistic" or mimetic representation of marital violence. A typical example is Barthel Beham's woodcut for Hans Sachs's broadsheet *The Nine Hides of an Angry Wife* (fig. 5.15).[32] In this case the image is a reversal of the

Die Meünerley hewt einer bösen frawen/sampt jren neün aygenschafften.

Als ich eins abents gieng spacieren
Ward einer sach nach fantasieren
Gieng auff vnd ab die Haller wiesen
Do gieng herein vom Püchsen schiessen
Mein gsellen einer der sich zwar
Verhayrat het in disem Jar
Der war zerckratzet vns zerckrelt
Den grüst ich vnd zü red jn stelt
Wo er gewest wer vntern katzen
Er sprach/du darffst mich nit seer fatzen
Die katzen haben mein nicht gfelt
Mein fraw die hat mir also gstrelt
Ich sprach/wie hat sich das begeben
Er sprach/nun hör vnd merck mich eben
Mein weyb ist nicht wie ander leut
Wann sie hat wol neünerley heut
O beinander/des hat sie pur
An jr auch neünerley natur
Des müß yegkliche haut allein
Besonderbar geschlagen sein
Es wil kein schlagen an jr klecken
Ich sprach thü mir die sach entecken
Das ichs verstee/ich bitt dich drum
Er sprach/in Summa summarum
Als ich am Montag kam vom wein
Vnd was ich fragt die Frawen mein
So wolt sie nur kein antwort geben
Do dacht ich bey mir selbert eben
Ich hab offt ghört von alten leuten
Etlich weyber sind von neün heuten
Der mir zü teyl ist eine woren
Also ergrimet ich in zoren
Vnd thet jr die Stockfisch haut plewen
Zum nechsten sich vor mir zü thewen
Antwort zü geben auff mein frag
So bald ich jr gab noch ein schlag
Do het ichs auff Bernhaut troffen
Do kam ein röt jr her geloffen
Vnd fieng beymlichen an zü prawmen
Wiewol ich kein wort hab vernumen
Gab ich jr noch ein güts an schlaff
Vnd sie gleich auff Genßhaut plaff
Erst fieng sie an ein solches schnadern
Ein schwatzen klapern vnd thadern
Ee ich ein wort antworten thet
Het sie die weyl wol siebne gredt
Thet mit hönworten mich fast essen
Erst thet ichs auff die Hundhaut treffen
Erst fieng sie hefftig an zü pellen
Vnd hieng mir an vil schamper schellen

Ich wer ein Esel/Narr vnd tropff
Ich gab jr noch ein güts an kopff
Do traff ichs auff den Hasen palck
Sie loff darvon vnd schray du schalck
Du Hüren jeger vnd Eebrecher
Du Spilgur vnd du wein zecher
Stach mit der gleich worten spitzig
Ich luff jr nach wurd wider hitzig
Vnd stach sie wider zü den oren
Traff sie gleich auff die roßhaut voren
Do schlugs auff samber windt her wehet
Vnd stieß mich das ich mich verdrehet
Erst traff ichs auff die haut der katzen
Do fiels auff mich mit kreln vnd kratzen
Also wolt sie mich zü flecken reissen
Das schryen kundt ich kaum verpeissen
Ich zuckt ein prügel lanck genüg
Damit ichs auff die Sew haut schlüg
Tantzt jr auff dem rück vnd den armen
Das sie sich selbert thet erbarmen
Vnd fieng an zü greynen vnd röln
Als ich sie war noch baser knüln
Erst traff ichs auff die menschen haut
Do rüfft sie vmb gnad gar laut
Vnd sprach mein hertz lieber Man
Hör auff ich wil sein nymmer than
Mich hat ein nachpawrin verfürt
Zü handeln das sich nicht gebürt

Der wil ich volgen nymmer mer
Hab dir zü pfandt mein weyblich eer
Vnd fiel mir weynend vmb den hals
Ich sprach/es sey vergeben als
Doch kum nymmer das rat ich dir
Dich auff zübaumen gegen mir
So machs wir mit einander seide
Wie lang es wert das waiß ich nit
So hat der hader sich angspunnen
Wie wol ich hab die schlacht gewunnen
Ist mir mein teyl auch tückisch woren
Im angsicht hals vnd vmb die oren
Das ich der schlacht nicht laugnen mag
Ich sprach/mein gsell merck was ich sag
Jr jungen Eemänner seyt zü gech
Zü mütwillig/doll/drum vnd frech
Wenn euch ein weyb nit schön ansicht
Oder nach ewerm sinn zü spricht
Oder mit aller sach recht geyt
Wenn jr schon gar vnheuflich seyt
Wölt jrs mit schlagen als auß richten
Das zimpt ein biderman mit nichten
Vngeraten Ee werden darauß
Man müß mit krieg nit halten hauß
Sonder mit frid vnd freundtschafft mer
Paulus vns mannen geyt ein ler
Die weyb mit vernunfft zü regieren
Mit pollern/grob tyrannisieren

Weyl sie der schwechst werckzeug sein
Derhalben straff dein weyb allein
Mit vernünfftigen güten worten
Zwischen euch beyden an den orten
Mein liebes weyb/das sol nicht thon
Vnd jhenes steet dir übel an
Schaw diß ist schand/vnd jhens ist schad
Wilt haben mein gunst vnd genad
So stee des müssig/vnd volg mir
Dargegen wil ich volgen dir
Wo mir ein ding steet übel an
Wil handlen als ein redlich Man
Vnd wil kein böß wort dir mer geben
So müg wir wol vnd freundlich leben
Bey leyb laß niemandt dich verhetzen
Das du dich gegen mir wölst setzen
Der gleich sol niemandt mich verfüren
Zü handlen das nicht thü gepüren
Was dir felt soltu klagen mir
Was mir bricht wil ich sagen dir
Du darffst dich vor mir gar nicht schewen
Kein mesch maint vns mit gantze trewen
Als wir zwey gbören ye zü samen
Was wolt wir zancken vnd grif gramen
Füren ein solch Teuffelisch leben
Vnd vns vnter die leut auff geben
Die halten dann nichts von vns beyden
Schaw also straff dein weyb bescheyden
Ist denn ein eer in jrem leyb
So zeuchst auß jr ein ghorsam weyb
Wie man den spricht ein ein frumer Man
Ein frumes weyb im ziehen kan
Wo sie aber blieb aygenwillig
Nicht handlet das wer gleich vnd billig
Wolt dir gar nicht sein vnthenig
Vngehorsam vnd widerspennig
Wo sie rümoret noch dar gegen
So magstu straffen sie mit schlegen
Doch mit vernunfft vnd wol bescheyden
Das es vnschedlich sey euch beyden
Also wendt süß vnd sawers für
Wie einem biderman gepür
Biß jr zü letzt eins synnes werdt
Dardurch euch hie in zeyt auff erdt
Frid/freüd vnd freündtligkeyt erwachs
Im Keling standt / das wunscht Hans
(Sachs

Gedruckt durch Hans
Guldenmundt.

iconography of the "battle for the pants" (see fig. 5.7). Instead of depicting female insubordination in terms of an allegory of the crime, the artist affords the viewer an image of its punishment whose impact depends on its function as an illustration of the text. No longer is the man subjected to the unlikely form of maltreatment illustrated by Erhard Schön (fig. 5.1). Instead, the woman is represented as the victim of a much more probable and all too familiar form of domestic violence. There is a movement, in other words, from allegory to narrative. The ambiguity of the "battle for the pants" iconography, in which it was always possible to view the triumphant woman as victor rather than accepting her triumph as a manifestation of improper behavior, has been decisively rejected.[33] The message of this broadsheet was to be univocal.

As we turn to the text of this broadsheet the brutality of the image becomes more comprehensible, for the story of the *Nine Hides* is one of the more sadistic products of a misogynist fantasy. Returning one evening from an inn where he has been drinking with his friends, a young husband finds that his wife refuses to speak to him. On beating her for this "insubordination," he receives no response and comments that his wife's skin feels like that of a codfish. When he strikes her a second time, she reacts like a raging bear; on receiving a third blow she resembles a hissing goose, on the fourth a barking dog, and so forth until when he reaches the ninth skin he wife becomes human once more and implores his forgiveness, promising never again to question his authority. Despite the fact that Sachs closes the poem advising against such violence and argues that women must be ruled with reason rather than with force, the appeal of the broadsheet undoubtedly lay in the sadistic humor with which this account of marital strife is described. The ambiguity of the poet's position is perhaps best discerned by examining his own words:

So punish your wife modestly,
And if there is any honor in her
She will become an obedient wife.
As one says, "A devoted husband
Can bring forth a devoted wife."
But if she remains self-willed
And refuses you in all your requests,
Ever disobedient and rebellious,
On those occasions when she spurns cooperation
You may punish her with blows.
Yet do it still with reason and discretion
So that no harm is done to either of you.
Use both carrot and stick

To bring about companionship
As befits an honorable man.[34]

What did Sachs mean when he advised "punishing" one's wife "modestly"? How were "blows" to be administered with "reason and discretion"? How were "carrot and stick" to bring about "companionship"? The tone of disinterested concern masks a defense of physical violence.

A variation on the composition Barthel Beham adopted in his woodcut for the *Nine Hides* is found in a broadsheet with the title *The Twelve Properties of an Insanely Angry Wife,* also written by Hans Sachs and illustrated by Erhard Schön (fig. 5.16).[35] Like the illustration to the *Nine Hides,* Schön's image is dominated by a troubling scene of domestic violence. The text narrates how, while walking by the river one day, the poet encountered a man who is contemplating throwing himself into the water. Asked why he is considering this desperate act, the man replies that his wife refuses to look after his house, neglects their children, drinks, spends his money on clothes, chases his friends from the house, alienates the neighbors, and is generally contrary, disobedient, and insubordinate. When he attempts to correct her behavior by beating her, she takes him before a judge, whom she persuades that she has been maltreated. All the man's woes are attributed to the woman's anger, which consists in her inability to bow to his authority. Sachs has no advice to offer the man other than to "console" him with the thought that he will soon be separated from his wife by death.

Sachs's texts for marriage broadsheets are typical of the misogynist humor developed in the rest of his literary production.[36] For example, the leading character of his carnival play *The Angry Wife* of 1533 insists on quarreling with her maid, a young artisan, and a neighbor in addition to her husband. The neighbor advises the husband that the only solution to the discontent she causes is for him to assert his authority:

Go ahead and act like a man!
Otherwise she'll end up riding you,
And before long she'll
Deprive you of your pants, your purse, and your sword,
Which will make us all ashamed of you.
Do not give her too much rein,
But rather take an oak cudgel
And beat her soundly between the ears![37]

Another of Sachs's plays, the moralizing allegory entitled *About an Innkeeper and Two Peasants Who Wanted to Take the Sausage from "the German Court"* (1539), is based on the proverbial inability of husbands to control their

5.16. Erhard Schön, *The Twelve Properties of an Insanely Angry Wife*, woodcut, 1530. (Photo, Gotha, Schlossmuseum.)

Die Zwölff Eygenschafft eines boßhafftigen verruchten weybs.

Die Erste Eygenschafft.

Die Ander Eygenschafft.

Die Dritt Eygenschafft.

Die Vierd Eygenschafft.

Die Fünfft Eygenschafft.

Die Sechst Eygenschafft.

Die Sibend Eygenschafft.

Die Achte Eygenschafft.

Die Newndt Eygenschafft.

Die Zehend Eygenschafft.

Die Eilfft Eygenschafft.

Die Zwelfft Eygenschafft.

Gedruckt zu Nürenberg bey Niclas Meldeman an der Lugenbrucken.

wives. An enormous sausage kept at an inn called "the German Court" can be taken home only by a man who is truly head of his household. As a consequence it has remained undisturbed for over two hundred years. The peasants who attempt to claim it must give up when they confess to being ordered about by their wives. One of them has abandoned the marital struggle since his wife beat him with one of the wooden laundry aids illustrated in figures 5.1 and 5.9, causing his jaw to swell. The other continues the contest without success and provides lurid descriptions of the violence that characterizes his home:

When my wife is angry, I get rough,
And when she throws filth at me,
I throw plates back at her.
As a result we often wound each other,
So that we both bleed like pigs.[38]

Among Sachs's many variations on this theme is a reworking of Hans Folz's play *The Evil Smoke* (see fig. 5.6).[39] Like its predecessor, this play was provided with a woodcut frontispiece representing a man and a woman fighting for a pair of pants (fig. 5.17). In contrast to the earlier work, however, this is no longer an allegorical "power of women" theme whose intellectual point depends on the inversion of actual relationships; it approaches the emotional significance of the issue more directly by purporting to represent the status quo. The play concerns a henpecked husband who is determined to end his wife's insubordination. A neighbor urges him to challenge his wife to a battle for the pants in which he can reassert his authority:

Now put a manly heart in your chest
And challenge your wife to a fight.
You must beat each other resolutely
So that you can establish
Who should wear the pants;
And whoever loses the battle
Must give the other the prize and the victory,
And they become the lord and man of the house![40]

The realization of this plan leads to a violent confrontation in which the husband and wife beat each other with cudgels. The man is quickly defeated, and the wife triumphantly pulls on the pants. Unlike the woodcut frontispiece, which eschewed the ambiguities of the "world upside down," Sachs's play ends with the "woman on top." On the other hand, ambiguity is minimized by means of the moralizing conclusion in which Sachs instructs husbands to train their wives to obey them. While this should preferably be done with words, physical punishment is appropriate if the wife proves recalcitrant.

There was nothing new about the misogynist humor described above. Such themes were, as we have seen, a commonplace of late medieval art and literature. One of the late fifteenth-century Nuremberg carnival plays, for example, is entitled *A Good Play about How to Make Angry Wives Obedient*.[41] According to this narrative, a young wife rebels against the authority of her husband on her mother's advice. The husband consults a doctor, who recommends the following "cure." The young man is to beat his wife until she bleeds, then rub ashes in her wounds and sew her inside a salted horsehide for three days and

5.17. Anonymous, *Battle for the Pants*, woodcut frontispiece to Hans Sachs's play *The Evil Smoke*. (Photo, Nuremberg, Stadtgeschichtliche Museen, *Die Welt des Hans Sachs* [exhibition catalog, Nuremberg, 1976], cat. no. 243.)

nights. Not surprisingly, the wife's attitude is transformed by this treatment, and on being released she promises to respect and obey her husband for evermore. However, the satirical imagery of the battle of the sexes, which had been developed in an age that regarded marriage as spiritually inferior to celibacy, had different implications in a context that regarded marriage as the most desirable form of social life.

In contrast to the orthodox church, Luther believed that no form of life on earth could lead to spiritual perfection. Since he regarded the sexual drive as an overpowering force from which no human being was exempt, the association of sex with lust brought about as a consequence of the Fall meant there was no escape from sin. These views led him to reject the church's regard for celibacy as the highest form of the Christian life. If human nature was in its essence sinful, then there was no possibility of living a wholly virtuous life. Rather than pursue a hopelessly flawed ideal, it was better that Christians should consider the married rather than the celibate life as the natural condition of human existence.[42] "For this word which God speaks, 'Be fruitful and multiply,' is not a command. It is more than a command, namely, a divine ordinance which it is not our prerogative to hinder or ignore. Rather, it is just as necessary as the fact that I am a man, and more necessary than sleeping and waking, eating and drinking and emptying the bowels and bladder."[43] Although the married state did not eliminate sin from sexual relations, it provided a context in which lust could be contained. In Luther's eyes the function of marriage as a way the sinful power of the sexual drive could be restrained and controlled was as important as its role in procreation: "Therefore [because of the Fall], the married state is now no longer pure and free of sin. The temptation of the flesh has become so strong and consuming that marriage may be likened to a hospital for incurables which prevents the inmates from falling into graver sin."[44]

If God's punishment of Adam and Eve was responsible for calling the institution of marriage into existence, it also determined its structure. Like the medieval theologians before him, Luther regarded the wife's subordination to her husband as God's curse on the female of the species for the sin of Eve.[45] "Hence it follows that if the woman had not been deceived by the serpent and had not sinned, she would have been the equal of Adam in all respects. For the punishment that she is now subjected to the man, was imposed on her after sin and because of sin, just as the other hardships and dangers were: travail, pain and countless other vexations."[46] As a consequence of this punishment the wife was to view her husband as her superior and should be prepared to obey him in all matters:

Therefore in the state of marriage the wife should not only love her husband but should be obedient and subservient to him so that she allows herself to be ruled by him, bowing before him. In short, she should follow him and pay attention to him not only because of the respect she owes him as a man and as her ruler but because of this example. She should always remember to think: "My husband is an image of the true high ruler Christ himself so that I will honor him and do what is pleasing to him in the same spirit as I would for Christ himself."[47]

Luther's views regarding the role of women in marriage were incorporated in the reformed wedding ceremony. In "The Order of Marriage," Luther ordained that the following words be included in the minister's blessing of the couple before the altar: "Wives submit yourselves unto your own husbands, as unto the Lord. For the husband is head of the wife, even as Christ is the head of the church: and he is the Saviour of the body. Therefore as the church is subject to Christ, so let wives be subject to their husbands in everything."[48] The subordination of women as a consequence of original sin was regarded by Luther not only as the justification of her inferior position in marriage, but as the foundation of all wordly authority. According to his "two world" theory, secular authority was a part of the natural law to which man was subject in the temporal world. Just as wives were subject to their husbands, so men were subject to the secular authorities.[49] Commenting on the fourth commandment, "Honor thy father and mother," Luther described the relationship in the following terms:

Therefore everything that one calls master stands in the place of the parents and must draw from them their power to rule. It is for this reason that according to Scripture they are all called fathers whenever they fill the post of father in their governments and must carry a fatherly heart toward their subjects. Just as since antiquity the Romans and other peoples called the lord and mistress of the house *patres et matres familias*, which means housefather and mother, therefore they also called their princes and rulers *patres patriae*, that is, father of their country. It is a great shame that we who want to be Christians do not do the same or at least regard and honor them in that way.[50]

Luther saw in the hierarchical structure of the family a model for the organization of the state. In promoting the creation of Lutheran drama, he expressly praised plays dealing with marriage because of their social implications:

Roman comedies please me very much, for their most important idea, *causa finalis*, and final cause was that by these means, as with a painting or a living example, they attracted men to marriage and drew them away from harlotry. For order and worldly authority cannot exist without marriage. Therefore those gifted men attempted to persuade their youth to enter marriage by means of comedies as well as paintings.

The single state, celibacy, and harlotry are a pestilence and poison to both the government and the world.[51]

Luther's teaching on marriage was made known in Nuremberg not only by the preaching of Lutheran ministers but by a variety of publications. These publications, which ranged from theological treatises to manuals of religious instruction, presented his views in various ways. Generally speaking this literature is engaged in a polemic against monasticism, so marriage is presented in a favorable light.[52] It is significant, however, that Luther's use of the sexual hierarchy of marriage as a metaphor of the social hierarchy should have played a central role in one of the earliest examples of this genre to be published in Nuremberg. Justus Menius's treatise the *Oeconomia Christiana, das ist von Christlicher Haushaltung*, which appeared in 1529,[53] contains a preface by Luther instructing parents not to bring up their children merely with a view to their being able to make a living. Instead, reformed parents should take every opportunity to further their children's education so that they may occupy responsible positions in both church and state: "If one does not bring children up to learning and art but merely raises lazy gluttons and good-for-nothings [literally, 'piglets'] concerned only about food, where will one find ministers, preachers, and others to spread God's word, fill church offices, and serve God? Where will kings, princes and lords, cities and counties, find chancellors, councillors, clerks, and other officials?"[54] Menius begins his treatise by stating that the secular sphere of Luther's "two world" distinction is itself constituted by two forms of government, that of the household and that of the state, "because there is no doubt that the *politia* or government of the state comes from or flows from the *oeconomia* or government of the household, as from a spring."[55] The duties of those that constitute the household—that is, the duty of the husband to his wife and family as well as the duty of the wife to her husband, of the children to their parents, and of the servants to the head of the household—should be viewed as Christian obligations. The implication is that recognizing the hierarchical organization of the family represents a willingness to obey God's will. Since the family is the model for society, obedience to secular authority is thus equated with an acknowledgment of divine order.

The consequences of Luther's teaching on marriage made themselves felt in Nuremberg in the mid-1520s. After the Religious Disputation of March 1525, when Lutheran ministers debated representatives of the orthodox church, the town council took measures to ensure that the city's monastic institutions were closed.[56] Although most of the monastic orders had been dissolved and their property placed at the disposal of the city's poor relief during the course of that year, the Franciscans, together with the convents of Saint Clare and Saint Catherine, held out. The surviving orders were prohibited from taking novices, from preaching, and from celebrating the Catholic mass. As a consequence they gradually died out over the sixteenth century.[57] In addition, the town council took the administration of marriage law out of the hands of the ecclesiastical authorities. Instead of forwarding marital cases to the episcopal court in Bamberg, the council referred them to the city courts.[58] The new marriage ceremony, commissioned by the council from Andreas Osiander, gave new importance to this rite. Whereas orthodox marriages had in most instances been blessed outside the church doors, a symbol of the church's unwillingness to accept full responsibility for what it regarded as a secular institution,[59] the marriage ordinance of 1525 decreed that the ceremony was now to take place inside the church, before the altar.[60] Unlike the orthodox church, which still recognized the validity of marriage vows taken outside the church even though it disapproved of them, the Lutherans were determined to make the religious ceremony the only recognized form of marriage. In contrast to the rest of Lutheran Germany, however, which tended to follow the pattern set in Wittenberg according to which marriage law was administered by a religious court composed of ministers, in Nuremberg legal control remained in the hands of the secular authorities.[61] The new faith thus enhanced the powers of the town council as custodians of the spiritual welfare of the community. The degree to which the interests of church and state intersected on this matter may be gauged by the fact that by 1537 the council no longer recognized marriages that had not been performed in church.[62]

What significance does the use of marriage broadsheets to validate the religious and political order of Nuremberg society have for the ongoing debate about the Reformation's consequences for the status and role of women?[63] First, the role that marriage broadsheets played in the construction of an orderly Lutheran society must have had an adverse effect on women's economic independence. During the course of the sixteenth century, women in Nuremberg were gradually but systematically excluded from the world of employment.[64] Whereas women had once been represented in a wide variety of occupations, sometimes constituting half the membership of certain guilds, a slow "professionalization" is discernible in which the highest-paying positions became the posts from which women were barred.[65] This process ultimately confined women to occupations that were low in both status and pay. This decline took place against a demographic background in which women heavily outnumbered men in a rising total population.[66] This disproportion must have been further increased by the closing of the convents. Although the historical forces responsible for these developments were undoubtedly complex and certainly included the effects of the general rise in population as well as the erosion of real wages as a consequence of inflation,[67] the persistent assertion that the subordination of women to male authority in marriage constituted a metaphor of the proper social order must be viewed as a justification of the economic oppression to which women were being subjected. The "battle of the sexes" represented in the marriage broadsheets not only may have fostered the competition for jobs but must also have exacerbated tensions arising from changes in the age of marriage. Historical demographers have shown that marriage took place progressively later over the sixteenth and seventeenth centuries. The medieval pattern of marriage at puberty was replaced by one in which partners married when both were in their late twenties or early thirties—the man usually being older than the wife.[68] This change, which has been associated with the need for families of all classes to ensure their social status by accumulating capital, would have enhanced the husband's authority at the expense of the wife's. The violence of the broadsheet imagery would thus have promoted male supremacy in a situation that was psychologically loaded. It seems unlikely that women who were entering marriage at a mature age would have found that their personal and social views coincided with their husband's in every respect. As a consequence of their maturity, as well as the difference in age that separated them from their husbands, the potential for conflict must have increased.

The social implications of the marriage broadsheets appear to have greater potential significance for the middle and lower classes than for those at the top of the social spectrum. Broadsheets were first of all the cheapest of the woodcuts discussed here. Unlike the "giant" woodcuts, they did not depend for their effect on the juxtaposition of a number of single-leaf woodcuts. Another indication of the milieu in which they were displayed is provided by Hans Sachs in his poem *The Young Man Who Fell through the Basket*.[69] Sachs recounts how he saw on the wall of an inn a broadsheet representing a young man being pulled up to a window for a rendezvous with his sweetheart; the man suddenly fell through the basket in which he was being lifted—much to the amusement of the passersby. In the text printed above the image, the young man expressed his shame and remorse, warning viewers against illicit love affairs. Sachs's conclusion makes use of the fictive image to advocate that young men arrange their marriages openly and publicly rather than engaging in secret liaisons. Whether or not his poem depended on his actually having seen a marriage broadsheet in an inn, it indicates that its presence in such a context was not unlikely. Such public calls for the subordination of women must have had special meaning for those artisans who had suffered from a capitalist organization of labor. In the increasingly difficult economic situation, these images would have reinforced the attitude of those who wished to eliminate women from the job market altogether by confining their sphere of activity to the home.

Conclusion

This attempt to see past the blinkers imposed on our sensibilities by traditional formalist notions of "aesthetic" value or their binary opposite, "folk art" or "mass art," suggests that the woodcuts Albrecht Dürer described as "simple" or "modest" cannot be regarded as unworthy of art historical interpretation or as a manifestation of the proverbial "simplicity" of the people. Rejecting the Kantian aesthetic tradition provides us with other choices. The character of these prints must be understood in terms of the artistic traditions they derived from as well as the social function they were meant to serve. Among the formative traditions were the devotional woodcuts of the fifteenth century, which were simple designs created by unskilled artisans and intended for mass reproduction. Rather than offering an illusionistic account of the deity, they were merely a means by which their prototype, whether a much venerated image or the supernatural being, could be made accessible to the devout worshiper. The tradition of illustrating all but the most expensive books was also noted for its simplicity. The illustration's dependence on the text was exploited to radically reduce the complexity of the image. The reader was expected to fill out the suggestions offered by the visual sign system by using the information found in the primary or linguistic sign system. And the images used in the imperial propaganda produced for Maximilian I depended not on the visual interest or complexity of the individual prints but on the repetition of similar elements. The individual woodcuts of the *Triumphal Arch* and the *Triumphal Procession* of Maximilian are quite similar; indeed, they were standardized to a particular pattern so as to work effectively within the context of a much larger composition. Since the function of this imagery was to impress, scale was an important consideration. In view of the reproductive quality of the medium, scale was most easily achieved by repetition.

Of the traditions cited above, the "giant" woodcuts such as *A Column of*

Mercenaries or *The Church Anniversary Holiday at Mögelsdorf* owed their inspiration to the imperial propaganda. As in the works executed for Maximilian, their visual effect depends on the repetition of relatively simple units. Some of the single-leaf woodcuts, such as the series of single standing mercenaries, also seem to depend on this tradition. It is likely that they were also meant to be collected and assembled in large compositions, even though they are visually and textually autonomous. In this case the scale achieved by means of repetition allowed them to be used in interiors as decorative friezes. A "giant" woodcut that does not belong in this category is Sebald Beham's *Large Peasant Holiday.* While the foreground of this print is to be "read" in much the same way as those just mentioned, there are no texts, and the background is filled with interest that can only be called "pictorial" in nature.

Broadsheets, on the other hand, are most closely related to the illustration of printed books. Like them, these images eschew any attempt at illusionism and present the figures referred to in the text as two-dimensional outlines. The function of these broadsheets, in which even the secular subjects are most often moralizing or instructional, would have been analogous to that of early printed books, whose production exploded with the coming of the Reformation.[1] On the other hand, the suggestion that such images played a role similar to that of fifteenth-century devotional woodcuts seems unfounded.[2] Although the spectator was expected to learn from the broadsheets, that learning did not depend on the image's ability to afford access to a magical or supernatural being.

Like the media that shaped their forms and functions, images of the woodcuts and broadsheets of the Reformation belong to what Norman Bryson has termed a "discursive" rather than a "figurative" category.[3] Discursive images are said to display their dependence on the texts they were associated with. They do not assert their autonomy by providing any information that might distract the reader from the text. The elaborate avoidance of naturalism by artists who in other media reveal themselves as masters of the illusionistic techniques of the Italian Renaissance indicates that the "simple" mode was a deliberate choice. The simplicity of these media is therefore not to be attributed to the failings of the artists or to the lack of sophistication of their audience; it reflects their role in the production of cultural meaning. The abstraction with which the themes they illustrate are handled prevented the image from gaining its independence and permitted an audience composed of all classes to fill them out with the values in the accompanying texts as well as with those found in sign systems of very different orders. It was the simplicity of these images that enabled them to be incorporated in an ideology determined by the sign systems that structured activities as disparate as dancing, army life, and family relations. Whereas the complexity of the illusionism of Renaissance art, patronized by the members of Nuremberg's incipient humanist culture, enabled artists to develop visual sign systems marked by a self-referentiality that was capable of being appreciated only by the members of a sophisticated, cultured elite, the simplicity of woodcut and broadsheet imagery allowed it to cut across class boundaries to articulate the cultural values on which Nuremberg society depended.

If we accept the status of works of art as cultural sign systems, they must be regarded as important in the construction of social "reality" as the class system, the organization of labor, the nature of religious belief, the *Schembartlauf,* and the carnival plays. The images of peasants, warriors, and wives discussed in the preceding chapters helped mold a world picture, one that determined social experience. What sort of culture did these images articulate? As we have seen, they illustrate the ambivalence of Lutheran social teaching. The Reformation had preached a new order, one based on the freedom of the individual conscience. This freedom was to enable men and women to determine moral values based on their understanding of the Bible rather than on unquestioning acceptance of the views of the orthodox church. Yet when the peasants sought to put these ideas into effect, they were disavowed as revolutionaries who had failed to understand that Luther's claims for the individual conscience had little to do with life in society. The iconography of the peasant as the "common man," a figure at whom early Lutheran propaganda was aimed, was transformed into an iconography of satire and contempt. Where once this figure had been used as a symbol of the need for change, the Peasants' War transformed it into an illustration of the need for subordination and passivity.

Like Erasmus, Luther was deeply concerned with the problem of war, which he regarded as a moral and social disaster. Yet in his concern to support the existing social order he found himself required to insist that Christians should heed the orders of their temporal rulers over the spiritual concerns of their own consciences. In terms of numbers, the iconography of the warrior as heroic defender of the empire far outweighed the iconography that satirized his antisocial behavior. Similarly, Luther taught that while all human beings were sinful in the eyes of God, women bore a greater burden as a consequence of Eve's responsibility for original sin. Woman was incorporated in a "myth of origin" in which secular authority found its legitimation. Just as woman was subject to man as a consequence of sin, so men were subject to their divinely appointed rulers. The relation of wife to husband is explicitly assimilated to the relation between subject and ruler. In the iconography of the Reformation this meant the wife was shown either beating her husband and thus as the embodiment of the "world upside down" or experiencing the consequences of insubordination by being beaten herself.

The culture these woodcuts and broadsheets helped to build was one in which spiritual considerations were compromised by an overriding preoccupation with observing the dictates of secular authority. They articulated a network of social relations in which an individual's spiritual life was private and personal and where the attitude toward secular power was one of subservient passivity. By insisting on interpreting the "natural law," or the social arrangements on which the status quo depended, as an expression of "divine law," Luther's "two world" teaching effectively rejected the revolutionary implications of his challenge to the Catholic church. The signifying structures of the secular world were invested with a spiritual significance that served to underwrite and guarantee their existence. The material signifiers of established cultural practice were endowed with a conceptual signified that enhanced and enobled them in such a way as to put them beyond the power of human reason to question or challenge. The consequences of this type of indoctrination were given dramatic expression long ago by Ernst Troeltsch:

The practice of government and the administration of justice are offices appointed by Divine command, and Luther describes with great rigour the contrast between the system of law which is carried out from the ruling prince down to the gaoler, the hangman, in which the work of government administration and punishment, including hanging, breaking on the wheel and beheading is all service to God, and the non-official purely personal morality, in which, on the other hand, the true service of God consists of loving one's enemies, in sacrifice, renunciation and endurance, in loving care for others and self sacrifice.[4]

While the woodcuts and broadsheets discussed here express the attitudes of the patriciate that was responsible for introducing the Reformation into Nuremberg, they cannot simply be regarded as art produced for the masses by the upper classes. Those responsible for producing these images belonged to the middle class. They were artisans whose wealth or education enabled them to identify with the values of the ruling patriciate. The *Formschneider* and *Briefmaler* had the capital to finance publishing houses. The writers and artists belonged to occupations that were in transition. Although still regarded as artisans by most of their contemporaries, they were aware that humanist culture ascribed them a far more exalted status. Nevertheless, the images themselves were marketed and priced to be accessible to all classes. Their cultural significance was not an inherent characteristic but depended upon the way it was incorporated into the outlook of members of different groups. Insofar as these images were the site for the creation of meaning by all classes, it is difficult to define them as examples of the exploitation of one class by another. In the absence of an alternative ideology, the public expression of views such as the social and moral inferiority of the peasant, the glorification of the imperial warrior, and the necessity that wives be subject to their husbands must be regarded as statements of values that bound the Nuremberg community together. In other words, the social values expressed by the visual sign systems of these media cannot be distinguished from some underlying reality that they are assumed to "reflect." To all intents and purposes, these systems constituted the society whose values they articulated.

Notes

INTRODUCTION

1. See Kant's *Critique of Aesthetic Judgment*, trans. James Meredith (Oxford, 1911). For a critique of Kant's aesthetic from a sociological viewpoint see Pierre Bourdieu, *Distinction: A Social Critique of the Judgment of Taste*, trans. Richard Nice (Cambridge, Mass., 1984).

2. For the privileging of the notion of style in the creation of the discipline of art history see Michael Podro, *The Critical Historians of Art* (New Haven, 1982).

3. The standard monograph on Albrecht Dürer was written by Erwin Panofsky, a historian whose thought was decisively shaped by neo-Kantian philosophy. See his *Albrecht Dürer,* 2 vols. (Princeton, 1943). For Panofsky's intellectual background see Michael Holly, *Panofsky and the Foundations of Art History* (Ithaca, N.Y., 1984).

4. Ernst H. Gombrich, *Aby Warburg: An Intellectual Biography* (Chicago, 1986; 1st ed. London, 1970), p. 210.

5. See, for example, Arnold Hauser, *The Philosophy of Art History* (New York, 1959; 1st German ed. Munich, 1958), pp. 281, 283–84, 351.

6. Ibid., p. 361; Lenz Kriss-Rettenbeck, "Der Hund 'Greif' und die Frage 'Was ist Volkskunst,'" *Pantheon* 33(1975): 145–52, esp. 148; Ewa Chojeka, "Zur Stellung des gedruckten Bildes im 15. und 16. Jahrhundert: Zwischen Kunstwerk und 'Massenmedium,'" in *Reform, Reformation, Revolution*, ed. S. Hoyer (Leipzig, 1980), pp. 123–27.

7. For a review of some of these theories see Kriss-Rettenbeck, "Hund 'Greif.'"

8. Karl Schottenloher, *Flugblatt und Zeitung* (Berlin, 1922); Hans Fehr, *Massenkunst im 16. Jahrhundert* (Berlin, 1924).

9. Maurice Gravier, *Luther et l'opinion publique* (Paris, 1942); Robert Scribner, *For the Sake of Simple Folk: Popular Propaganda for the German Reformation* (Cambridge, 1981).

10. Paul Kristeller, "The Modern System of the Arts," in *Renaissance Thought II* (New York, 1965), pp. 163–227, esp. 163–64.

11. Rosario Assunto, *Die Theorie des Schönen im Mittelalter* (Cologne, 1981; 1st ed. 1963), pp. 18–19, 24–26.

12. See Johannes Kollwitz, "Bild und Bildertheologie im Mittelalter," in *Das Gottesbild im Abendland* (Berlin, 1957), pp. 109–38.

13. Moshe Barasch, *Theories of Art: From Plato to Winckelmann* (New York, 1985), p. 64.

14. Assunto, *Theorie des Schönen*, p. 25.

15. For the variety see Max Geisberg, *The German Single Leaf Woodcut*, 4 vols., trans. Walter Strauss (New York, 1974; 1st German ed. Munich, 1923–30).

16. William Ivins, *Prints and Communication* (Cambridge, Mass., 1955).

17. See Svetlana Alpers, *The Art of Describing: Dutch Art in the Seventeenth Century* (Chicago, 1983); idem, *Rembrandt's Enterprise: The Studio and the Market* (Chicago, 1988); Michael Fried, *Absorption and Theatricality: Painting and Beholder in the Age of Diderot* (Berkeley, 1980); idem, *Realism, Writing, Disfiguration: On Thomas Eakins and Stephen Crane* (Chicago, 1987); David Summers, *Michelangelo and the Language of Art* (Princeton, 1981); idem, *The Judgement of Sense: Renaissance Naturalism and the Rise of Aesthetics* (New York, 1987); Michael Baxandall, *Painting and Experience in Fifteenth Century Italy: A Primer in the Social History of Pictorial Style* (Oxford, 1972); idem, *Patterns of Intention: On the Historical Explanation of Pictures* (New Haven, 1985); T. J. Clark, *Image of the People: Gustave Courbet and the 1848 Revolution* (London, 1973); idem, *The Painting of Modern Life: Paris in the Art of Manet and His Followers* (New York, 1985); Norman Bryson, *Word and Image: French Painting of the Ancien Régime* (Cambridge, 1981); idem, *Vision and Painting: The Logic of the Gaze* (New Haven, 1983); Linda Nochlin, *Women, Art, and Power* (New York, 1988); Griselda Pollock and Rozsicka Parker, *Old Mistresses: Women, Art and Ideology* (London, 1981); Griselda Pollock, *Vision and Difference: Femininity, Feminism and the Histories of Art* (London, 1988).

18. For Panofsky's remarks about the role of "tradition" in determining the canon, see his essay "The History of Art as a Humanistic Discipline," in *Meaning in the Visual Arts* (Garden City, New York, 1955), p. 18. n. 13. For his subscription to the values of humanist art theory see Keith Moxey, "Panofsky's Concept of 'Iconology' and the Problem of Interpretation in the History of Art," *New Literary History* 17(Winter 1986): 265–74.

19. Adolf Vogt, "Panofskys Hut," in *Architektur und Sprache: Gedenkschrift für Richard Zürcher*, ed. C. Braegger (Munich, 1982), pp. 279–96; Georges Roque, "L'iconologie selon Magritte," in *Pour un temps: Erwin Panofsky*, ed. Jacques Bonnet (Paris, 1983), pp. 167–83.

20. Jean Arrouye, "Archéologie de l'iconologie," in Bonnet, *Pour un temps*, pp. 71–83, esp. 73–74.

21. See especially Ernst Gombrich, *Art and Illusion: A Study in the Psychology of Pictorial Representation* (Oxford, 1977; 1st ed. 1960).

22. See Nelson Goodman, *Languages of Art* (Indianapolis, 1976); Bryson, *Vision and Painting*; W. J. T. Mitchell, *Iconology: Image, Text, Ideology* (Chicago, 1986).

23. See Goodman, *Languages of Art*, p. 5.

24. See Bryson, *Vision and Painting*, chap. 2: "The Essential Copy." The term "reality effect" is derived from an essay by Roland Barthes, "The Reality Effect" (1968), in *French Literary Theory Today: A Reader*, ed. Tzvetan Todorov, trans. R. Carter (Cambridge, 1982), pp. 11–17.

25. Hubert Damisch, "Sémiologie et iconographie," in *La sociologie de l'art et sa vocation interdisciplinaire: L'oeuvre et l'influence de Pierre Francastel* (Paris, 1976), pp. 29–39; Christine Hasenmueller, "Panofsky, Iconography, and Semiotics," *Journal of Aesthetics and Art Criticism* 36(1978): 289–301.

26. Louis Althusser, "Ideology and Ideological State Apparatuses," in *Lenin and Philosophy and Other Essays*, trans. Ben Brewster (New York, 1971), pp. 127–86.

27. For the difficulties raised by the "base/superstructure" distinction for Marxist cultural criticism, see Raymond Williams, "Base and Superstructure in Marxist Cultural Theory," *New Left Review* 82(1973): 3–16.

28. Erwin Panofsky, "Iconography and Iconology: An Introduction to the Study of Renaissance Art," in *Meaning in the Visual Arts*, p. 41.

29. Norman Bryson, "Semiology and Visual Interpretation," in *Visual Theory*, ed. Norman Bryson, Michael Holly, and Keith Moxey (Cambridge, 1989).

30. Hayden White, "The Burden of History," in *Tropics of Discourse: Essays in Cultural Criticism* (Baltimore, 1978), pp. 27–50, esp. 41.

1. For the history of Nuremberg in the fifteenth and sixteenth centuries see Emil Reicke, *Geschichte der Reichsstadt Nürnberg* (Nuremberg, 1896); Gerhard Pfeiffer et al., *Nürnberg: Geschichte einer europäischen Stadt* (Munich, 1971); and Gerald Strauss, *Nuremberg in the Sixteenth Century* (Bloomington, Ind., 1976).

2. Rudolf Endres, "Zur Einwohnerzahl und Bevölkerungsstruktur Nürnbergs im 15/16. Jahrhunderts," *Mitteilungen des Vereins für Geschichte der Stadt Nürnberg* 57(1970): 242–71.

3. Rudolf Endres, "Zur Lage der Nürnberger Handwerkerschaft zur Zeit von Hans Sachs," *Jahrbuch für Fränkische Landesforschung* 37(1977): 107–23.

4. Ibid., p. 121.

5. Endres, "Einwohnerzahl," pp. 267–68.

6. See Strauss, *Nuremberg*, pp. 58–64.

7. Ibid., p. 97.

8. Ibid, pp. 98–105.

9. Endres, "Zur Lage," pp. 115–18.

10. Strauss, *Nuremberg*, pp. 154–60; Imgard Höss, "Das religiöse Leben vor der Reformation," in Pfeiffer et al., *Nürnberg*, pp. 137–46.

11. See Bernd Moeller, "Imperial Cities and the Reformation," in *Imperial Cities and the Reformation: Three Essays*, ed. E. Midelfort and M. Edwards (Philadelphia, 1972), pp. 41–115.

12. Strauss, *Nuremberg*, pp. 174–79.

13. See Hans-Joachim Gänssler, *Evangelium und weltliches Schwert* (Wiesbaden, 1983), pp. 99–104. The "two world" teaching has been much discussed. See Franz Lau, *Luthers Lehre von der beiden Reichen* (Berlin, 1953); Johannes Heckel, *Im Irrgarten der Zwei-Reiche-Lehre Luthers* (Munich, 1957); idem, *Lex charitatis: Eine juristische Untersuchung über das Recht in der Theologie Martin Luthers* (Cologne, 1973); Heinrich Bornkamm, *Luthers Lehre von den zwei Reichen in Zusammenhang seiner Theologie* (Gütersloh, 1960); Gunther Wolf, ed., *Luther und die Obrigkeit* (Darmstadt, 1972); Erwin Iserloh and Gerhard Müller, *Luther und die politische Welt* (Stuttgart, 1984).

14. Bernd Hamm, "Stadt und Kirche unter dem Wort Gottes: Das reformatorische Einheitsmodell des Nürnberger Ratsschreiber Lazarus Spengler (1479–1534)," in *Literatur und Laienbildung im Spätmittelalter und in der Reformationszeit*, ed. L. Grenzmann and K. Stackmann (Stuttgart, 1984), pp. 710–29.

15. For an account of these controversies see W. Möller, *Andreas Osiander: Leben und ausgewählte Schriften* (Elberfeld, 1870), chap. 2.

16. See Samuel Sumberg, *The Nuremberg Schembart Festival* (New York, 1941); Hans Ulrich Roller, *Der Nürnberger Schembartlauf: Studien zum Fest und Maskenwesen des späten Mittelalters* (Tübingen, 1965); also Samuel Kinser, "Presentation and Representation: Carnival at Nuremberg, 1450–1550," *Representations* 13(1986): 1–41.

17. Roller, *Nürnberger Schembartlauf*, p. 33.

18. Ibid., p. 175.

19. Ibid., p. 38.

20. Möller, *Andreas Osiander*, pp. 180, 182.

21. Ibid., p. 188.

22. Excellent studies of the carnival plays are provided by Eckehard Catholy, *Das Fastnachtspiel des Spätmittelalters: Gestalt und Funktion* (Tübingen, 1961); Werner Lenk, *Das Nürnberger Fastnachtspiel des 15. Jahrhunderts* (Berlin, 1966); Hagen Bastian, *Mummenschanz: Sinneslust und Gefühlsbeherrschung im Fastnachtspiel des 15. Jahrrunderts* (Frankfurt am Main, 1983).

23. Lenk, *Nürnberger Fastnachtspiel*, pp. 60–92.

24. Johannes Merkel, *Form und Funktion der Komik im Nürnberger Fastnachtspiel* (Freiburg im Breisgau, 1971): Rüdiger Krohn, *Der unanständige Bürger: Untersuchungen zum Obszönen in dem Nürnberger Fastnachtspielen des 15. Jahrhunderts* (Kronberg, 1974); Bastian, *Mummenschanz.*

25. Johannes Janota, "Städter und Bauer in literarischen Quellen des Spätmittelalters," *Die alte Stadt* 6(1979): 225–42.

26. Julia Schnelbögl, "Die Reichskleinodien in Nürnberg, 1424–1523," *Mitteilungen der Verein für Geschichte der Stadt Nürnberg* 51(1962): 78–159.

27. See Nuremberg, Germanisches Nationalmuseum, *Albrecht Dürer, 1471–1971* (exhibition catalog, Nuremberg, 1971), cat. nos. 251, 252.

28. Albrecht Kircher, *Deutsche Kaiser in Nürnberg: Eine Studie zur Geschichte des öffentlichen Lebens der Reichsstadt Nürnberg von 1500–1612* (Nuremberg, 1955); Fritz Schnelbögl, *Der Kaiser in Nürnberg: Archivalienaustellung des Staatsarchivs Nürnbergs* (exhibition catalog, Nuremberg, 1962).

29. Eugen Franz, *Nürnberg, Kaiser und Reich: Studien zur Reichstädtischen Aussenpolitik* (Munich, 1930); Hans Baron, "Religion and Politics in the German Imperial Cities during the Reformation I and II," *English Historical Review* 52(1937): 405–37, 614–33; Gerald Strauss, *Nuremberg.*

30. See Georg Ludewig, *Die Politik Nürnbergs im Zeitalter der Reformation (von 1520–1534)* (Göttingen, 1893), chap. 10; K. Schornbaum, "Zur Politik der Reichsstadt Nürnberg vom Ende des Reichstages zu Speier 1529 bis zum übergabe der Augsburgischen Konfession 1530," *Mitteilungen des Vereins für Geschichte der Stadt Nürnberg* 17(1906): 178–245.

31. For this policy see Stephen Fischer-Galati, *Ottoman Imperialism and German Protestantism: 1521–1555* (Cambridge, Mass., 1959); also A. Engelhardt, *Die Reichstag zu Augsburg, 1530* (Nuremberg, 1929), p. 142.

32. A. Westermann, "Die Türkenhilfe und die politische-kirchlichen Parteien auf dem Reichstag zu Regensburg 1532," *Heidelberger Abhandlungen zur Mittleren und Neueren Geschichte* 25(1910): 1–237, esp. 89–90; Wolfgang Steglich, "Die Reichstürkenhilfe in der Zeit Karls V," *Militärgeschichtliche Mitteilungen* 11(1972): 7–55.

33. See Baron, "Religion and Politics," pp. 619–20; Franz, "Nürnberg, Kaiser und Reich," pp. 134–36, 149.

34. Max Herrmann, *Die Reception des Humanismus in Nürnberg* (Berlin, 1898); Pfeiffer et al., *Nürnberg,* pp. 127–37; Strauss, *Nuremberg,* chap. 6.

35. Paul Joachimsen, *Geschichtsauffassung und Geschichtschreibung in Deutschland unter dem Einfluss des Humanismus* (Leipzig, 1910); Hedwig Riess, *Motive des patriotischen Stolzes bei den deutschen Humanisten* (Berlin, 1934).

36. Joachimsen, *Geschichtsauffassung,* p. 32. H. Tiedemann, *Tacitus und das Nationalbewusstsein der deutschen Humanisten Ende des 15. und Anfang des 16. Jahrhunderts* (Berlin, 1913); Ulrich Paul, *Studien zur Geschichte des deutschen Nationalbewusstseins im Zeitalter des Humanismus und der Reformation* (Berlin, 1936), pp. 25ff.

37. See Adrian Wilson, *The Making of the Nuremberg Chronicle,* intro. Peter Zahn (Amsterdam, 1976).

38. For Celtis see Lewis Spitz, *Conrad Celtis: The German Arch-humanist* (Cambridge, 1957); idem, *The Religious Renaissance of the German Humanists* (Cambridge, 1963); Gerald Strauss, *Sixteenth Century Germany: Its Topography and Topographers* (Madison, 1959); Kurt Adel, *Konrad Celtis: Poeta laudatus* (Graz, 1960).

39. It is of interest that Spengler locked horns with Osiander on this issue as well. See Ludwig Cardauns, *Die Lehre vom Widerstandsrecht des Volks gegen die rechtmässige Obrigkeit im Luthertum und in Calvinismus des 16. Jahrhundert* (Darmstadt, 1973; 1st ed. 1903); Heinz Schei-

ble, *Das Widerstandsrecht als Problem der deutschen Protestanten, 1523–1546* (Gütersloh, 1969), pp. 29–39, 51–56; Cynthia Grant Schoenberger,, "The Development of the Lutheran Theory of Resistance: 1523–1530," *Sixteenth Century Journal* 8(1977): 61–76; Harold Grimm, *Lazarus Spengler: A Lay Leader of the Reformation* (Columbus, Ohio, 1978).

CHAPTER TWO

1. See Adolf Spamer, *Das kleine Andachtsbild vom XIV bis zum XX Jahrhundert* (Munich, 1930), amd more recently Horst Appuhn and Christian von Heusinger, "Der Fund kleiner Andachtsbilder des 13. bis 17. Jahrhunderts in Kloster Wienhausen," *Niederdeutsche Beiträge zur Kunstgeschichte* 4(1965): 157–238.

2. Anton Mayer, "Die heilbringende Schau in Sitte und Kult," in *Heilige Überlieferung: Ausschnitte aus der Geschichte des Mönchtums und des heiligen Kultes. Festschrift Idelfons Herwegen* (Münster, 1938), pp. 234–62.

3. Sixten Ringbom, *Icon to Narrative: The Rise of the Dramatic Close-up in Fifteenth-Century Devotional Painting* (Abo, 1965), pp. 23–30.

4. See Christiane Andersson and Charles Talbot, *From a Mighty Fortress: Prints, Drawings and Books in the Age of Luther, 1483–1546* (exhibition catalog, Detroit: Institute of Arts, 1983), cat. no. 139.

5. For the early history of woodcut and its relation to printing see Arthur Hind, *An Introduction to the History of Woodcut*, 2 vols. (New York, 1963; 1st ed. 1955), vol. 1. See also Horst Kunze, *Geschichte der Buchillustration in Deutschland: Das 15. Jahrhundert*, 2 vols. (Leipzig, 1975).

6. Rainer Schoch, "A Century of Nuremberg Printmaking," in *Gothic and Renaissance Nuremberg, 1300–1550* (exhibition catalog, New York: Metropolitan Museum of Art, 1986), pp. 93–99.

7. Adrian Wilson, *The Making of the Nuremberg Chronicle*, intro. Peter Zahn (Amsterdam, 1976).

8. The *Formschneider* originally cut blocks for textile printing and in that capacity had belonged to either painters' or carpenters' guilds. See Hind, *History of Woodcut*, 1:89.

9. W. L. Schreiber, "Die Briefmaler und ihrer Mitarbeiter," *Gutenberg Jahrbuch*, 1932, pp. 53 ff.; Hind, *History of Woodcut*, 1:81; Lore Sporhan-Krempel, "Kartenmaler und Briefmaler in Nürnberg," *Philobiblon* 10(1966): 138–49; Bruno Weber, *Wunderzeichen und Winckeldrucker, 1543–1586: Einblattdrucke aus der Sammlung Wikiana in der Zentralbibliothek Zürich* (Zurich, 1972), p. 32; Alison Stewart, "Early Woodcut Workshops," *Art Journal* 39(1980): 189–94.

10. See Hellmut Rosenfeld, "Sebastian Brants 'Narrenschiff' und die Tradition der Ständesatire, Narrenbilderbogen und Flugblätter des 15. Jahrhunderts," *Gutenberg Jahrbuch*, 1965, pp. 242–48.

11. Hellmut Rosenfeld, "Die Rolle des Bilderbogens in der deutschen Volkskultur," *Bayerisches Jahrbuch für Volkskunde*, 1955, pp. 79–85.

12. See Larry Silver, "Prints for a Prince: Maximilian, Nuremberg and the Woodcut," in *New Perspectives on the Art of Renaissance Nuremberg: Five Essays*, ed. Jeffrey Chipps Smith (Austin, Tex., 1985), pp. 7–21; also E. Chmelarz, "Die Ehrenpforte des Kaisers Maximilian I," *Jahrbuch der Kunsthistorischen Sammlungen des Allerhöchsten Kaiserhauses* 4(1886): 289–319.

13. Silver, "Prints for a Prince"; Franz Shestag, "Kaiser Maximilian I Triumph," *Jahrbuch der Kunsthistorischen Sammlungen des Allerhöchsten Kaiserhauses* 1(1883): 154–81; Emile Mâle, "Les triomphes," *Revue de l'Art Ancien et Moderne* 19(1906): 111–26; Werner Weisbach, *Trionfi* (Berlin, 1919); Stanley Appelbaum, ed., *The Triumph of Maximilian I: 137 Woodcuts by Hans Burgkmair and Others* (New York, 1964).

14. Karl Giehlow, "Die Hieroglyphenkunde des Humanismus in der Allegorie der Renaissance, besonders der Ehrenpforte Kaiser Maximilian I," *Jahrbuch der Kunsthistorischen Sammlungen des Allerhöchsten Kaiserhauses* 32(1915): 1–232.

15. Silver, "Prints for a Prince."

16. See Jan Dirk Müller, *Gedechtnus: Literatur und Hofgesellschaft um Maximilian I* (Munich, 1982), p. 77.

17. Müller, *Gedechtnus*, pp. 77–79. See also Peter Diederichs, *Kaiser Maximilian I als politischer Publizist* (Jena, 1933); Georg Wagner, "Maximilian I und die politische Propaganda," in *Maximilian I* (exhibition catalog, Innsbruck, 1969).

18. Lucien Febvre and Henri-Jean Martin, *The Coming of the Book: The Impact of Printing, 1450–1800*, trans. David Gerard (London, 1976), pp. 216–19.

19. Hind, *History of Woodcut*, 1:280.

20. Weber, *Wunderzeichen*, p. 27; Gisela Ecker, *Einblattdrucke von den Anfängen bis 1555: Untersuchungen zu einer Publikationsform literarischer Texte*, 2 vols. (Göppingen, 1981), p. 50; Robert Scribner, *For the Sake of Simple Folk: Popular Propaganda for the German Reformation* (Cambridge, 1981), p. 5.

21. For the use of woodcuts in the houses of the patriciate see chapter 3 below; in the houses of the peasantry see Pieter Brueghel the Elder's painting *The Peasant Wedding*, Kunsthistorisches Museum, Vienna; in the interiors of inns see chapter 4, n. 56, and chapter 5 below.

22. Robert Scribner, "Flugblatt und Analphabetum: Wie kam der gemeine Mann zu reformatorischen Ideen?" in *Flugschriften als Massenmedium der Reformationszeit*, ed. Hans-Joachim Köhler (Stuttgart, 1981), pp. 65–76.

23. Febvre and Martin, *Coming of the Book*, pp. 113–14.

24. Rolf Engelsing, *Analphabetum und Lektüre: Zur Sozialgeschichte des Lesens in Deutschland zwischen feudaler und industrieller Gesellschaft* (Stuttgart, 1973), p. 8.

25. Weber, *Wunderzeichen*, n. 71. During his visit to the Netherlands in 1520, Albrecht Dürer sold the woodcuts of the *Large Passion* at approximately five pfennig apiece. See Michael Baxandall, *The Limewood Sculptors of Renaissance Germany* (New Haven, 1980), p. ix.

26. For the early history of print collecting see E. M. Hajos, "The Concept of an Engraving Collection in the Year 1565: Quiccelberg, *Inscriptiones Vel Tituli Theatri Amplissimi*," *Art Bulletin* 40(1958): 151–56; William Robinson, "'This Passion for Prints': Collecting and Connoisseurship in Northern Europe during the Seventeenth Century," in *Printmaking in the Age of Rembrandt*, ed. Clifford Ackley (exhibition catalog, Boston: Museum of Fine Arts, 1981); Peter Parshall, "The Print Collection of Ferdinand Archduke of Tyrol," *Jahrbuch der Kunsthistorischen Sammlungen in Wien* 78(1982): 139–84; Iain Buchanan, "Dürer and Abraham Ortelius," *Burlington Magazine* 124(1982): 734–41; Jan van de Waals, "The Print Collection of Samuel Pepys, *Print Quarterly* 1(1984): 236–57. For Nuremberg see Wilhelm Schwemmer, "Aus der Geschichte der Kunstsammlungen der Stadt Nürnberg," *Mitteilungen des Vereins für Geschichte der Stadt Nürnberg* 40(1949): 97–133 (I am grateful to Peter Parshall for this reference); Jeffrey Chipps Smith, "The Transformations of Patrician Tastes in Renaissance Nuremberg," in *New Perspectives on the Art of Renaissance Nuremberg: Five Essays*, ed. Jeffrey Chipps Smith (Austin, Tex., 1985), pp. 83–100; Stephen Goddard, "The Use and Heritage of the Small Engraving in Renaissance Germany," in *The World in Miniature: Engravings by the German Little Masters, 1500–1550*, ed. Stephen Goddard (exhibition catalog, Lawrence, Kans.: Spencer Museum of Art, 1988), pp. 13–29.

28. Engelsing, *Analphabetum und Lektüre*, p. 32.

29. Natalie Zemon Davis, "Printing and the People," in *Society and Culture in Early Modern France* (Stanford, 1965), pp. 189–226, esp. 201–2; Scribner, *Simple Folk*; Engelsing, *Analphabetum und Lektüre*, pp. 22–24.

30. Engelsing, *Analphabetum und Lektüre*, p. 38.

31. For sixteenth-centure Nuremberg censorship see August Jegel, "Altnürnberger Zensur vor allem des 16. Jahrhunderts," in *Festschrift Eugen Stollreither*, ed. Fritz Redenbacher (Erlangen, 1950), pp. 55–64; Arnd Müller, "Zensurpolitik der Reichsstadt Nürnberg," *Mitteilungen des Vereins für Geschichte der Stadt Nürnberg* 49(1959): 66–169; Christiane Andersson, "Polemical Prints during the Reformation," in *Censorship: Five Hundred Years of Conflict*, ed. William Zeisel (New York, 1984), pp. 34–51.

32. Jegel, "Altnürnberger Zensur," p. 57.

33. Theodor Hampe, *Nürnberger Ratsverlässe über Kunst und Künstler im Zeitalter der Spätgotik und Renaissance* (Vienna, 1904), no. 1380.

34. Sporhan-Krempel, "Kartenmaler," p. 143; Weber, *Wunderzeichen*, p. 43.

35. For an account of this production see Scribner, *Simple Folk*; Christiane Andersson, "Popular Imagery in German Reformation Broadsheets," in *Print and Culture in the Renaissance: Essays on the Advent of Printing in Europe*, ed. G. Tyson and W. Wagonheim (Newark, N.J., 1986), pp. 120–50.

36. Scribner, *Simple Folk*, pp. 70–71, 161–63.

37. Scribner, *Simple Folk*, pp. 100–104. For the date see Heinrich Röttinger, *Die Bilderbogen des Hans Sachs* (Strasbourg, 1927), cat. no. 1224. See also Georg Stuhlfauth, "Drei zeitgeschichtliche Flugblätter des Hans Sachs mit Holzschnitten des Georg Pencz," *Zeitschrift für Bücherfreunde*, n.s., 10, 2(1919): 233–48.

38. Müller, "Zensurpolitik," pp. 79–80.

39. The text was actually taken from an early sixteenth-century Italian publication of eschatological prophecies attributed to the twelfth-century monk Jacopino dal Fiore. See Roland Bainton, "Eyn wunderliche Weyssagung: Osiander, Sachs, Luther," *Germanic Review* 21(1946): 161–64, and Aby Warburg, "Heidnisch-Antike Weissagung in Wort und Bild zu Luthurs Zeit," in *Gesammelte Schriften*, 2. vols., ed. G. Bing and F. Rougemont (Leipzig, 1932), 2:520–21, 652–53.

40. Müller, "Zensurpolitik," pp. 84–85.

41. Herbert Zschelletschky, *Die "drei gottlosen Maler" von Nürnberg* (Leipzig, 1975).

42. For the Beham brothers see A. Rosenberg, *Sebald und Barthel Beham, zwei Maler der deutschen Renaissance* (Leipzig, 1875); G. K. Seibt, *Hans Sebald Beham, Maler und Kupferstecher* (Frankfurt am Main, 1882); Alfred Bauch, "Der Aufenhalt des Malers Sebald Beham während der Jahre 1525–1535," *Repertorium für Kunstwissenschaft* 20(1897): 194–205; Theodor Kolde, "Zum Prozess des Johann Denck und der 'drei gottlosen Maler' von Nürnberg," in *Kirchengeschichtliche Studien Hermann Reuter zum 70. Geburtstag gewidmet* (Leipzig, 1888), pp. 228–50; idem, "Hans Denck und die gottlosen Maler von Nürnberg," *Beiträge zur Bayerischen Kirchengeschichte* 8(1902): 1–31, 49–72; H. W. Singer, *Die Kleinmeister* (Bielefeld, 1908); Emil Waldmann, *Die Nürnberger Kleinmeister* (Leipzig, 1911); Zschelletschky, *"Drei gottlosen Maler"*; Goddard, *World in Miniature*.

43. For an account of their interrogation see Kolde, "Zum Prozess" and "Hans Denck."

44. Zschelletschky, *"Drei gottlosen Maler,"* pp. 31–55.

45. See Georg Baring, "Hans Denck und Thomas Müntzer in Nürnberg, 1524," *Archiv für Reformationsgeschichte* 50(1959): 145–81.

46. Günter Vogler, *Nürnberg, 1524–1525: Studien zur Geschichte der reformatorischen und sozialen Begwegungen in der Reichstadt* (Berlin, 1982), p. 301.

47. J. J. Kiwiet, "The Theology of Hans Denck," *Mennonite Quarterly Review* 32(1958): 3–27.

48. See Charles de Tolnay, *Pierre Bruegel l'ancien*, 2 vols. (Brussels, 1935).

49. For this declaration see Kolde, "Hans Denck," pp. 52–59.

50. Vogler, *Nürnberg*, p. 302.

51. Ibid., p. 106.

52. Ibid., p. 116.

53. Joseph Kurthen has shown that Sebald's system of proportions was in fact different from that used by Dürer. See his "Zum Problem der Dürerschen Pferdekonstruktion: Ein Beitrag zur Dürer und Behamforschung," *Repertorium für Kunstwissenschaft* 44(1924): 77–99.

54. See A. Biermann, "Die Miniaturenhandschriften des Kardinals Albrecht von Brandenburg (1514–1545)," *Aachener Kunstblätter* 46(1975): 232–39.

55. See Edgar Wind, "Studies in Allegorical Portraiture, 2: Albrecht von Brandenburg as St. Erasmus," *Journal of the Warburg and Courtauld Institutes* 1(1937): 142–62.

56. Patricia Emison, "The Little Masters, Italy and Rome," in Goddard, *World in Miniature,* pp. 30–39.

57. Jayney Levy, "The Erotic Engravings of Sebald and Barthel Beham: A German Interpretation of a Renaissance Subject," in Goddard, *World in Miniature,* pp. 40–53.

58. See, for example, his interpretation of the engraving *The Way of the World,* Zschelletschky, *"Drei gottlosen Maler,"* pp. 67–77.

59. Andersson and Talbot, *From a Mighty Fortress.*

CHAPTER THREE

1. Treatments of the peasant as an iconographic theme in late medieval art are numerous: see Reinhold Freiherr von Lichtenberg, *Über den Humor bei den deutschen Kupferstechern und Holzschnittkünstlern des 16. Jahrhunderts* (Strasbourg, 1897); Adolf Bartels, *Der Bauer in der deutschen Vergangenheit* (Leipzig, 1900); Berthold Haendcke, "Der Bauer in der deutschen Malerei von ca. 1470 bis ca. 1550," *Repertorium für Kunstwissenschaft* 35(1912): 385–401; R. van Marle, *Iconographie de l'art profane,* 2 vols. (The Hague, 1931), vol. 1, chap. 8; P. Strieder, *Das Volk auf deutschen Tafelbildern des ausgehenden Mittelalters* (Munich, 1939); Jozef de Coo, *De boer in de kunst* (Rotterdam, 1946); Renate Maria Radbruch and Gustav Radbruch, *Der deutsche Bauernstand zwischen Mittelalter und Neuzeit* (Göttingen, 1961); M. Pianzola, *Bauern und Künstler* (Berlin, 1961); Ingrid Möller, *Der Bauer in der Kunst* (Leipzig, 1973); S. Epperlein, *Der Bauer im Bild des Mittelalters* (Leipzig, 1975); Dresden, Albertinum, *Der Bauer und seine Befreiung. Kunst vom 15. Jahrhundert bis zur Gegenwart* (exhibition catalog, Dresden, 1975). The article by Konrad Renger, "Bettler und Bauern bei Pieter Bruegel d. Ä.," *Sitzungsberichte: Kunstgeschichtliche Gesellschaft zu Berlin* 31(1971–72): 9–16, which also traces the graphic tradition of peasant satire back to its roots in medieval literature, came to my attention only after I completed this chapter. Since I wrote this essay, a version of which was published in *Simiolus* 12(1982): 107–30, the literature on the imagery of the "festive" peasant has been significantly enriched by Paul Vandenbroeck, "Verbeeck's Peasant Weddings: A Study of Iconography and Social Function," *Simiolus* 14(1984): 79–124, and Hans-Joachim Raupp, *Bauernsatiren: Enstehung und Entwicklung des bäuerlichen Genres in der deutschen und niederländischen Kunst ca. 1470–1570* (Niederzier, 1986). These studies confirm and elaborate upon the interpretation proposed here. Alison Stewart's "The First 'Peasant Festivals': Eleven Woodcuts Produced in Reformation Nuremberg by Barthel and Sebald Beham and Erhard Schön, ca. 1524 to 1535" (Ph.D. diss., Columbia University, 1986), and Margaret Carroll's "Peasant Festivity and Political Identity in the Sixteenth Century," *Art History* 10(1987): 289–314, on the other hand, take issue with it on a number of points. These interpretations suggest that, far from passing satirical commentary on peasant mores, prints such as those analyzed here represent a celebration of peasant life with which the viewer was intended to identify.

2. See J. C. Webster, *The Labors of the Months in Antique and Medieval Art* (Princeton, 1938).

3. Examples are found in the work of Master E. S., Master B. R., Dürer, Hans Weiditz, Niklaus Manuel Deutsch, Urs Graf, and Hans Holbein.

4. Gustav Pauli, *Hans Sebald Beham: Ein kritisches Verzeichnis seiner Kupferstiche, Radierungen und Holzschnitte* (Strasbourg, 1901), cat. no. 1245. The print is made from four blocks and measures 36.2 × 114.0 cm (14¼ × 44⅞ in). Its date was read as 1539 by Max Geisberg, *The German Single Leaf Woodcut, 1500–1550*, trans. Walter Strauss, 4 vols. (New York 1974), vol. 1, cat. nos. G251–54. Geisberg's reading was repeated by F. W. H. Hollstein, *German Engravings, Etchings and Woodcuts, ca. 1400–1700*, 28 vols. (Amsterdam 1954–), 3:255. The later date would place the work in Sebald's Frankfurt period, following his departure from Nuremberg in 1535. Not only would the subject be unique in the production of his later years, but it would be isolated from the intense interest displayed in the theme by both Sebald and his brother Barthel in the late 1520s and early 1530s.

5. Radbruch and Radbruch, *Deutsche Bauernstand*, pp. 85–86. "Naturalistisch ist der Stil dieser Kunst, nicht karikierend, ihre Absicht die Darstellung einer robusten, brutalen und obszönen Wirklichkeit, ohne Ekel vor den naturalia non turpia, ohne Kritik, Satire, Sittenrichterei, eher mit Wohlgefallen am Natürlichen, Derben, wohl auch Unanständigen. Der Bauernstand hatte sich im Bauernkriege wenigstens dies erwungen: gesehen zu werden, wie er war." This and the following translations are my own.

6. H. Zschelletschky, *Die "Drei gottlosen Maler" von Nürnberg* (Leipzig, 1975), pp. 302–3: "Die Blätter wirken nicht als Ergebnis mühsamer Werkstatterfindung, sondern als auf Streifzügen mit dem Skizzenbuche in Nürnbergs Ländlicher Umgebung gewonnene frische Wiedergabe mit offenen Sinnen erlebter Wirklichkeit."

7. Ibid., p. 333: "*In dieser Erfassung der massenhaften Existenz des Bauern dürfen wir auch eine Widerspiegelung des . . . Grossen Deutschen Bauernkrieges erkennen der erst eigentlich die Bauern auch als Masse ins Bewusstsein all übrigen Stände treten liess*" (author's italics).

8. Bartels, *Bauer*, p. 98: "dennoch verraten die Künstler der Zeit alle bürgerlichen Ursprungs, . . . stets die satirische Absicht: es ist ihnen darum zu thun, die Üppigkeit und Tölpelhaftigkeit der Bauern möglich drastisch, zur Ergötzung der Bürgerstandes vorzufuhren."

9. Kurt Uhrig, "Der Bauer in der Publizistik der Reformation bis zum Ausgang der Bauernkrieges," *Archiv für Reformationsgeschichte* 33(1936): 70–125, 165–225, esp. 224: "Den breiten Raum nehmen nach der Niederschlagung des Bauernkrieges die Spottbilder der Bauernfiguren ein. . . . Alles, was in der Literatur der vergangenen Zeit an Hohn und Spott über den Bauern lebendig war, wird nun von der darstellenden Kunst aufgenommen und gezeichnet, und in der vollen Bewusstseinskraft der neuaufstrebenden jungen Kunst werden mit einer erstaunlichen Frische und Lebendigkeit die Typen des verfressenen, versoffenen, plumpen, derben, gemeinen, sich ewig prugelnden Bauern bildhaft dargestellt."

10. Erika Kohler, *Martin Luther und der Festbrauch* (Cologne, 1959), p. 140; also Hans Sachs, *Sämtliche Fabeln und Schwänke*, ed. E Goetze (Halle, 1893–1913), vol. 4, no. 393a: *Der Kirchfannen Ursprung*.

11. Emil A. Friedberg, *Das Recht der Eheschliessung* (Aalen, 1965; 1st ed. Weimar, 1875); R. Sohm, *Das Recht der Eheschliessung* (Aalen, 1966; 1st ed. Weimar, 1875); K. Weinhold, *Die deutschen Frauen in dem Mittelalter*, 2 vols. (Vienna, 1882), vol. 1; H. Bächtold, *Die Gebraüche bei Verlobung und Hochzeit* (Basel, 1914). During the course of the sixteenth century, Lutheran communities increasingly adopted a marriage ceremony performed before the altar (see Sohm, *Recht*, p. 172).

12. August Jegel, "Altnürnberger Hochzeitsbrauch und Eherecht, besonders bis zum Aus-

gang de 16. Jahrunderts," *Mitteilungen des Vereins für Geschichte der Stadt Nürnberg* 44(1953): 238–74, esp. 252; Andreas Osiander, "Die Nürnberger Trauordnung," ed. Gerhard Simon, in *Andreas Osiander d. Ä. Gesamtausgabe,* ed. Gerhard Müller, 6 vols. (Gütersloh, 1975–81), 2:290–95, esp. 290.

13. For a discussion of Luther's attitude toward ecclesiastical art, see Carl Christensen, *Art and the Reformation in Germany* (Detroit, 1979), chaps. 2 and 3.

14. Ibid., p. 75.

15. The inscription on the dentist's sign reads: "Hi guet thiriact und wuermsam" (good "theriak" and parasite medicine for sale here). According to Luis de Avila, physician to Charles V, whose book *Bancket der Hofe und Edelleut: Des Gesundenn Lebens Regiment* was published in Frankfurt in 1551 with illustrations by Sebald Beham, Avicenna recommended that "theriak" be taken once a week together with pomegranate juice as a protection against poison. See Adolf Rosenberg, *Sebald und Barthel Beham: Zwei Maler der deutschen Renaissance* (Leipzig, 1875), p. 63, n. 2.

16. His garb may be compared, for example, with that of Sebald's figure illustrating the "priesthood" in his woodcut representing the members of the various clerical and monastic orders; Geisberg, *Woodcut,* vol. 1, cat. nos. 226–33, esp. 228.

17. For the use of garlands at peasant weddings see R. Frenzel, "Der deutsche Bauer in der ersten Hälfte des 16. Jahrhunderts," *Heimat und Volkstum,* 1962–63, pp. 65–183, esp. 118–19. The significance of the garland in marriage rituals stems from its significance as a symbol of virginity; see Jacob Grimm and Wilhelm Grimm, *Deutsches Wörterbuch,* vol. 5 (Leipzig, 1873), s.v. "Kranz"; E. Hoffman-Krayer and H. Bächtold-Stäubli, *Handwörterbuch des deutschen Aberglaubens,* vol. 5 (Berlin, 1932), s.v. "Kranz."

18. G. Pauli, *Hans Sebald Beham: Nachträge zu dem kritischen Verzeichnis seiner Kupferstiche, Radierungen und Holzschnitte* (Strasbourg, 1911), cat. no. 1246. (Cited hereafter as *Nachträge.*)

19. Pauli, *Nachträge,* cat. no. 1246a, as by Sebald Beham. The print was taken from four blocks and measures 38.0 × 110.1 cm (14^{15}/₁₆ × 43⅜ in). The work was reattributed to Barthel Beham by H. Röttinger, *Die Holzschnitte Barthel Behams* (Strasbourg, 1921), cat. no. 4, an attribution that has been generally accepted. Both Barthel's original and Sebald's copy are thought by Röttinger to date before 1534.

20. Pauli, *Hans Sebald Beham,* cat. no. 1247, as by Sebald Beham. The print was taken from six blocks and measures 17.8 × 238.3 cm (7 × 94⅛ in). Röttinger, *Holzschnitte Barthel Behams,* cat. no. 3, reattributed this work to Barthel Beham, suggesting that Erhard Schön may have been responsible for certain parts of the composition. He then attributed a copy of the print to Sebald. According to Röttinger, Barthel's version was executed before 1528, the date of Hans Sachs's text. He suggests a date of ca. 1531–34 for Sebald's copy on stylistic grounds.

21. "Eins tags ich auff ein kirchwey kam / Gen Megeldorff da ich vernam / In einem grossen Wirtes haus / Die Pauren leben in dem sauss."

22. Grimm and Grimm, *Deutsches Wörterbuch,* vol. 5, s.v. "Kirchweih"; E. Hoffman-Krayer and H. Bächtold Stäubli, *Handwörterbuch des deutschen Aberglaubens,* vol. 4 (Berlin, 1931–32), s.v. "Kirchweih."

23. "Der Weyn wart also knollet drunken / Das jr vil unther Penck suncken / Sich hüben gross gröltzen und speyen / Ein kallen singen, Juchtzen, schreyen."

24. "Vom Potenstain de Esel miller / Der war am dysch der gröst fuller / Mit mayer Gred auch umhim nülpt / Und herzet sie das sie ergülpt."

25. Pauli, *Hans Sebald Beham,* cat. no. 1250. The print is taken from a single block and measures 39.3 × 36.3 cm (15½ × 14⁵/₁₆ in). It is dated on the basis of Hans Sachs's poem. For a discussion of the relation of text and image see Mary Beare, "Observations on Some of the

Illustrated Broadsheets of Hans Sachs," *German Life and Letters* 16 (1962–63): 174–85, 175–76.

26. "Eins tags vil kurtzweyl ich vernam / Und auff ein Pawren Kirchtag kam / In ein dorff Gümpels prunn genant / Da ich vil volle Pawren fandt / Schreyend all stedel vol gesessen / Da war ein trincken und essen / Die Mayd in die Sackpfeyffen sungen / Die Pawren knecht lüffen und rungen / Warffen ein einander auff der semper / Das manchem kracht im leib der gemper."

27. "Her drungen Pawren und jr Basen / Unzal, mit also grossen nasen / Lang, dick, und krum, hencket, und pucklet / Murrett, muncket, preyt, pflunscht, und hucklet / Zincket, hacket, knorret und knollet / Dreyeyckicht, viereckicht, und drollet / Gleyssent und rot, küpffren und högret / Vol engerling, wimeret und knögret / So unfüg, das ich auff den tag / Tantzens und kleynat gar verwag / In dem die Pfeyffer beyd auff pfiffen / Einander sie zun nasen griffen / Zogen einander an den rayen."

28. Lutz Röhrich, *Lexikon der sprichwörtlichen Redensarten*, 2 vols. (Freiburg, 1973), vol. 2, s.v. "Nase."

29. "Und als der tanz am besten war / Do erhüb sich ein grosses schlagen / Am kugelplatz, die wurden jagen / Einander her in dem gedöss / Word ein gelauff und gross gestöss / All liessen sie am rayen faren."

30. See Franz M. Böhme, *Geschichte des Tanzes in Deutschland*, 2 vols. (Leipzig, 1866), vol. 1, chaps. 7 and 8; Kent R. Greenfield, *Sumptuary Law in Nürnberg: A Study in Paternal Government* (Baltimore, 1918), p. 93.

31. Sebastian Brant, *Ship of Fools*, ed. Edwin Zeydel (New York, 1944), p. 205; see also Geiler von Kaisersberg's sermon on this text in Johann Scheible, ed. *Das Kloster* (Stuttgart 1845), 1:553–57.

32. See Jacob Grimm and Wilhelm Grimm, *Deutsches Wörterbuch*, 2d ed., vol. 10 (Munich, 1984). For the use of the cock as a symbol of lust see Carl Nordenfalk, "The Five Senses in Late Medieval and Renaissance Art," *Journal of the Warburg and Courtauld Institutes* 48(1985): 1–22, esp. 3–4, fig. 1b; Dirk Bax, *Hieronymus Bosch: His Picture Writing Deciphered* (Rotterdam, 1979), pp. 190–91. For the origins of this usage see Lorraine Baird, "*Priapus Gallinaceus*: The Role of the Cock in Fertility and Eroticism in Classical Antiquity and the Middle Ages," *Studies in Iconography* 7/8(1981–82): 81–111.

33. Heinrich Adelbert von Keller, ed., *Fastnachtspiele aus dem fünfzehnten Jahrhundert*, 4 vols. (Darmstadt, 1965; 1st ed. Stuttgart, 1853–58), vol. 2, cat. no. 67; *Vasnachtspil: Der alt Hannentanz*.

34. Ibid., vol. 2, cat. no. 89: *Der kurz Hannentanz*.

35. Geisberg, *Woodcut*, vol. 3, cat. nos. 1001–3, 1064–79. While the attribution of most of the series to Schäufelein is uncontested, those now given to Pencz were formerly attributed to Sebald Beham and Peter Flötner; see Cambell Dodgson, *Catalogue of the Early German and Flemish Woodcuts in the British Museum*, 2 vols. (London, 1903–11), 1:477, 540–41, 2:50–53; H. Röttinger, *Die Holzschnitte Georg Pencz* (Leipzig, 1914), pp. 39–40.

36. "Lass uns den Reyen langsam füren / Als es dem Adel thüt gebüren."

37. Sachs, *Sämtliche Fabeln und Schwanke*, vol. 2, no. 230: *Der purger Dancz*: "Die zwen fordanczer sagen / Las uns den rayen sitlich füren / Wie es den purgern thuet gepüeren."

38. F. W. H. Hollstein, *Dutch and Flemish Etchings, Engravings and Woodcuts, ca. 1450–1700*, 25 vols. (Amsterdam, 1949–), vol. 4, cat. nos. 17–21. Hollstein's claim that the image depends on Sebald Beham's *Large Peasant Holiday* is incorrect. The peasant dancers are copies from a cycle by Christoph Murer executed in the late sixteenth century. See Walter L. Strauss, *The German Single-Leaf Woodcut, 1550–1600*, 3 vols. (New York, 1975), 2:776.

39. (*a*) Hîc púdor, hîc morum probitas hîc aúlica suada, / Et lepor, & vitae generosa modestia gliscit. / Qúid mirúm, divas ultrò si diâ seqúantúr. (*b*) Qúantúm aúla à Caúla: tantúm qúoq

distat agresti / Aulicús: hoc presens te laxa Chorea docebit / Sed bene, sic variae liqúeant discrimina vitae. (I am grateful to Edwin Carawan and David Summers for their assistance with this translation.)

40. Hollstein, *Dutch and Flemish Etchings*, vol. 9, cat. no. 31.

41. (My translation.) "Meester Ian Slecht Hoot, wilt miin luiite versnaren. Ick en sal Vrouw Langnuese, laet mii ongequelt. Want ick moetse, voor Modder Muiilken bewaren. Die hadde haer luiite, oock seer geerne gestelt."

42. See Karl Filzeck, *Metaphorische Bildungen im älteren deutschen Fastnachtsspiel* (Würzburg, 1933), p. 46; Lutz Röhrich, "Das verführte und das verführende Mädchen," in *Festschrift für Siegfried Gutenbrunner*, ed. O. Bandle et al. (Heidelberg, 1972), pp. 183–93.

43. Hollstein, *German Engravings*, 3:94, 95, 98, 99.

44. See Hans Hubert Hoffmann, "*Nobiles Norimbergenses*: Beobachtungen zur Struktur der reichstädtischen Oberschicht," *Zeitschrift für Bayerische Landesgeschichte* 28(1965): 114–50, esp. 136–37; Gerhard Hirschmann, "Das Nürnberger Patriziat," in *Deutsches Patriziat, 1430–1740*, ed. Hellmuth Rössler (Limburg, 1968), pp. 257–76, esp. 265; Werner Schultheiss, "Die Mittelschicht Nürnbergs im Spätmittelalter," in *Städtische Mittelschichten*, ed. Erich Maschke and Jürgen Sydow (Stuttgart, 1972), pp. 135–49, esp. 138.

45. J. P. Filedt Kok, *Lucas van Leyden-Grafiek* (exhibition catalog, Amsterdam: Rijksprentenkabinet, 1978), p. 161, cat. no. B157.

46. Geisberg, *Woodcut*, vol. 1, cat. no. 139.

47. Heinrich Adelbert von Keller and E. Goetze, eds., *Hans Sachs*, 26 vols. (Hildesheim, 1964; 1st ed. Stuttgart, 1870), 23:458: *Der zanprecher*. For the attribution of these verses to Sachs, see Nuremberg, Stadtgeschichtlichen Museen, *Die Welt des Hans Sachs* (exhibition catalog, Nuremberg, 1976), cat. no. 4.

48. L. Lier, "Studien zur Geschichte des Nürnberger Fastnachspieles," *Mitteilungen des Vereins für Geschichte der Stadt Nürnberg* 8(1889): 87–160, esp. 116–18, 147–52. For Sachs's attitude see also his poem *Der bawrn aderlass samt eynen zanbrecher* in Keller and Goetze, *Hans Sachs*, 5:273–75.

49. Pauli, *Hans Sebald Beham*, cat. no. 1245b: "Aspice qùam suaeves quaerat sibi turba levésque / Rustica delicias, celebrans Encaenia Baccho. / Nulla Sacerdoti reverentia, nulla Dynastae, / Cum quovis jugiter potius sua Gretula saltat." I am indebted to David and Nancy Summers for their assistance with this translation. The word *encaenia* was used to refer to festivals commemorating the foundation of churches. Cf. *Thesaurus linguae latinae*, vol. 5 (Leipzig, 1931).

50. Hollstein, *Dutch and Flemish Etchings*, vol. 3, cat. no. 467. There is a close, large-scale sixteenth-century Flemish copy of Sebald's print bearing the name and address of an Antwerp publisher; see Pauli, *Hans Sebald Beham*, cat. no. 1245a. It is of interest that this artist should have interpreted Beham's print as a comment upon peasant life rather than a record of it. Instead of duplicating the inscription on the dentist's signboard, with its advertisement for bogus remedies, he substituted the words "Wilde boeren salve" (wild peasant ointment).

51. "De dronkarts verblijen hem in sulcken feesten / Kijven en vichten en dronken drincken als beeste / Te kermissen te ghaenne tsij mans oft vrouwen / Daer ome laet de boeren haer kermisse houwen."

52. Hollstein, *Dutch and Flemish Etchings*, vol. 3, cat. no. 208: "De boeren verblijen hem in sulcken feesten / Te dansen springhen en droncken-drincken als beesten / Sij moeten die kermissen onderhouwen / Al souwen sij vasten en sterven van kouwen" (The peasants rejoice at such festivals / to dance, jump and drink themselves drunk as beasts / They must observe the church festivals / Even if they fast and die of cold). For other prints in which the peasant holiday theme is used to pass moralizing comment on the nature of the action represented, see

Hessel Miedema, "Realism and the Comic Mode: The Peasant," *Simiolus* 9(1977): 205–19, esp. 212–13, and idem, "Feestende boeren—lachende dorpers: Bij twee recente aanwinsten van het Rijksprentenkabinet," *Bulletin van het Rijksmuseum* 29(1981): 191–213.

53. Pauli, *Hans Sebald Beham*, cat. nos. 192–98.

54. Ibid., cat. no. 1197.

55. Uhrig, *Bauer*, pp. 211–23: "Die Bilddarstellung des reformatorischen Bauern"; Paul Böckmann, "Der gemeine Mann in den Flugschriften der Reformation," *Deutsche Viertel-jahrschrift für Literaturwissenschaft und Gestesgeschichte* 22(1944): 186–230; Karl-Heinz Klingenburg, "Die Wandlung des Bildes vom 'gemeinen Mann' als Ausdruck der gesellschaftlichen Rangerhöhung der unteren Volksschichten," in *Lucas Cranach, Künstler und Gesellschaft* (Wittenberg, 1972), pp. 145–49; Werner Lenk, "Das Bild des Bauern in Literatur and Publizistik im Zeichen der frühburgerlichen Revolution," in *Der Bauer im Klassenkampf: Studien zur Geschichte des deutschen Bauernkrieges und der bäuerlichen Klassenkämpfe im Spätfeudalismus*, ed. Gerhard Heitz, Adolf Laube, Max Steinmetz, and Günther Vogler (Berlin, 1975), pp. 279–302; R. W. Scribner, "Images of the Peasant, 1514-1525," *Journal of Peasant Studies* 3(1975–76): 29–48.

56. See Otto Clemen, *Flugschriften aus den ersten Jahren der Reformation*, 4 vols. (Nieuwkoop, 1967; 1st ed. Halle, 1907–11): vol. 4, *Karsthans*, ed. Herbert Burckhart, pp. 1–33. For a discussion of the importance of this figure in the pamphlet literature of the Reformation, see Böckmann, *Gemeine Mann*, pp. 194 ff.

57. J. Pelikan and H. Lehmann, eds., *Luther's Works*, 55 vols. (Philadelphia, 1955-), vol. 46, ed. R. Schultz, pp. 5–43. Luther's reaction to the Peasants' War has been much discussed. See, for example, Paul Althaus, *Luther's Haltung im Bauernkrieg* (Darmstadt, 1969; 1st ed. Tübingen, 1952); M. Greschat, "Luthers Haltung im Bauernkrieg," *Archiv für Reformationsgeschichte* 56(1965): 31–47; H. Kirchner, *Luther and the Peasants' War*, trans. Darrell Jodock (Philadelphia, 1972; 1st ed. 1967); Robert N. Crossley, *Luther and the Peasants' War* (New York, 1974).

58. Pelikan and Lehmann, *Luther's Works*, 46: 50.

59. For the history of the revolt in Nuremberg and its territories see Lawrence Buck, "The Containment of Civil Insurrection" (Ph.D. diss., Ohio State University, 1971); Günter Vogler, "Ein Vorspiel des deutschen Bauernkrieges im Nürnberger Landgebiet, 1524," in Heitz et al., *Bauer im Klassenkampf*, pp. 49–81; idem, *Nürnberg, 1524-25: Studien zur Geschichte der reformatorischen und sozialen Bewegungen in der Reichstadt* (Berlin, 1982).

60. Baptista Mantuanus, *Eclogues*, ed. Wilfred P. Mustard (Baltimore, 1911). For a history of the theme in German literature of the sixteenth century, see J. Winzer, *Die ungleichen Kinder Evas in der Literatur des 16. Jahrhunderts* (Greifswald, 1908).

61. Winzer, *Kinder Evas*, pp. 16–36. For Melanchthon's social philosophy see W. Sohm, "Die Soziallehren Melanchthons," *Historische Zeitschrift*, 3d ser., 19(1916): 64–76; Guido Kisch, *Melanchthons Recht und Sozaillehre* (Berlin, 1967).

62. A. Kellner, "Ueber 'Die ungleichen Kinder Evä' von Hans Sachs," *Zeitschrift für den Deutschen Unterricht* 24(1910): 417–40.

63. Winzer, *Kinder Evas*, pp. 36–42.

64. Edith C. Rodgers, *Discussion of Holidays in the Late Middle Ages* (New York, 1940), pp. 19–20, 107–9.

65. Pelikan and Lehmann, *Luther's Works*, vol. 44, ed. J. Atkinson, pp. 182–83. For a general discussion of Luther's attitude to church festivals see Kohler, *Martin Luther*.

66. Pelikan and Lehmann, *Luther's Works*, 44: 183.

67. *D. Martin Luthers Werke: Kritische Gesamtausgabe*, vol. 17 (Weimar, 1927), p. 501: "Wenn in disem tempel kirchweyhung ist, da klingt man nit mit glocken noch Zimbaln, da

pfeifft man nitt auff der Orgel da höret man kainen schalmeyen, da steckt man kaine fanne züm thurn auss sondern dz ist ein verborgner tempel," cited by Kohler, *Martin Luther*, p. 140.

68. *Ain Sermo von der kyrchweyche* (Basel [?], 1522). I am indebted to Alison Stewart for a photocopy of this pamphlet.

69. Sebastian Franck, *Weltbuch: Spiegel uñ bildtniss des gantzen erdbodens* (Tübingen, 1534), fol. 132v; "Darnach kumpt die heylig kirchweihe daran ein gross gefress ist under den leyen unnd pfaffen die eynander weit darzu laden. Die Bawren laden gemeyglich jren Pfarrer zu jn in das wirtzhauss mit seiner köchin oder kellerin (dann er darff keyn eeweib haben). Ettwan wirt der pfarrer voll so füren jn die baurn heym ettwan hebt der pfarrer eynen baurn den kopff bis er sich überwirfft und gespeiet."

70. G. Seebass, *Das reformatorische Werk Andreas Osiander* (Nuremberg, 1967), pp. 179–80; Emil Sehling, *Die evangelischen Kirchenordnungen des 16. Jahrhunderts*, 14 vols. (Leipzig, 1902–69), 11:140 ff.

71. See Raupp, *Bauernsatiren*, pp. 178–84, who provides some examples I was unaware of when I wrote this chapter.

72. Hilde Hügli, *Der deutsche Bauer im Mittelalter* (Bern, 1929); Fritz Martini, *Das Bauerntum im deutschen Schrifttum* (Halle, 1944); H. Möller, *Die Bauern in der deutschen Literatur des 16. Jahrhunderts* (Berlin, 1902).

73. George Fenwick Jones, *Wittenwiler's Ring and the Anonymous Scots Poem Colkelbie Sow* (Chapel Hill, N.C., 1956). The poem develops the theme of the peasant wedding already established as a literary subject in the fourteenth century. See E. Wiessner, *Der Bauernhochzeitsschwank: Meier Betz und Metz Hochzit* (Tübingen, 1956).

74. See Hans-Ulrich Roller, *Der Nürnberger Schembartlauf* (Magstadt, 1965), pp. 148–49.

75. For the analysis of peasant humor in the carnival plays see Werner Lenk, *Das Nürnberger Fastnachtspiel des 15. Jahrhunderts* (Berlin, 1966), pp. 20–92; Eckehard Catholy, *Fastnachtspiel* (Stuttgart, 1968), pp. 41–47; Johannes Merkel, *Form und Funktion der Komik im Nürnberger Fastnachtspiel* (Freiburg im Breisgau, 1971), pp. 243 ff.; Rüdiger Krohn, *Der unanständige Bürger: Untersuchungen zum Obszönen in den Nürnberger Fastnachtspielen des 15. Jahrhunderts* (Kronberg, 1974), pp. 64–120; Johannes Janota, "Städter und Bauer in literarischen Quellen des Spätmittelalters," *Die alte Stadt* 6 (1979): 225–42; Hagen Bastian, *Mummenschanz: Sinneslust und Gefühlsbeherrschung im Fastnachtspiel des 15. Jahrhunderts* (Frankfurt am Main, 1983). For an opposing point of view—that the peasant humor of the carnival plays was not hostile—see Ulrich Zahn, "Die Darstellung des Bauern in den Nürnberger Fastnachtspielen des 15. Jahrhunderts" (M.A. thesis, University of Texas at Austin, 1968); John Tailby, "Peasants in Fifteenth Century *Fastnachtspiele* from Nuremberg: The Problems of Their Identification and the Significance of Their Presentation," *Daphnis* 4(1975): 172–78.

76. Barbara Könnecker, "Die Ehemoral in den Fastnachtspielen von Hans Sachs: Zum Funktionswandel des Nürnberger Fastnachtspiels im 16. Jahrhundert," in *Hans Sachs und Nürnberg*, ed. H. Brunner, G. Hirschman, and F. Schnelbögl (Nuremberg, 1976), pp. 219–44; Bastian, *Mummenschanz*, pp. 114–16.

77. Samuel Sumberg, *The Nuremberg Schembart Festival* (New York, 1941), p. 180.

78. Franck, *Weltbuch*, fol. 131 r: "Nachmals kumpt fassnacht der Römischen Christen Bacchanalia. An disem fest pflegt man vil kurzweil, spectakel, spil zuhalten, mit stechen, thurnieren, tantzen, rockenfart, fassnachtspil. Do verkleyden sich die leüt, lauffen wie narren und unsinnigen in der statt umb, mit mancherley abentheur und fantasei, was sie erdencken mögen, wer etwas nerrisch erdenckt der ist meyster. Da sihet man in seltzamer rüstung seltzam mummerei, die frawen inn manns kleydern, und die mann in weiblicher waat, unnd ist fürwar scham, zucht, erbarkeyt, fromkeyt an disem Christlichen fest theür, uund geschicht vil büberei."

79. Horst Appuhn, "Papiertapeten, Riesenholzschnitte und ihre Verwendung im 16. Jahrhundert," in *Riesenholzschnitte und Papiertapeten der Renaissance*, ed. Horst Appuhn and Christian von Heusinger (exhibition catalog, Unterschneidheim, 1976), pp. 87–103, 102.

80. Ibid., p. 97.

81. Ibid., pp. 102–3.

82. See Aby Warburg, "Arbeitende Bauern auf Burgundische Teppichen," *Zeitschrift für bildende Kunst* 18(1906): 41–47.

83. See Adolf S. Cavallo, "The Garden of Vanity: A *Millefleurs* Tapestry," *Detroit Institute of Arts* 57(1979): 31–39.

84. It has recently been suggested that woodcuts of this type may have been used to decorate the interiors of inns. See Margaret Carroll, "Peasant Festivity," p. 294.

CHAPTER FOUR

1. For popular histories in which representations of soldiers are usually regarded as documents of sixteenth-century life see, for example, Gustav Freitag, *Bilder aus der deutschen Vergangenheit*, 4 vols. (Leipzig, 1874), vol. 2, part 1; J. E. Wessely, *Die Landsknechte: Eine culturhistorische Studie* (Berlin, 1877); Friedrich Blau, *Die deutschen Landsknechte: Ein Kulturbild* (Görlitz, 1882); Hans von Zwiedeneck-Südenhorst, *Kriegsbilder der deutschen Landsknecht* (Stuttgart, 1884): Georg Liebe, *Der Soldat in der deutschen Vergangenheit* (Jena, 1924); Hans Stöcklein, *Der deutsche Nation Landsknecht* (Leipzig, 1935): Heinrich Pleticha, *Landsknecht, Bundschuh, Söldner* (Würzburg, 1974): Douglas Miller, *The Landsknechts* (London, 1976). For a study of soldier imagery from the point of view of the history of costume see Graf Breunner-Enckevoerth, ed., *Römisch kaiserlicher Majestät kriegsvölker in Zeitalter der Landsknecht*, intro. Jakob von Falke (Vienna, 1883), and J. H. von Hefner-Alteneck, *Trachten, Kunstwerke und Geräthschaften vom frühen Mittelalter bis Ende des achtzehnten Jahrhunderts*, 2d ed., 10 vols. (Frankfurt, 1879–89), vols. 8, 9. The only iconographic studies of this theme I know are Helmut Schnitter, "Das Soldatenbild des deutschen Bauernkrieges," in *Der Bauer im Klassenkampf: Studien zur Geschichte des deutschen Bauernkrieges und der bäuerlichen Klassenkämpfe im Spätfeudalismus*, ed. Gerhard Heitz, Adolf Laube, Max Steinmetz, and Günther Vogler (Berlin, 1975), pp. 201–13; and Rainer Wohlfeil and Trudl Wohlfeil, "Landsknechte im Bild: Überlegungen zur 'Historische Bildkunde,'" in *Bauer, Reich und Reformation: Festschrift für Günther Franz zum 80. Geburtstag am 23 Mei, 1982*, ed. Peter Blickle (Stuttgart, 1982), pp. 104–19 (I am indebted to Dr. Leonie von Wilckens for this reference). I am grateful to Sir John Hale for sending me the text of a lecture "The Soldier in German Graphic Arts of the Renaissance," delivered at Johns Hopkins University in May 1983, which was later published in the *Journal of Interdisciplinary History* 17 (1986): 85–114.

2. See, for example, Master W⋀ Master P.W., Master B.M. and Master M.Z. in Max Lehrs, *Geschichte und kritischer Katalog des deutschen, niederländischen und französischen Kupferstichs im XV Jahrhundert*, 10 vols. (Nendeln, 1969; 1st ed. Vienna, 1908), vols., 6, 7, 8.

3. In contrast to Germany, the iconography of the soldier in Swiss art has been much written about. See Werner Weisbach, "'Ein Fuss beschuht, den andere nackt': Bemerkungen zu einigen Handzeichnungen des Urs Graf," *Zeitschrift für Schweizerische Archaeologie und Kunstgeschichte* 4(1942): 108–22; Franz Bächtinger, "Erörterungen zum 'Alten und Jungen Eidgenossen,'" *Jahrbuch des Bernischen Historischen Museums*, 1969–70, pp. 35–70; idem, "Andreaskreuz und Schweizerkreuz: Zur Feindschaft zwischen Landsknechten und Eidgenossen," *Jahrbuch des Bernischen Historischen Museums*, 1971–72, pp. 205–70; idem, "Marignano: Zum *Schlachtfeld* von Urs Graf," *Zeitschrift für Schweizerische Archaeologie und Kunstgeschichte* 31(1974): 31–54; idem, "Bemerkungen zum 'Widersacher' des Eidgenossen von 1529," *Zeit-*

schrift für Schweizerische Archaeologie und Kunstgeschichte 37(1980): 252–59; Christiane Andersson, "Popular Lore and Imagery in the Drawings of Urs Graf" (Ph.D. diss., Stanford University, 1977), pp. 206–20; idem, *Dirnen, Krieger, Narren: Ausgewählte Zeichnungen von Urs Graf* (Basel, 1978), pp. 41–46; Hans Christoph von Tavel, ed., *Niklaus Manuel Deutsch* (exhibition catalog, Bern: Kunstmuseum, 1979); idem, "Das Triumphbild als Memento," *Zeitschrift für Schweizerische Archaeologie und Kunstgeschichte* 37(1980): 238–44; Cäsar Menz, "Zum Bild des Reisläufers bei Niklaus Manuel," *Zeitschrft für Schweizerische Archaeologie und Kunstgeschichte* 37(1980): 245–51.

4. Heinrich Röttinger, *Erhard Schön und Niklas Stör, der Pseudo Schön: Zwei Untersuchungen zur Geschichte des alten Nürnberger Holzschnittes* (Strasbourg, 1925), cat. no. 236. The woodcut consists of nine prints taken from eight different blocks (one of the blocks being printed twice). It measures about 37.5 × 301.1 cm (14⅔ × 17½ in). The version illustrated here may have been part of the princely collection of the house of Braunschweig-Luneburg at Wolfenbüttel, which was formed in the late sixteenth and seventeenth centuries. It was transferred from Wolfenbüttel to the print room of the Herzog Anton-Ulrich Museum in Braunschweig in 1928. It is likely that it was hand colored in the sixteenth century. (I am indebted to Dr. Christian von Heusinger for this information.) This is the only one of three surviving impressions in which image and text were printed together.

5. For the history of this commission see Franz Shestag, "Kaiser Maximilian I Triumph," *Jahrbuch der Kunsthistorischen Sammlungen des Allerhöchsten Kaiserhauses* 1(1883): 154–81. The work, which was left unfinished at Maximilian's death in 1519 and was published only in 1526, is fifty-four meters long. The sections representing marching mercenaries are attributed to Leonhard Beck and Hans Schäufelein. The resemblance between the two works is closer than has hitherto been noted. The halberdiers (*Die mit Heller parten*) that follow the flag and the second of two groups of spear-carrying men identified as ordinary soldiers (*Die Gemaynen Knecht*) are based on two groups of figures by Hans Burgkmair in the section of the *Triumphal Procession* illustrating the weapons used in the form of tournament combat known as *Gefecht* (see Stanley Appelbaum, *The Triumph of Maximilian I* [New York, 1964], plates 35 and 36). The only difference is that weapons have been switched so that the halberdiers carry lances and the ordinary soldiers bear halberds. Although the 1526 edition of the *Triumphal Procession* was printed without texts, empty cartouches and banderoles appear above the heads of the figures. The resemblance between these texts (preserved in a manuscript in the Austrian National Library, Vienna, and translated by Appelbaum, *Triumph*, pp. 1–19) and those that accompany the *Company of Mercenaries*—a resemblance that depends on the way they both define the offices and ranks represented and praise the individuals who fill them—may indicate that they were available to Hans Sachs in some form while he was composing his own verses.

6. For this revival see Emile Mâle, "Les triomphes," *Revue de l'Art Ancien et Moderne* 19(1906): 111–26; Werner Weisbach, *Trionfi* (Berlin, 1919); Roy Strong, *Splendour at Court: Renaissance Spectacle and Illusion* (London, 1973); Francis Yates, *Astraea: The Imperial Theme in the Sixteenth Century* (London, 1975). For Maximilian's intentions in commissioning this work see Erich Egg, "Maximilian und die Kunst," in *Maximilian I* (exhibition catalog, Innsbruck, 1969), pp. 93–112, and Jan-Dirk Müller, *Gedechtnus: Literatur und Hofgesellschaft um Maximilian I* (Munich, 1982), pp. 77–78, 149–53.

7. See Jörg Breu, *The Entry of Charles V into Augsburg in 1530* (Max Geisberg, *The German Single-Leaf Woodcut, 1500–1550*, 4 vols., trans. Walter Strauss [New York, 1974], vol. 1, cat. nos. 357–66); Hans Schäufelein, *Triumphal Procession of Emperor Charles V* (ibid., vol. 3, cat. nos. 1080–88). This print is perhaps more indebted to Albrecht Dürer's *Large Triumphal Wagon*, a work originally intended for the *Triumphal Procession of Maximilian I*, but published separately in 1522, see Nuremberg, Germanisches Nationalmuseum, *Albrecht Dürer, 1471–1971*

[exhibition catalog, Nuremberg, 1971], cat. no. 264); anonymous Venetian artist, *Entry of Charles V into Bologna, 1529* (Strong, *Splendour at Court*, figs. 67–70); Robert Peril, *Triumphal Procession of Charles V after His Coronation in Bologna by Clement VII, 1530* (Walter Nijhoff, *Nederlandsche Houtsneden, 1500–1550*, 2 vols. [The Hague, 1933–36], plates 46–49).

8. For a discussion of the Burgundian insignia see Florens Deuchler, *Die Burgunderbeute* (Bern, 1963), pp. 361–62.

9. For the history of the *Landsknechte* see Herman Meynert, *Geschichte des Kriegswesens und der Heerverfassungen in Europa*, 3 vols. (Graz, 1973; 1st ed. Vienna, 1868–69), vol. 2, chaps. 2, 3; Max Jähns, *Geschichte der Kriegswissenschaften vornehmlich in Deutschland*, 3 vols. (Munich, 1889–91), vol. 1; Max Laux, "Der Ursprung der Landsknechte," *Zeitschrift für Kulturgeschichte* 8(1901): 1–27; Martin Nell, *Die Landsknechte: Enstehung der ersten deutschen Infanterie* (Vaduz, 1965; 1st ed. Berlin, 1914); Hans Delbrück, *Geschichte der Kriegskunst im Rahmen der politischen Geschichte*, 7 vols. (Berlin, 1964; 1st ed. Berlin, 1923), vols. 3, 4; Eugen von Frauenholz, *Entwicklungsgeschichte des deutschen Heerwesens*, 5 vols. (Munich, 1935–41), vol. 2; Günther Franz, "Von Ursprung und Brauchtum der Landsknechte," *Mitteilungen des Instituts für Österreichische Geschichtsforschung* 61(1953): 79–98; V. G. Kiernan, "Foreign Mercenaries and Absolute Monarchy," *Past and Present* 11(1957): 66–86; Fritz Redlich, *The German Military Enterpriser and His Work*, 2 vols. (Wiesbaden, 1964), vol.1; Rainer Wohlfeil, "Adel und neues Heerwesen," in *Deutscher Adel, 1430–1555*, ed. Hellmuth Rössler (Darmstadt, 1965), pp. 203–33; Hans-Michael Möller, *Das Regiment der Landsknechte: Untersuchung zu Verfassung, Recht und Selbstverständnis in deutschen Söldnerheeren des 16. Jahrhunderts* (Wiesbaden, 1976); Reinhard Baumann, *Das Söldnerwesen im 16. Jahrhundert im bayerischen und suddeutschen Beispiel: Eine gesellschaftsgeschichtliche Untersuchung* (Munich, 1978). The origins of the term *Landsknecht* have been much debated. The consensus today is that it was coined to refer to soldiers drawn from the German provinces and was meant to distinguish them from the more famous Swiss mercenaries of this period (Franz, "Ursprung und Branchtum," p. 87).

10. This and the following translations are my own: "Zu eym Fendrich byn ich bestelt / Vom Hellen hauffen ausserwelt / Weyl die das Fendleyn sehen flygen / Verhoffen sie noch ob zu sygen / Und sind beherzet in der Schlacht / Und weren sich mit ganzer macht / Darums lass ich meyn fendleyn schweben / Die weyl hie wert meyn leyb und leben / Setz ich hie keyn flüchtigen fuss / Drey Sold ich wol verdienen muss / Von eynem grossmechtigen Herren / Der kriegt nach preyss und grossen ehren."

11. For mercenary pay scales, see the rates provided by Reinhart Graf zu Solms, *Kriegsregierung* (Lich, 1559), book 3, p. 64, and Leonhart Fronsperger, *Kriegsbuch*, 3 vols. (Frankfurt am Main, 1565–73), vol. 1, fol. 145v.

12. See Ruth Bleckwenn, "Beziehungen zwischen Soldatentracht und ziviler modischer Kleidung zwischen 1500 und 1650," *Waffen und Kostumkunde* 16(1974): 107–18, esp. 108 (I am indebted to Dr. R. Wagner of the Lipperheidsche Kostumbibliothek, Berlin, for this reference); also Eva Nienholdt, "Die bürgerlicher Tracht in Nürnberg und Augsburg vom Anfang des 15. bis zur Mitte des 16. Jahrhunderts (ca. 1420–ca. 1550)" (Ph.D. diss., Leipzig University, 1925), p. 40. For an opposing view, that the upper classes imitated mercenary costume, see Paul Post, "Das Kostum der deutschen Renaissance, 1480–1550," *Anzeiger der Germanischen Nationalmuseums*, 1954–59, pp. 21–42, esp. 26 (I am grateful to Dr. Leonie von Wilckens for this reference).

13. Dresden, Staatliche Kunstsammlungen, 1975 cat. no. 1906G.

14. For the class composition of mercenary armies see Baumann, *Söldnerwesen*, pp. 49–54. The continuing role of the nobility has been documented by Wohlfeil, "Adel und neues Heerwesen," pp. 214–17, and by Hans-Achim Schmidt, "Landsknechtswesen und Kriegsführung in Niedersachsen, 1533–1545," *Niedersächsisches Jahrbuch* 6(1929): 167–223.

15. For Schön see Röttinger, *Erhard Schön und Niklas Stör*, cat. nos. 212, 213, 214, 215, 216, 217, 219, 220. For Beham consult Gustav Pauli, *Hans Sebald Beham: Ein kritisches Verzeichnis seiner Kupferstiche, Radierungen und Holzschnitte. Mit Nachträgen so wie Ergänzungen und Berichtigungen von Heinrich Röttinger* (Baden-Baden, 1974; 1st ed. Strasbourg, 1901), cat. nos. 1255a, 1255α, 1255β, 1255γ, 1255δ, 1255ε, 1255ξ, 1256a, 1257a, 1258a. Although none of these prints are dated, several were copied in etchings by Daniel Hopfer sometime before his death in 1536. Such series continued to be popular in Nuremberg for the rest of the century, being produced by Niklas Stör, Wolfgang Strauch, Hans Wandereisen, Hans Glaser, and Martin Weygel. Engraved series were also produced by Daniel Hopfer, Virgil Solis, Jakob Bink and Franz Brun.

16. For the influence of Tacitus see Paul Joachimsen, *Geschichtsauffassung und Geschichtschreibung in Deutschland unter dem Einfluss des Humanismus* (Leipzig, 1910); Hans Tiedemann, *Tacitus und das Nationalbewusstsein der deutschen Humanisten* (Berlin, 1913): Hedwig Riess, *Motive des patriotischen Stolzes bei den deutschen Humanisten* (Berlin, 1934).

17. W. Gerstenberg, *Zur Geschichte des deutschen Türkenschauspiels* (Meppen, 1902), 1:38–40.

18. Ibid., pp. 33–38.

19. See Rolf Brednich, *Die Liedpublizistik im Flugblatt des 15. bis 17. Jahrhundert*, 2 vols. (Baden-Baden, 1974); Gisela Ecker, *Einblattdrucke von den Anfangen bis 1555: Untersuchungen zu einer Publikationsform literarische Texte*, 2 vols. (Göppingen, 1981). I am grateful to Volker Honemann for the text of a lecture, "Das Historische Volkslied," delivered at the Freie Universität, Berlin, in March 1983.

20. Pauli, *Hans Sebald Beham*, cat. no. 1252α. For the text see Rochus von Liliencron, *Deutsches Leben im Volkslied um 1530* (Berlin, 1884), cat. no. 9: *Ain schönes Lied von der schlacht vor Pavia geschehen.*

21. Geisberg, *Woodcut*, vol. 4, cat. nos. 1460–62; Nuremberg Stadtgeschichtlichen Museen, *Die Welt des Hans Sachs* (exhibition catalog, Nuremberg, 1976), cat. no. 31; Heinrich Röttinger, *Die Bilderbogen des Hans Sachs* (Strasbourg, 1927), cat. no. 352; Heinrich Adelbert von Keller and E. Goetze, eds., *Hans Sachs*, 26 vols. (Hildesheim, 1964; 1st ed. Stuttgart, 1870), 21:151–54; *Ein Lob des frummen Landsknecht zu Wyen:* "Wach auff herz syn unnd freyer mut / hilff mir preysen die Landsknecht gut / yr ryterliche thatte / begangen yetz in Osterreych / zu Wyen in der statte." Sachs also included mercenaries in a song composed in 1532 urging the various estates of the empire to resist the Turks. See Rochus von Liliencron; *Die historische Volkslieder der Deutschen von 13. bis 16. Jahrhundert*, 4 vols. (Leipzig, 1856–69), vol. 4, cat. no. 439. For a song produced at this time in which praise of the mercenary is combined with suggestions that he mend his ways, see Liliencron, *Historische Volkslieder*, vol. 3, cat. no. 411.

22. Winfried Theiss, "Der Bürger und die Politik: Zu den zeitkritischer Dichtungen von Hans Sachs," in *Hans Sachs und Nürnberg*, ed. H. Brunner, G. Hirschmann, and F. Schnelbögl (Nuremberg, 1976), pp. 76–104.

23. See Albert Ritter von Camesina, "Fliegende Blätter über das Türkische Heer vor Wien im Jahre 1529," *Berichte und Mitteilungen des Alterthums Vereins zu Wien* 15(1875): 107–16; Heinrich Röttinger, "Die Zeichner der nürnbergischen Flugblätter zur Wiener Türkenbelagerung von 1529," *Mitteilungen der Gesellschaft für Vervielfältigende Kunst* 44(1921): 3–7; idem, *Erhard Schön und Niklas Stör*, p. 13, cat. nos. 238 (Schön) and 45 (Stör); Pauli, *Hans Sebald Beham*, cat. no. 1114 γ, 1–3 (Beham): Röttinger, *Bilderbogen des Hans Sachs*, cat. no. 352a; Nuremberg, Stadtgeschichtlichen Museen, *Welt des Hans Sachs*, cat. nos. 35–52; Walter Sturminger, *Bibliographie und Ikonographie der Türkenbelagerung Wiens 1529 und 1683* (Graz, 1955), cat. nos. 3368–85; Vienna, Historisches Museum, *Wien, 1529: Die erste Türkensbelagerung* (exhibition catalog, Vienna, 1980), cat. no. 151, 1–14.

24. Röttinger, *Erhard Schön und Niklas Stör*, cat. no. 238, 3.

25. Ibid., cat. no. 251. See also p. 9.

26. *Ernstlicher Bericht, wie sich ain frume Oberkayt Vor, In, und Nach, den gefarlichsten Kriegssnoten, mit klugem vortayl, zu ungezweyfeltem Sig, loblichen uben, un halten sol* (Augsburg, 1532); Nuremberg Germanisches Nationalmuseum, 8 Kr142 Postinc.

27. *Anschlag wider die grausamen und blutdürstigen Tyranney des Türgken* (n.p., 1542). This pamphlet, which was originally written in the fifteenth century, went through a number of editions in the sixteenth century. See A. Scholze, *Die orientalische Frage in der öffentlichen Meinung des sechszehnten Jahrhunderts* (Frankenberg, 1880), pp. 8–9; H. Ehrenfried, *Türke und Osmanenreich in der Vorstellung der Zeitgenossen Luthers* (Freiburg, 1961), pp. 355–56; John Bohnstedt, "The Infidel Scourge of God: The Turkish Menace as Seen by German Pamphleteers of the Reformation Era," *Transactions of the American Philosophical Society*, n.s. 58, part 9(1968):1–58, esp. 35–36, fig. 4.

28. For the history of this commission see J. Baader, *Beiträge zur Kunstgeschichte Nürnbergs*, 2 vols. (Nördlingen, 1860–62), 2:52; T. Hampe, *Nürnberger Ratsverlässe über Kunst und Kunstler*, 3 vols. (Vienna, 1904), 1:254, 255, 257, 258, 259; Pauli, *Hans Sebald Beham*, cat. no. 1114δ; Röttinger, "Zeichner der nürnbergischen Flugblätter," pp. 3–7; *idem, Erhard Schön und Niklas Stör*, pp. 14–15. The map was taken from six different blocks and measures 79.6 × 84.7 cm (31 × 33 in). Meldemann's competitor Hans Guldenmund attempted to market his own view of the siege but was prevented from doing so by direct intervention of the city council, which confiscated the woodblock.

29. For Spengler's role in the conduct of this policy see Heinz Scheible, *Das Widerstandsrecht als Problem der deutschen Protestanten, 1523–1546* (Gütersloh, 1969), pp. 29–39; Cynthia Grant Schoenberger, "The Development of the Lutheran Theory of Resistance: 1523–1530," *Sixteenth Century Journal*, 1977, pp. 61–76; Harold Grimm, *Lazarus Spengler: A Lay Leader of the Reformation* (Columbus, Ohio, 1978).

30. Horst Appuhn, "Papiertapeten, Riesenholzschnitte und ihre Verwendung im 16. Jahrhundert," in *Riesenholzschnitte und Papiertapeten der Renaissance*, ed. Horst Appuhn and Christian von Heusinger (exhibition catalog, Unterschneidheim, 1976), pp. 87–103, 97.

31. See Georg Ludewig, *Die Politik Nürnbergs im Zeitalter der Reformation (von 1520–1534)* (Göttingen, 1893), pp. 100–101; A. Westermann, "Die Türkenhilfe und die politische-kirchlichen Parteien auf dem Reichstag zu Regensburg 1532," *Heidelberger Abhandlungen zur Mittleren und Neueren Geschichte* 25 (1910): 146–47.

32. "Heirnach ziech wir mit freyen Sin / Hewt frue ist der fuerer hin / Das er beschlag das Leger heindt / So palt wir schlagen unser Feyndt / Das wir da tuen uber nacht / Die Wagenpurg wirt auch gemacht / Der Wachmaister unnd Quartirer / Wartten alda auff unser Heer."

33. Röttinger, *Erhard Schön und Niklas Stör*, cat no. 235. The woodcut is taken from four different blocks and measures 29.5 × 153.8 cm (11½ × 59⁹⁄₁₀ in). Only the title of Sachs's text, *Der dross sampt der dot*, has been preserved. See Röttinger, *Bilderbogen des Hans Sachs*, cat. no. 535; Nuremberg, Stadtgeschichtlichen Museen, *Welt des Hans Sachs*, cat. no. 120.

34. This section of the *Triumphal Procession* is attributed to Albrecht Altdorfer (see Franz Winzinger, *Albrecht Altdorfer: Graphik* [Munich, 1963], cat. nos. 76–81). Specific borrowings may be found in the depiction of the standard-bearer and his companion and the couple on horseback in front of them. The camel is borrowed from another section of the *Triumphal Procession* by Hans Burgkmair, representing a cart filled with musicians pulled by a dromedary (see Appelbaum, *Triumph*, pl. 23).

35. Nuremberg, Germanisches Nationalmuseum, box 1291 (HB 13098); "Wan nit wer das fressen un sauffen / Ja ich wolt dir nit lang nach lauffen. / Solt ich umb sunst lang naby trabe,

/ Liess dich wol die Frantzhosen haben. / Wolt wol dahaymen sein belyben, / Und wolt das neen haben tryben." The translation is adapted from that provided by Merry Wiesner Wood, "Birth, Death and the Pleasures of Life in Nuremberg, 1480–1620" (Ph.D. diss. University of Wisconsin, Madison, 1979), p. 283, fig. 14; this dissertation has now been published as *Working Women in Renaissance Germany* (New Brunswick, N.J., 1986), but without this illustration.

36. See chap. 3. n. 32.

37. Geisberg, *Woodcut*, vol. 4, cat. no. 1471: "Ich haiss und bin ain stoltzer hann / Mein hennen ich wol ziehen kan / Das sij nach meinen willen thon / Ich wach mit fleis und hiet ir schon / Sich mich oft um und habs in hut / Welcher man nit also thut / Der ist ain hen und nit ain han / Und soll die bruch nit tragen ann."

38. Schön had used the image of the camel (originally borrowed from the *Triumphal Procession*—see note 34) in a woodcut published to illustrate the plunder taken from the Turks at the relief of the siege of Vienna (see Geisberg, *Woodcut*, vol. 4, cat. no. 1248; Röttinger, *Erhard Schön und Niklas Stör*, cat. no. 242). Here it is given two humps instead of one, so as to represent a dromedary.

39. See Stephan Cosacchi, *Makabertanz: Der Totentanz im Kunst, Poesie und Brachtum des Mittelalters* (Meisenheim am Glan, 1965); Hellmut Rosenfeld, *Der mittelalterliche Totentanz: Enstehung, Entwicklung, Bedeutung* (Cologne, 1968).

40. Geisberg, *Woodcut*, vol. 4, cat. no. 1573: (*a*) "Wie wol du bist kun, stoltz starck und lang / Manch man hat von dre gelitten zwang / Dannocht must du von mir nider ligen / Ich hab dir lang dein hochmut vertzigen / Dein hellenbart wirt nit mer schnyden / Deine federn unnd dein tege mussend hie leyden / Das ich si will tretten in das kat / Dich hilfft nit dein fraidiger bart un grosse tat / Alle deine anschleg habent ain ennd / Schnell darvon unnd machs behennd." (*b*) "O du grymmer tod was tüst du hie / An dich hett ich kain glouben me / Bis ich sieh dem grewlichs gesicht / Ganntz alle vorcht hab ich vernicht / Manch grosse not hab ich bestannden / In walschen unnd in teutschen lannden / Nun hilfft mich nit mein tapffere wer / Ich ruffe an als himlisch her / Von mir wirff ich tegen und hellenbarten / Gottes und marie gnaden will ich warten." This image appears to have been the source for Dürer's broadsheet *Death and the Mercenary* of 1510, which is accompanied by a poem of his own composition. See Hans Rupprich, ed., *Dürer: Schriftliche Nachlass*, 3 vols. (Berlin, 1956), vol. 1, cat. no. 13. For other representations of this theme in this period see Franz Bächtinger, *Vanitas: Schicksaldeutung in der deutschen Renaissance graphik* (Zurich, 1970), pp. 122 ff.

41. Emil Mayor and Erwin Gradmann, *Urs Graf* (Basel, n.d.), cat. no. 151; Hans Koegler, *Beschreibendes Verzeichnis der Basler Handzeichnungen des Urs Graf* (Basel, 1928), cat. no. 178; Emil Gradmann, "Urs Graf: Zwei Krieger, Dirne und Tod," *Bericht der Gottfried Keller Stiftung*, 1950–51, pp. 20–22.

42. For these identifying characteristics see Bächtinger, "Andreaskreuz und Schweizerkreuz."

43. F. W. H. Hollstein, *Dutch and Flemish Etchings, Engravings and Woodcuts, ca. 1450–1700*, 25 vols. (Amsterdam, 1949–), vol. 4, cat. no. 28: "Procinctu tali gens forrea militiaj / Pergit, Equis, Scortis, Plaustris et cincta camelis / Vastatúra domos, Urbes et florida regna / Infelix certè númerus, furúmq maniplús / Cui ne perdendj et pereúndi occasio desit / Mors comes à tergo trahitúr frúce lúrida falce." (I am grateful to Hans Mielke for his assistance with this translation.)

44. Keller and Goetze, *Hans Sachs*, 5:208–14: *Ein kampffgesprech zwischen eyner haussmagd und eynem gesellen.*

45. Ibid., 9:242–50; *Vergleichung eines lantzknechts mit einem krebs.* Sachs continued to satirize the mercenaries in later works such as *Saint Peter and the Mercenaries*, in which Saint Peter's

mistake in allowing them into heaven enables them to take over (ibid., 5:117–20: *Sanct Peter mit den lands-knechten*) and *The Devil Refuses to Allow Any More Mercenaries into Hell*, in which the devil himself feels incapable of controlling them (ibid., 5:121–25: *Der teuffel lest kein landsknecht mehr in die helle faren*).

46. Liliencron, *Deutsches Leben*, cat. no. 117. This was published as a broadsheet in Nuremberg about 1530 but presumably was composed before the death of Maximilian in 1519, since he is mentioned in the first verse. For Graff, who served as a mercenary himself, see Theodor Hampe, "Der blinde Landsknecht-Dichter Jörg Graff und sein Aufenthalt in Nürnberg (1517–1542)," *Euphorion* 4(1897): 457–72; idem, "Volkslied und Kriegslied im alten Nürnberg," *Mitteilungen des Verein für Geschichte der Stadt Nürnberg* 23(1919): 3–54; Alfred Goetze, "Jörg Graff, Landsknecht und Poet," *Zeitschrift für den Deutschen Unterricht* 27(1913): 81–107; Wolfgang Stammler and K. Langosch, eds., *Die deutsche Literatur des Mittelalters: Verfasserlexikon*, 5 vols. (Berlin, 1933–55), 2:86–94; Gerhard Hirschmann, "Todestag und Herkunftsort des Jörg Graff," *Mitteilungen des Verein für Geschichte der Stadt Nürnberg* 60(1973): 304 ff.

47. Liliencron, *Deutsches Leben*, cat. no. 118.

48. Ibid., cat. no. 120.

49. Röttinger, *Erhard Schön und Niklas Stör*, cat. nos. 25, 24. These prints are usually dated in the 1530s: (*a*) "Ey geb dem schühmachen den rüten / Ich hab mich lang darmit gelitten / Ee ich wochenlon gewynn / So ist das ander gar dahin / Ich wil ein anders fahen an / In hosen wammes wallen an / Ob ich im krieg möcht gelt gewynnen / Allde güt gsell ich far von hinnen." (*b*) "Halt güt gsell ich will mit dir / Gleich wies dir gat also auch mir / Lanng sitzen und ein klainer Lon / Do mit ich nyndert kan beston / Dess muss ein anders ich an fanngen / Und neen mit der hopffen stanngen / In freyen Felld mit pfeyffen Trummen / Ob ich auch gelt möcht über kummer."

50. See Redlich, *German Military Enterpriser*, p. 127. For the worsening economic situation of Nuremberg's artisans, see Rudolf Endres, "Zur Lage der Nürnberger Handwerkerschaft zur Zeit von Hans Sachs," *Jahrbuch für Fränkische Landesforschung* 77(1977): 107–23, esp. 121.

51. Röttinger, *Erhard Schön und Niklas Stör*, cat. no. 22: (*a*) "Wol auff du schönes Urschelein / Ihn Frigaul [Friuli] wöllen wir hinein / Schüch machen wil ich lassen ligen / Wann ich hab vor in manchen kriegen / Gewunnen Eer und grosses güt / Wer waiss wembs gelucken thut." (*b*) "Mein hans so wil ich mit dir lauffen / Ihn Frigaul zu dem hellen hauffen / Villeicht mag ich so vil gewinnen / Das ich die weyl nit möcht erspinnen / An dem nee garen unnd zwyren / Wirt dannoch wol ein Schüsters dyren."

52. Geisberg, *Woodcut*, vol. 4, cat. no. 1518. The print is dated 1521: (*a*) "Ich haiss Mair ülin von der linden / Wa mecht ma bösser kriegsma finden / Bin wol gerist mit spies und stangen / Mei harnasch hab ich an mir hange." (*b*) "Dar zu trag ich gut wein und ganss / Und sieg gar wol zü dissen hans / Damit vul ich in seinen kropf / Das er mich dester basser schop."

53. Röttinger, *Erhard Schön und Niklas Stör*, cat. no. 211. Dated in the 1530s: "Ich pin genent Valtein Schramhanns / In Dennmarck wert ich mich des mans / In den Wirtzhawss auff dem umplatz / Lig ich noch tag und nacht im hatz / Und welcher mich unlustig macht / Der muss pald liefferen mir ein Schlacht."

54. Berlin, Staatliche Museen Preussischer Kulturbesitz, *Catalogue of Paintings, 13th to 18th Centuries*, trans. L. Parshall (Berlin, 1978), cat. no. 558; Dietrich Schubert, *Die Gemälde des Braunschweiger Monogrammisten* (Cologne, 1970), cat. no. 26.

55. Konrad Renger, *Lockere Gesellschaft: Zur Ikonographie des verlorenen Sohnes und von Wirtshausszenen in der niederländischen Malerei* (Berlin, 1970).

56. See Shakespeare, *Henry IV, Part Two*, 2.1.147–51, where Falstaff recommends that Mistress Quickly decorate her tavern with woodcuts. Cited by Margaret Carroll, "Peasant Festivity and Political Identity in the Sixteenth Century," *Art History* 10(1987): 289–314, esp. 294.

57. For the doctrine of the "just war" see Robert Regout, *La doctrine de la guerre juste* (Aalen, 1974; 1st ed. Paris, 1934); Frederic Russell, *The Just War in the Middle Ages* (Cambridge, 1975).

58. Margaret Mann Phillips, *Erasmus on His Times: A Shortened Version of the Adages* (Cambridge, 1967), p. 116. The essay first appeared in the 1515 edition of the *Adages*. It was also printed separately on numerous occasions. Phillips mentions nineteen Latin, two German, and one English editions during the sixteenth century. Erasmus's most famous critique of war is *The Complaint of Peace*, which first appeared in 1517 and went through thirty-two editions in the sixteenth century, including French, Spanish, Dutch, German, and English translations. See Roland Bainton, "*The Complaint of Peace* of Erasmus: Classical and Christian Sources," in *Collected Papers in Church History*, 3 vols. (Boston, 1962-64), 1: 217-35. For a discussion of Erasmus's attitude, see Adriana de Jongh, *Erasmus Denkbeelden over Staat en Regeering* (Amsterdam, 1927): Inez Thuerlemann, *Erasmus von Rotterdam und Johannes Ludovicus Vives als Pazifisten* (Freiburg, 1932).

59. Phillips, *Erasmus*, p. 126.

60. Desiderius Erasmus, *The Education of a Christian Prince*, ed. Lester Born (New York, 1973), p. 250. The work was first published in Louvain in 1515. Other editions appeared shortly thereafter in Venice (the same year) and in Basel (1516). German translations were published in Augsburg and Zurich in 1521. See Desiderius Erasmus, *Fürstenerziehung. Institutio Principis Christiani: Die Erziehung eines christlichen Fürsten*, trans. Anton Gail (Paderborn, 1968). For the consequences of Erasmus's attitude for the mercenary profession in Switzerland see Gary Klumker, "Mercenaries and the Reformation: Zürich's Opposition to Mercenary Service and Its Impact on the Zwinglian Reformation to 1533" (Ph.D. diss., Brigham Young University, 1976).

61. Johann Eberlin von Günzburg, *Sämtliche Schriften*, ed. Ludwig Enders (Halle, 1902), 3:150. "Ein untzelich gelt hat vertzert das kriegen K. Maximilian im Nyderlant, in Ungern, in Italia, in Frankreich, und zu seinen zeitten ist erwachsen ein newer orden der seelossen leuth, genant die Landsknecht welche on alles auffsehen auf ehre oder billigkeit, luffent an die ort, do sie hoffen gut zu uberkommen, geben sich mutwilliglich in geferligkeit yrer selen, und in verderbniss angeborner erberkeit, und guten landsitten, so sie lernen und gewonen aller untzucht in schetten, schweren, schandworten, fluchen etc., ya in hurerey, ehebruch, iungfrawschendung, fullerey, zusauffen, ya zu gantz vihischen sachen, stelen, rauben, mörden ist bey ynen wie teglich brot, und das thun sie ihenen armen leuthen, welche sie die landsknecht nie beleidigt haben. Kurtz, sie stehen ganz gebunden im gewalt des teuffels, der zeucht sie wohin er wil."

62. For Luther's attitude toward armed resistance to the Turkish invasions see Richard Lind, *Luthers Stellung zum Kreuz- und Türkenkrieg* (Giessen, 1940); Helmut Lamparter, *Luthers Stellung zum Türkenkrieg* (Munich, 1940); George Forell, "Luther and the War against the Turks," *Church History* 14(1945): 256-71; Harvey Buchanan, "Luther and the Turks, 1519-1529," *Archiv für Reformationsgeschichte* 47(1956): 145-60; Kenneth Setton, "Lutheranism and the Turkish Peril," *Balkan Studies* 3(1962): 133-68; Carl Göllner, *Turcica*, 3 vols. (Bucharest, 1961-78), 3:181-98.

63. The importance of Luther's "two world" theology for his attitude toward war has been brought out by Douglas Overmyer, "The Concept of Christian Militancy in the First Decade of the German Reformation" (Ph.D. diss., Princeton University, 1972), pp. 191-92.

64. Martin Luther, *Ob Kriegsleute auch in seligem Stande sein können, 1526*, in *Martin Luthers Werke: Kritische Gesamtausgabe*, vol. 19 (Graz, 1964; 1st ed. Weimar, 1897), pp. 616-62. See also Gustav Kawerau, "Luthers Gedanken über den Krieg," *Schriften des Vereins für Reformationsgeschichte* 124(1916): 37-56.

65. Martin Luther, *Vom Kriege wider die Türken, 1529,* in *Martin Luthers Werke,* vol. 30 (Weimar, 1909), pp. 81–148; *Heerpredigt wider den Türken,* in ibid., pp. 149–97.

66. Johannes Brenz, *Zwo und zwaintzig Predig den Türckischen Krieg, und ander zufallend unfäll betreffend* . . . (Nuremberg, 1532). Brenz was also responsible for several other works on the same subject, such as *Wie sich Prediger und Leyen halten sollen, so der Turck das deutscheland uberfalle würde* (Wittenberg, 1531). For his life see Julius Hartmann, *Johannes Brenz: Leben und ausgewählte Schriften* (Elberfeld, 1862): Alfred Brecht, *Johannes Brenz der Reformator Württembergs* (Stuttgart, 1949); James Estes, *Christian Magistracy and State Church: The Reforming Career of Johannes Brenz* (Toronto, 1982).

67. See Bohnstedt, "Infidel Scourge of God," pp. 15–16; Bernhard Klaus, *Veit Dietrich: Leben und Werk* (Nuremberg, 1958), pp. 190–93; Wilhelm Möller, *Andreas Osiander: Leben und ausgewählte Schriften* (Elberfeld, 1870), pp. 245–46.

68. Veit Dietrich, *Der XX Psalm Davids, wie man für unser Kriegsvolck recht betten, und sie Christlich wider den Türcken schicken, und glückselig kriegen sollen* (Nuremberg, 1542); idem, *Wie man das volck zur Buss, und ernstlich gebet wider den Türcken auff der Cantzel vermanen sol* (Nuremberg, 1542); Andreas Osiander, *Unterricht, und vermanung, wie man wider den Turcken peten und streyten soll* (n.p., 1542).

69. *Ein Christenlicher zug, wider den Türcken* (Mainz, 1532; Nuremberg, Germanisches Nationalmuseum, G12707 Zug). Another edition with no place of publication is dated 1542 (Wolfenbütel, Herzog August Bibliothek, T450 Helmst. 4 [6]).

70. *Der Allermechtigste und unüberwindtlichste keyser, vermant seine gelobte und geschworne haubtleut, das sie auffs fürderlichst, on alle hindernuss gerüst und auff seyen,* (n.p., n.d.; Wolfenbüttel, Herzog August Bibliothek, K285 Helmst. 4 [5]).

CHAPTER FIVE

1. See Heinrich Röttinger, *Die Bilderbogen des Hans Sachs* (Strasbourg, 1927).

2. Max Geisberg, *The German Single Leaf Woodcut,* 4 vols., trans Walter Strauss (New York, 1974), vol. 3, cat. no. 1176. In this case the publisher was also the author of the text.

3. Hans Moser, "Die Geschichte der Fastnacht im Speigel von Archivforschungen: Zur Bearbeitung bayerische Quellen," in *Fasnacht,* ed. Hermann Bausinger (Tübingen, 1964), pp. 15–41; idem, "Städtische Fasnacht des Mittelalters," in *Masken: Zwischen Spiel und Ernst,* ed. Hermann Bausinger (Tübingen, 1967), pp. 135–202, esp. 186–89.

4. Geisberg, *Woodcut,* vol. 3, cat. no. 1181. Heinrich Röttinger, *Bilderbogen,* cat. no. 561. For the text see Heinrich Adelbert von Keller and E. Goetze, eds., *Hans Sachs,* 26 vols, (Hildesheim, 1964; 1st ed. Stuttgart, 1870), 5:179–83.

5. See Bob Scribner, "Reformation, Carnival and the World Turned Upside Down," *Social History* 3(1978): 303–29.

6. Sebastian Brant, *The Ship of Fools,* trans. and ed. Edwin Zeydel (New York, 1944), p. 170.

7. Jan Piet Filedt Kok, ed., *Livelier Than Life: The Master of the Amsterdam Cabinet or the Housebook Master* (exhibition catalog, Amsterdam, Rijksmuseum, 1985), cat. no. 54. The Housebook Master was active on the Middle Rhine in the late fifteenth century. The engraving is usually dated in the 1480s.

8. For the iconography of the "power of women" in the late Middle Ages see Friedrich Maurer, "Der *Topos* von den Minnesklaven: Zur Geschichte eine thematischen Gemeinschaft zwischen bildenden Kunst und Dichtung im Mittelalter," *Deutsche Vierteljahrschrift für Literaturwissenschaft und Geistesgeschichte* 27(1953): 182–206; and Susan Smith, "'To Woman's Wiles

I Fell': The Power of Women *Topos* and the Development of Medieval Secular Art" (Ph.D. diss., University of Pennsylvania, 1978).

9. Filedt Kok, *Livelier Than Life*, cat. no. 89. For other examples see the engravings by Master b. x. g. in ibid., cat. nos. 95, 102.

10. For the text of this poem see Heinrich Adelbert von Keller, ed., *Fastnachtspiele aus dem fünfzehnten Jahrhundert*, 4 vols. (Stuttgart, 1853–58), 2:1278–82. The poem was first published about 1480.

11. The theme of the battle for the pants is already found in a French tale dating from the thirteenth century. See Theodore Neff, *La satire des femmes dans la poésie lyrique française du Moyen-Age* (Geneva, 1974; 1st ed. Paris, 1900), p. 21. The metaphor is widely used in European literature from at least the fourteenth century. Among its earliest occurrences in German literature is the following passage from Heinrich Wittenwiler's poem the *Ring* of about 1400 (my translation): "Be master in your house / If your wife wears the pants / She'll be your scourge and your curse / Since this defies God and his law / You will become a laughing-stock" ("Bis du herr in deinem haus! / Wiss, und trayt dein weib die pruoch, / Sey wirt dein hagel und dein fluoch / Wider got und sein gepott; / Hier zuo wirst der leuten spott"). Quoted by Franz Brietzmann, *Die böse Frau in der deutschen Litteratur des Mittelalters* (Berlin, 1912), p. 128. In the Middle Ages, pants seem to have been exclusively a male garment (see C. Willet and P. Cunnington, *The History of Underclothes* [London, 1981; 1st ed. 1951], chap. 1).

12. See Lené Dresen-Coenders, "De strijd om de broek: De verhouding man/vrouw in het begin van de moderne tijd (1450–1630)," *De Revisor* 4(1977): 29–37, 77; also Walter Gibson, "Some Flemish Popular Prints from Hieronymus Cock and His Contemporaries," *Art Bulletin* 60(1978): 673–81.

13. Max Lehrs, *Geschichte und kritischer Katalog des deutschen, niederländischen und französischen Kupferstichs im XV Jahrhundert*, 10 vols. (Nendeln, 1969; 1st ed. Vienna, 1908), vol. 9, cat. no. 504. Israhel van Meckenem was active at Bocholt at the end of the fifteenth century.

14. Hans Walther, ed., *Proverbia sententiaeque latinitatis medii aevii: Lateinische Sprichwörter und Sentenzen des Mittelalters*, 6 vols. (Göttingen, 1959–67), vol. 3, part 2b, cat. no. 9016: "Femina demonio tribus assibus est mala peior."

15. W. L. Schreiber, *Handbuch der Holz und Metallschnitte des XV Jahrhunderts*, 8 vols. (Leipzig, 1926–30), vol. 4, cat. no. 1974m. See also Walter Gibson, "Bruegel, Dulle Griet and Sexist Politics in the Sixteenth Century," in *Pieter Bruegel und seine Welt*, ed. O. von Simson and M. Winner (Berlin, 1979), pp. 9–16.

16. Jacob Grimm and Wilhelm Grimm, *Deutsches Wörterbuch*, vol. 30 (Munich, 1984; 1st ed. Leipzig, 1960), s. v. "Windelwascher."

17. Geisberg, *Woodcut*, vol. 3, cat. no. 1107; Röttinger, *Bilderbogen*, cat. no. 719; Nuremberg, Stadtgeschichtlichen Museen, *Die Welt des Hans Sachs* (exhibition catalog, Nuremberg, 1976), cat. no. 168. The broadsheet was probably published in 1536.

18. Proverbs 30:10. Sebastian Franck, *Sprichwörter, Schöne, Weise, Klugreden . . .* (Frankfurt am Main, 1548), cited by Joyce Irwin, *Womanhood in the Radical Reformation, 1525–1675* (New York, 1979), p. 69.

19. I have adapted this translation from that provided by Steven Ozment, *When Fathers Ruled: Family Life in Reformation Europe* (Cambridge, Mass., 1983), pp. 52–53.

20. See Keith Moxey, "Master E. S. and the Folly of Love," *Simiolus* 11(1980): 125–48.

21. Lehrs, *Katalog*, vol. 2, cat. no. 213. Master E. S. was active on the Upper Rhine from about 1450 to 1466.

22. Ibid., vol. 9, cat. no. 481.

23. Max Lehrs, *Late Gothic Engravings of Germany and the Netherlands*, ed. A. Hyatt Major

(New York, 1969), p. 650: "Ich varen usz mit vogelen Ind mit winden / of ich rechte trouve mochte finden. Jungfrou tzart ind reyn / die vindent ir by goede alleyn."

24. For medieval views regarding the intellectual and moral inferiority of women see Ian Maclean, *The Renaissance Notion of Woman: A Study in the Fortunes of Scholasticism and Medieval Science in European Intellectual Life* (Cambridge, 1980).

25. Geisberg, *Woodcut*, vol. 4, cat. nos. 1352 and 1353. The texts are anonymous.

26. See Johannes Bolte, "Doktor Siemann und Doktor Kolbmann, zwei Bilderbogen des 16. Jahrhundert," *Zeitschrift für Volkskunde* 12(1902): 296–307. The term *Siemann* could also be used to refer to men who refused to "rule" their families.

27. Röttinger, *Bilderbogen*, cat. no. 659. Röttinger mistakenly identified the woodcut to this broadsheet as the illustration to Sachs's poem *Hans Unfleiss*, which is dated 1534. For the text printed with this image see Geisberg, *Woodcut*, vol. 1, cat. no. 160, and Bolte, *Doktor Siemann und Doktor Kolbmann*, pp. 306–7.

28. Ruth Mellinkoff, "Riding Backwards: Theme of Humiliation and Symbol of Evil," *Viator* 4(1973): 153–76.

29. Ibid., pp. 163–64; Natalie Davis, "The Reasons of Misrule," in *Society and Culture in Early Modern France* (Stanford, 1975), pp. 95–123, n. 34, and p. 116; E. P. Thompson, "'Rough Music': Le charivari anglais," *Annales, Economies, Sociétés, Civilisations* 27(1972): 285–312.

30. Mellinkoff, "Riding Backwards," p. 163; Jakob Grimm, *Deutsche Rechtsaltertümer*, 2 vols. (Leipzig, 1926), 2:318.

31. See Alwyn Schultz, *Deutsches Leben im XIV und XV Jahrhundert* (Vienna, 1892), pp. 491–92.

32. Geisberg, *Woodcut*, vol. 1, cat. no. 158; Röttinger, *Bilderbogen*, cat. no. 900. Sachs's text, which was entered into his collected works with the date 1539, is thought by Röttinger to have been composed earlier.

33. For a discussion of the way the image of the unruly woman was used for revolutionary purposes in this period see Natalie Davis, "Women on Top," in *Society and Culture*, pp. 124–51, esp. 131.

34. This translation is based on that provided by Ozment, *When Fathers Ruled*, pp. 76–77.

35. Geisberg, *Woodcut*, vol. 3, cat. no. 1179.

36. For this literary genre see Waldemar Kawerau, *Die Reformation und die Ehe* (Halle, 1892); idem, "Lob und Schimpf des Ehestandes in der Litteratur des sechzehnten Jahrhunderts," *Preussische Jahrbucher* 69(1892): 760–81; Brietzmann, *Frau*, chap. 6; Rudolf Schmidt, *Die Frau in der deutschen Literatur des 16. Jahrhundert* (Strasbourg, 1917), chap. 2; H. Gattermann, *Die deutsche Frau in den Fastnachtspielen* (Greifswald, 1911); Robert Bilka, "A Functional Definition of Satire Applied to Women in the *Fastnachtspiele* of Hans Sachs" (Ph.D. diss., Brigham Young University, 1975).

37. Keller and Goetze, *Hans Sachs*, 5:64. This and the following translations are my own: "So nimb an dich eins mannes mut! / Sie würd zu-letzt gar auff dir reyten / Und würd dir noch in kurtzen zeyten / Bruch, daschen und das messer nemen, / Das müssen wir uns für dich schemen. / Das lass ir nicht zu lang den zügel, / Sondern nimb einen aichen prügel / Und schlag sie waidlich zwischn die ohren!"

38. Ibid., 5: 42: "Mein fraw ist böss, so bin ich grob, / Wann sie würfft offt mit hefn nach mir, / So schmitz ich denn mit dellern zu ir, / Und reissen auch offt an einander, / Dar wir blutn, wie die sew, baidsander."

39. The play takes its title from a late medieval proverb that listed the three things that drove a good man from his home: a roofless house, a smoking chimney, and a quarrelsome wife. For a fourteenth-century French example see Julia O'Faolain and Lauro Martinez, *Not*

in God's Iamge (London, 1973), pp. 168–69. The expression was also known in England in the fifteenth century; see Francis Lee Utley, *The Crooked Rib: An Analytical Index to the Argument about Women in English and Scots Literature to the End of the Year 1568* (Columbus, Ohio, 1944), p. 263.

40. Keller and Goetze, *Hans Sachs*, 5:109–10; "Nimb ein manns-hertz in deinen leib / Und bewt ein kampff an deinen weib, / Du wöllst dich weidlich mit ir schlagen. / Wellichs sol die bruch antragen; / Und welches in dem kampff erlieg / Das das ander gewinn und sieg / Und sey dem herr und mann im hauss!"

41. Keller, *Fastnachtspiele*, 2:969–86.

42. For Luther's views on marriage see Kawerau, *Reformation;* Reinhold Seeberg, "Luthers Anschauung von den Geschlechtsleben und der Ehe und ihre geschichtliche Stellung," *Luther Jahrbuch* 7(1925): 72–122; Lilly Zarnke, "Die naturhafte Eheanschauung des jungen Luther," *Archiv für Kulturgeschichte* 25(1935): 281–305; idem, "Der geistliche Sinn der Ehe bei Luther," *Theologische Studien und Kritiken* 106(1934): 20–39; Olavi Lähteenmäki, *Sexus und Ehe bei Luther* (Turku, 1955); Roland Bainton, "Changing Ideas and Ideals in the Sixteenth Century," in *Collected Papers in Church History*, 3 vols. (Boston, 1962–64), 1:154–82; Klaus Suppan, *Die Ehelehre Martin Luthers* (Salzburg, 1971).

43. "The Estate of Marriage," 1530, trans. Walter Brandt in *Luther's Works*, vol. 45, ed. J. Pelikan and H. Lehmann (Philadelphia, 1962), p. 18.

44. "A Sermon on the Estate of Marriage," 1519, trans. James Atkinson, in *Luther's Works*, vol. 44 (Philadelphia, 1966), p. 9.

45. For medieval teaching on this subject see Kari Elisabeth Borresen, *Subordination et équivalence: Nature et rôle de la femme d'après Augustin et Thomas d'Aquin* (Oslo, 1968).

46. "Lectures on Genesis," 1535–36, trans. George Schick, in *Luther's Works*, vol. 1 (Saint Louis, 1958), p. 115.

47. "Hochzeitspredigt," 1536, in *Luthers Werke*, ed. D. Buchwald et al. (Leipzig, 1924), 5:501: "Demnach soll auch im ehelichen Stande das Weib den Mann nicht allein lieben, sondern auch gehorsam und unterthan sein, dass sie sich lasse regieren und vor ihm bücke und kurz, sich allein an ihn halte und nach ihm richte und nicht allein des Mannes Hut, ihres Hauptes, ansehe, sondern an demselben dies Exempel sich vorbilde, das sie erinnere, also zu denken: Mein Mann ist ein Bild des rechten hohen Hauptes Christi, um desselben willen will ich ihn ehren und thun, was ihn gefällig ist."

48. "The Order of Marriage," 1529, trans. Paul Zeller Strodach and Ulrich Leupold, in *Luther's Works*, vol. 53 (Philadelphia, 1965), p. 114.

49. See Franz Lau, *"Äusserliche Ordnung" und "Weltlich Ding" in Luthers Theologie* (Göttingen, 1933); Johannes Heckel, *Lex charitatis: Eine juristische Untersuchung über das Recht in der Theologie Martin Luthers* (Cologne, 1973).

50. "Der Grosse Katechismus," 1529, ed. D. Albrecht, D. Brenner, and J. Luther, in *D. Martin Luthers Werke: Kritische Gesamtausgabe*, vol. 30, part 1 (Graz, 1964; 1st ed. Weimar, 1910), p. 152, "Also das alle die man herrn heisset an der eltern stad sind und von yhn krafft und macht zuregieren nemen müssen. Daher sind auch nach der schrifft alle Veter heissen, als die ynn yhrem regiment das vater ampt treiben und veterlich hertz gegen den yhren tragen sollen. Wie auch von alters her die Römer und andere sprachen herrn und frawen ym haus Patres et matres familias, das ist haus veter und haus mutter, genennet haben. Also auch yhre landsfursten und oberherrn haben sie Patres patriae, das ist veter des gantzen lands geheissen und die wir Christen sein wöllen, zu grossen schanden, das wir sie nicht auch also heissen oder zum wenigsten dafur halten und ehren."

51. Anthony Lauterbach's "Diary," 29 May 1538, quoted by Hugo Holstein, *Die Reformation im Spiegelbilde der dramatischen Litteratur des sechzehnten Jahrhunderts* (Nieuwkoop, 1967;

1st ed. Halle, 1886), pp. 19–20, "Komödien gefallen mir sehr wohl bei den Römern, welche fürnemste Meinung, *causa finalis* und endliche Ursache ist gewest, dass sie damit als mit einem Gemälde und lebendigem Exempel zum Ehestand locken und von Hurerei abziehen. Denn Polizei und weltliche Regiment können nicht bestehen ohne den Ehestand. Deshalb suchten jene geistreichen Männer aufs trefflichsten die Jugend durch Komödien wie durch Gemälde zur Ehe zu bewegen. Eheloser Stand, der Cölibat und Hurerei sind der Regiment und Welt Pestilenz und Gift."

52. For accounts of this literature see Kawerau, *Reformation*, chap. 3; idem. "Lob und Schimpf"; Julius Hoffman, *Die "Hausväterliteratur" und die "Predigten über den christlichen Hausstand": Lehre vom Hause and Bildung für das hausliche Leben im 16, 17, und 18. Jahrhundert* (Weinheim, 1959); Ozment, *When Fathers Ruled*, chaps. 1 and 2.

53. Justus Menius, *An die hochgeborne Fürstin Fraw Sibilla Hertzogin zu Sachsen, Oeconomia Christiana, das ist von Christlicher Haushaltung* (Nuremberg, 1529).

54. Ibid., fol. Aiiir: "Wen man nit kinder zeucht zur lere und kunst sonder eytel fresslinge und sewfferckel machet, die allein nach dem füter trachten, wo wil man pfarher, prediger un ander personen, zum wort gottes, zum kirchen ampt, zur seelen sorgen und Gottes dienst nemen? So wolle König, Fürsten un herren, stedte unnd lender nemen Cantzler, rethe, schreyber, amptleut?"

55. Ibid., fol. Biiir: "Denn daran ist kein zweiffel, aus der Oeconomia oder hausshaltung, müs die Politia oder landregierung, als aus eine brunguel, entspringen und herkummen."

56. Gerhard Pfeiffer, "Entscheidung zur Reformation," in *Nürnberg: Geschichte eine europäischer Stadt* (Munich, 1971), pp. 152–54.

57. For the history of the order of Saint Clare see Nuremberg, Kaiserburg, *Caritas Pirckheimer, 1467–1532* (exhibition catalog, Nuremberg, 1982).

58. For an account of these developments see the excellent commentary on Osiander's role in creating a new wedding ceremony in Gerhard Müller, ed. *Andreas Osiander d. Ä. Gesamtausgabe*, 6 vols. (Gütersloh, 1975–81), 2:195 ff., 290 ff.

59. For the situation before the Reformation see Rudolph Sohm, *Das Recht der Eheschliessung* (Aalen, 1966; 1st ed. Weimar, 1875), chap. 5; Richard Köbner, "Die Eheauffassung des ausgehenden deutschen Mittelalters," *Archiv für Kulturgeschichte* 9(1911): 136–98, 279–318; August Jegel, "Altnürnberger Hochzeitsbrauch und Eherecht besonders bis zum Ausgang des 16. Jahrhunderts," *Mitteilungen des Verein für Geschichte der Stadt Nürnberg* 44(1953): 238–74.

60. Judith Harvey, "The Influence of the Reformation on Nürnberg Marriage Laws, 1520–25" (Ph.D. diss., Ohio State University, 1972), p. 55.

61. Hartwig Dieterich, *Das protestantische Eherecht in Deutschland bis zur Mitte des 17. Jahrhunderts* (Munich, 1970), pp. 92–93.

62. Harvey, "Influence of the Reformation," p. 60.

63. For recent evaluations see Natalie Davis, "City Women and Religious Change in Sixteenth Century France," in *A Sampler of Women's Studies*, ed. Dorothy McGuigan (Ann Arbor, Mich., 1973), pp. 18–45; Jane Dempsey Douglass, "Women and the Continental Reformation," in *Religion and Sexism: Images of Women in the Jewish and Christian Traditions*, ed. Rosemary Ruether (New York, 1974), pp. 292–318; Eleanor McLaughlin, "Male and Female in Christian Tradition: Was There a Reformation in the Sixteenth Century?" in *Male and Female: Christian Approaches to Sexuality* (New York, 1976), pp. 39–52; Lawrence Stone, *The Family: Sex and Marriage in England, 1500–1600* (London, 1977), chap. 5: "The Reinforcement of Patriarchy"; Ozment, *When Fathers Ruled*.

64. Karl Bücher, *Die Frauenfrage im Mittelalter* (Tübingen, 1910); Luise Hess, *Die deutsche Frauenberufe des Mittelalters* (Munich, 1940); Merry Wiesner Wood, *Working Women in Renais-*

sance Germany (New Brunswick, N.J., 1986); Martha Howell, *Women, Production, and Patriarchy in Late Medieval Cities* (Chicago, 1986).

65. Wood, *Working Women*, pp. 189–90.

66. For the population of Nuremberg see Rudolf Endres, "Zur Einwohnerzahl und Bevölkerungstruktur Nürnbergs im 15. und 16. Jahrhundert," *Mitteilungen des Verein für Geschichte der Stadt Nürnberg* 57(1970): 242–71. For the overrepresentation of women see Bücher, *Frauenfrage*.

67. M. J. Elsas, *Umriss einer Geschichte der Preise und Löhne in Deutschland vom ausgehenden Mittelalter bis zum Beginn des neunzehnten Jahrhunderts*, 2 vols. (Leyden, 1936–49), 2:8 ff.; Rudolf Endres, "Zur Lage der Nürnberger Handwerkerschaft zur Zeit von Hans Sachs," *Jahrbuch für Fränkische Landesforschung* 37(1977): 107–23, 121.

68. J. Hajnal, "European Marriage Patterns in Perspective," in *Population in History*, ed. D. Glass and D. Eversley (London, 1965), pp. 101–43.

69. Keller and Goetze, *Hans Sachs*, 21: 259–61: *Schwanck: Der jung gesell fellet durch den korb*. The description of the image is clearly indebted to representations of "Virgil in the Basket," one of the favorite illustrations of the evil "power of women" theme. For the medieval Virgil legends see John Spargo, *Virgil the Necromancer* (Cambridge, Mass., 1934). For the use of woodcuts in the decoration of inns, see Margaret Carroll, "Peasant festivity and Political Identity in the Sixteenth Century," *Art History* 10(1987): 289–314, esp. 294.

CONCLUSION

1. Rolf Engelsing, *Analphabetum und Lektüre: Zur Sozialgeschichte des Lesens in Deutschland zwischen feudaler und industrieller Gesellschaft* (Stuttgart, 1973), p. 26.

2. Hellmut Rosenfeld, "Die Rolle des Bilderbogen in der deutschen Volkskultur," *Bayerisches Jahrbuch für Volkskunde*, 1955, pp. 79–85.

3. Norman Bryson, *Word and Image: French Painting of the Ancien Régime* (Cambridge, 1981), chap. 1.

4. Ernst Troeltsch, "The Social Ethic of Lutheranism," in *Reformation and Authority: The Meaning of the Peasants' Revolt*, ed. Kyle Sessions (Lexington, Mass., 1968), p. 71.

Index

Page numbers in **bold** refer to illustrations.